AMPHIBIOUS OPERATIONS IN THE SOUTH PACIFIC IN WORLD WAR II

VOLUME I

THE AMPHIBIANS ARE COMING!

EMERGENCE OF THE 'GATOR NAVY AND ITS REVOLUTIONARY WWII LANDING CRAFT

William L. McGee

BMC PUBLICATIONS
Santa Barbara, California
2000

LIBRARY OF CONGRESS Control Number: 00-091391
McGee, William L., 1925-
   The Amphibians are Coming! Emergence of The 'Gator Navy and Its Revolutionary Landing Craft in World War II/William L. McGee.
   Includes appendices, bibliographical references, notes, and index
   ISBN 0-9701678-6-5 (Volume I)
   ISBN 0-9701678-9-X (3-Volume Set)
   1. World War, 1939-1945—Amphibious operations. 2. United States Navy—History—1939-1945. 3. World War, 1939-1945—Campaigns—Solomon Islands—Guadalcanal. 4. WWII Amphibious Operations in the South Pacific. 5. World War, 1939-1945—Amphibious Training Bases. 6. Landing Ships and Craft—Design and construction—History. 7. World War, 1939-1945—Equipment and supplies.

Printed in the United States of America on acid-free paper

First printing

Published by BMC Publications—
(A BMC Communications Company)
        P.O. Box 5768
        Santa Barbara, California 93150
        Tel: (805) 969-5970   FAX: (805) 969-4402
        E-mail: BMCpublications@aol.com
        www.BMCpublications.com

Front Cover Illustration: U.S. Army Troops storm Omaha Beach on 6 June 1944 during initial landings. They were hauled ashore by a U.S. Coast Guard-manned LCVP. (Courtesy U.S. National Archives, Washington, D.C.)
Amphibious Patches: See page x for description.

Dedication

❖ *To the hundreds of thousands of home-front warriors who built the amphibious ships and craft—or supplied the shipyard industry with everything from steel to propulsion equipment*

❖ *To the largely forgotten crews—from skippers to assault boat coxswains—who were trained to run their craft at full throttle toward a fiercely defended beach*

❖ *And to the Marine Corps and Army troops who stormed ashore—especially those who made the ultimate sacrifice for our country—and to their families*

Books by William L. McGee

Bluejacket Odyssey 1942-1946—Guadalcanal to Bikini.
 Naval Armed Guard in the Pacific

First printing, 1997
Revised Edition, 2000

World War II Amphibious Operations in the South Pacific

Vol. I: *The Amphibians Are Coming! Emergence of the 'Gator Navy*
 and its Revolutionary Landing Craft

Third printing, 2001

Vol. II: *The Solomons Campaigns 1942-1943*
 From Guadalcanal to Bougainville—Pacific War Turning Point

First printing, 2002

Vol. III: *Pacific Express—America's World War II Military Supply System*

First printing, 2003

Meet the Author

B ill McGee, a Montana country boy, joined the U.S. Navy in 1942 on his 17th birthday, after serving six months as a welder in Kaiser's Vancouver, Washington Shipyards building Liberty ships and LSTs. He was assigned to the Naval Armed Guard, the navy branch that protected Merchant Marine ships and their valuable cargo and crews from enemy attacks and sabotage.

After gunnery training, McGee's "Kid's Cruise" threw him in the middle of air attacks at Guadalcanal and torpedoings in the South Pacific; carried him through the action in the Western Pacific; and ended in peacetime on the cruiser USS *Fall River* with the atomic bomb tests at Bikini.

After his "Kid's Cruise" (1942-1946), McGee attended Montana State College, established an import-export company, and later began a long and successful career in broadcasting. He is also the author of nine books on retail advertising and broadcast advertising sales. He and his wife Sandra live in Santa Barbara.

His previous book, *Bluejacket Odyssey,* now available in paperback, is a close-up view of a defining period in our nation's history as experienced from the unique perspective of a volunteer enlisted man. McGee is already deep into his next two military histories on amphibious operations in the South Pacific during WWII.

Through the unfathomable process whereby the official mind finally emerges from darkness into light, the Navy eventually decided to standardize on the 36-foot Higgins boat.

—General Holland M. Smith, USMC

Contents

List of Maps and Charts

About the Amphibious Patches

The patch with the eagle over the gun and anchor on the front cover was reportedly made by Lord Louis Mountbatten for his Special Operations Executive (SOE). The U.S. Army liked it so much that they obtained permission from Mountbatten to use it for their elite Rangers. The Army version is the same as Mountbatten's, but with a *blue* background. Then the Navy got hold of it and decided to use it for their Amphibious Forces. Since the Army was using a blue field, the Navy put theirs on a *red* field.

The 'gator patch on the back cover was created by Commander, Amphibious Force Atlantic Fleet, circa 1942-44, and was to be used only by landing ships and craft.

Source: John C. Reilly, Head, Ships Histories Section, Naval Historical Center, Washington, D.C.

Acknowledgments

Many people have contributed to the completion of this work, either by information, suggestions or critique.

Lists of interviewees and contributors of privately published memoirs are included in the Bibliography, but I would especially like to thank the following amphibians who shared their memories with me:

> Charles Adams, Herb Alhgren, Jim Cogswell, Read Dunn, Harry Frey, "Bo" Gillette, Gerhard Hess, Bill Jayne, "Cookie" Johnson, Bob Kirsch, John McNeill, Martin Melkild, "Monty" La Montagne, Tom Mulligan, Al Ormston, Elmo Pucci, Rogers Aston*, Bob Sahlberg, Don Sterling*, Anthony Tesori, and Austin Volk.

I also had the help of some very talented professionals.

Samuel Loring Morison, accomplished naval historian and nonpareil researcher, provided me with microfilmed action reports and other valuable documentation from our nation's archives.

Richard F. Cross III, Washington, D.C.-based historian and photo consultant, supplied me with many photos to choose from for this book and other "works in progress."

A special thanks to Mr. Bernard Cavalcante, Mrs. Cathy Lloyd and the staff at the U.S. Navy Department's Naval Historical Center; Mr. Gary Morgan and his staff of the Textural Reference Division, Suitland Reference Branch (both part of the National Archives and Records Administration) for their collective research and encouragement.

---

* Sad to report, these men have crossed over the bar since our interviews.

I would also like to thank the many individuals and organizations who filled my photo requests, especially the Still Photo Sections of the National Archives and the Naval Historical Center. Special thanks are due Chuck Harberlein, Ed Finney, Jack Green, and Pamela Overman at the latter facility for putting up with my requests during a week long search of their files.

Special thanks to John A. Lorelli, author of *To Foreign Shores—U.S. Amphibious Operations in World War II* (Annapolis: Naval Institute Press, 1995) for writing the Foreword. John served with the U.S. Navy from 1966 to 1968, including one deployment to Vietnam on the USS *Ramsey*. His book is a valuable reference source on amphibious operations world-wide.

Thanks are also extended to Jan Adelson for the long hours of manuscript typing and interview transcription, and to Jeremy Adelson for his microfiche/film research.

A very special thanks to my beautiful wife, Sandra, for the hundreds of hours of proofreading and editing she endured on my behalf. Finally, there would not be a book without the talented Ms. Jaye Carman who edited and designed this book—the first in a trilogy covering South Pacific operations during World War II.

William L. McGee

Santa Barbara, California

Foreword

As the commercial success of several recent books and a continual flow of documentaries on the History Channel have shown, the long ago days of World War II continue to fascinate us. We have fought many wars in our history, but when was the last time that two books about the Civil War were Top Ten sellers across the country? Most Americans under the age of 30 are hazy about the outcome of the war in Vietnam but probably all of them know who won World War II.

Our interest in the biggest and most terrible war ever fought is somewhat of an irony. We are a country built on the promise of tomorrow and compared to many other peoples, have a generally cursory knowledge of our history. We celebrate Memorial Day, the 4th of July and Veterans Day without much real knowledge of why we do so. Nonetheless, of the many wars fought by Americans, we are most interested in the one that came to America on a quiet Sunday in 1941 and ended in the searing flash of an atomic bomb forty-four months later.

Many reasons for our interest have been given voice. The war has been likened to a Crusade. It was the last time Americans fought for an unequivocal right: we had to defeat Nazism or see the world ruled by a new barbarism. We like to believe that we set aside our differences, put on our uniforms and fought with clear-eyed unity of purpose. We take justifiable pride in the fact that 12.5 million of us served in every corner of a world at war, and that the American economic engine powered the allied victory. Today we live in a world fraught with moral ambiguity and in a country that often seems to be speaking with a modern Babel of voices, each trying to outshout the other. The certitude of a war being fought for all the right reasons by a country united in purpose beckons to us as an example of what we might be. I like to think that the children and grandchildren of the World War II generation have come to recognize that we owe them our world and all the freedom we often take for granted.

We are also motivated by another very real fact: time is taking its inevitable toll. Of the millions of men and women who served in the war, more than half are gone and according to recent news reports, are passing at a rate of 1,000 per day. Soon we will have no direct link with the event that defined America in the 20th century. With all the millions of words that have been written about the war, it doesn't seem possible that there can be anything left to record. Nonetheless, and thankfully, many stories previously untold are making their way into print. Bill McGee has taken the time to add to the record.

Of all military enterprises, amphibious warfare is often called the most difficult. An invader has to bring all the wherewithal of war with him, get it ashore often in the face of terrific opposition, and then maintain his lodgment, sometimes many thousands of miles away from a base of supply. World War II saw amphibious warfare fought on a scale no one could have imagined in 1939 when German panzers flooded into Poland. Midway through 1942, with the German-Japanese axis at the height of conquest, mastery of amphibious warfare was clearly the only avenue through which the Anglo-American alliance could carry the war to their enemies.

Americans went to war with only a small investment in the resources that would be needed. The first tentative steps toward an amphibious doctrine had been hammered out by some dedicated marine and naval officers. The initial trials of landing craft had been conducted but the war would bring a proliferation of needs: specialized ships by the score, landing craft by the thousands, operating techniques, and sailors by the hundreds of thousands. They had to learn the intricacies of loading and sailing unwieldy, slow, slab-sided, flat-bottomed ships like the LST into every corner of the world's oceans. They had to learn the skills needed to put a fully loaded landing craft smoothly onto a beach and then get it off again. They had to do this coming from every possible background and with most of them never having been in even a rowboat. They had to do it quickly and quite often, when they got to their eventual destination, they practiced their new skills under heavy fire from a determined and courageous enemy.

The price was high: more than 1,000 marines and sailors of the amphibious force died in three dreadful days at Tarawa in November 1943. Cinema-goers got a graphic representation of an amphibious assault in the wonderfully done movie *Saving Private Ryan* which depicted the morning of 6 June 1944 when the amphibious forces broke open the door to Hitler's Festung Europa. No finer ode to American military skills can be found than the events of 19 February 1945 when the combined navy-marine amphibious team stormed the heavily defended island of Iwo Jima. If the Americans had learned from previous assaults, so had the Japanese. The combination of terrain, sea conditions, and a tenacious defense has given us some of the most enduring images of amphibious warfare in World War II.

The amphibians of World War II are long gone. A fleet of six thousand ships and landing craft like the one that lay off the beaches of Normandy in 1944 will never be seen again. Amphibious warfare is still an integral part of American military doctrine but the machines are vastly different. Marines are now transported to the beach in 60-knot air cushion landing craft and 200 miles-per-hour airplanes that transition to helicopters. An amphibious assault force may contain two or three landing ships instead of the hundreds that were the hallmark of the World War II fleets. Still, the sailors and marines of today stand in a direct line with their accomplished grandfathers of more than 50 years ago.

Bill McGee, himself a veteran of the World War II navy, has not only done some exhaustive research into the documentation of how the amphibious forces were built, but has added the words of the men who took the theory and the new machines to sea. His dedicated work will surely help keep the day-to-day naval record of the "Greatest Generation" from being lost.

Ventura, California

June 6, 2000

John A. Lorelli

Author, *To Foreign Shores—*
U.S. Amphibious Operations
in World War II

Before the present war I had never heard of any landing craft except a rubber boat. Now I think about little else.

—General George C. Marshall, USA

Preface

It's been almost eight years since I started researching *Bluejacket Odyssey* which was to be a single chapter in a "family history." It evolved into a factual account within a naval history of my four-year "Kid's Cruise" during World War II. By the time *Odyssey* was first published in 1997, I had become a military history buff searching for answers. For this reason, I decided to take a closer look at the early amphibious operations in the South Pacific—arguably the most important turning point in the Pacific War. That "closer look" gradually evolved into this three-volume series. Here's why and how.

My initial *Odyssey* research encompassed numerous supply runs to the South Pacific area (Solomon Islands); the Southwest Pacific Area (New Guinea and the Philippines); and the Central Pacific Area (Marshalls and Mariana Islands). See "Pacific and Adjacent Theaters" map on page 44. During this research I was constantly reminded of how little we knew about the war around us, let alone the big picture. Research findings usually trigger further research. For example, in *Bluejacket Odyssey* (Chapters 6-8), I describe my first trip to the South Pacific in the SS *Nathaniel Currier* and the 120-plane air raid on 16 June 1943 off Guadalcanal followed by the torpedo attack of 23 June while part of Task Unit 32.4.4. The date, time, and place were fixed in my memory. Research filled in the blanks, such as what ships were in the Task Unit, which ships were bombed and beached during the air raid, and which ships were torpedoed in the dark of night June 23rd.

Thanks to the help of several veterans magazines and newsletters,

I was able to locate and interview more than forty survivors off the two ships that were torpedoed. These interviews, some fifty years later, revealed that both ships went down and that sharks began savaging the oil-soaked men in the water. That's researching the past to update the historical records. So you see, historical research is never-ending. It also mounts up!

Here's a partial list of subjects I commissioned Samuel L. Morison to research for this trilogy:

- The new shore-to-shore landing ships and crafts and their crews.
- Amphibious operations from Guadalcanal to Bougainville.
- Seabee construction and stevedore battalions.
- Marine Corps engineers and pioneer battalions.
- Emergency shipbuilding under the Maritime Commission.
- Logistical challenges in the Pacific.
- Naval service squadrons.
- Manning the long-, medium- and short-haul vessels with U.S. Navy, Coast Guard, Merchant Marine, and Army crews to keep the "Pacific Express" pipeline filled.

In *Bluejacket Odyssey* I described our first encounter with the new amphibians (LCTs and LSTs) during a big air raid. The 1st Special (Seabee) Battalion was unloading us at the time. Well…you get the picture. *The Amphibians Are Coming!* is based on archival research and more than one hundred interviews with amphibious veterans who were there. Welcome aboard!

William L. McGee
Santa Barbara, California
June 2000

Introduction

Today, if one could ask famed Rear Admiral Richmond Kelly Turner, the brilliant Commander of Amphibious Force South Pacific (ComPhibForSoPac) to bottom-line an amphibious operation—the most difficult problem in warfare—he would probably respond something like this:

"D-Day is the moment of truth for the Amphibians. When the order 'Land the Landing Force' is passed, combat troops will climb down the nets of the big transports into assault boats, or directly storm the beaches in the new specialized landing ships and craft, such as LCTs, LSTs and LCIs, to commence the invasions.

"Getting the Landing Force ashore in an assault against the enemy—with calculated risk held to a minimum—is the culmination of an immensely complex planning process.

"The factors that must be considered include knowing the condition of the assault beaches, enemy strength and disposition of his units, tides and weather forecasts, and the size and attitude of the civilian population in the objective area. Equally important factors include plans for supplying the Landing Force ashore, evacuation and treatment of casualties, and the provision for replacements (men and equipment) as required on the beach.

"These and many more questions are considered by Navy-Marine planners in developing the operation orders for the assault landing. Once the objective has been selected, mission assigned, and ships and units designated for the operation, embarkation planning begins, designed to ensure that units are properly loaded aboard amphibious assault shipping. Screening forces are organized to protect the Amphibious Task Force from enemy air, surface and subsurface attack. Naval gunfire and aviation planners schedule the neutralization of beaches and landing zones. Underwater Demolition Teams plan the elimination of natural and man-made beach obstacles.

"The preface to D-Day is R-Day, a rehearsal on a friendly beach to make certain that any flaws in the planned assault are identified and corrected prior to execution of the real thing.

"H-Hour on D-Day is the moment of truth when the success or failure of the operation will largely depend on the intelligence available, the expertise of the planning staff, and the courage and ability of the Navy and Marine officers and men of the Amphibious Task Force."

The primary objective of this book—the first of three volumes on the amphibious operations in the South Pacific—is to provide an insider's view of the new World War II shore-to-shore landing craft and the unsung crews that manned them—the revolutionary LCTs (Landing Craft, Tank), LSTs (Landing Ship, Tank) and LCIs (Landing Craft, Infantry) that were specifically designed and built to speed assault troops directly to the beach.

This book can be divided into two parts. Chapters 1 and 2 provide a brief American history of amphibious warfare, from the Revolutionary War to the 1942 Guadalcanal and North Africa campaigns of World War II, followed by a profile of the famed "Green Dragons," the APD high-speed destroyer transports which filled a pressing Marine Corps need for ship-to-shore delivery prior to the availability of the new landing craft.

We then focus in on Flotilla Five crews and their new ships in Chapters 3 to 5—from amphibious training and crew formations in the States, to on-the-job training in the southern Solomons in preparation for Operation TOENAILS, their first invasion of enemy-held territory.

There are several reasons why I feature the Flotilla Five LCTs, LSTs and LCIs in this book. Consider this:

• On my first supply run to Guadalcanal—as a member of the U.S. Navy's gun crew aboard merchantman *Nathaniel Currier*— Seabee stevedores discharged our cargo into Flot Five LCTs and LSTs. Even though I had helped build them in Kaiser's Vancouver, Washington, shipyard in 1942 prior to joining the Navy, it was my first opportunity to see an LST in action and to talk to some Flot Five crew members.

• The Flot Fives were the first to arrive in the Solomon Islands in the South Pacific (19 December 1942 -10 April 1943).

• The Flot Five LCTs were the first to see action and to get their bottoms crinkled (February 1943).

• Flot Five LST-340 was the first LST battle casualty of World War II (June 1943).

• Flot Five LCTs, LSTs and LCIs were the first of the larger U.S.-built shore-to-shore landing craft to be integrated into an amphibious attack force in World War II (Solomons – Operation TOE-NAILS, June 1943).

The biographies in Chapters 3 through 5 appear in the same order as the flotilla arrivals in the South Pacific. I believe the pioneering efforts of these "earlybird crews" are representative of the struggles faced by 'Gator Navy sailors the world over during World War II.

I make every effort to convey the reality of shipboard life: the tedious voyage to Guadalcanal with its drills, breakdowns, and more drills, and the endless waiting while riding the "hook" in Purvis Bay, followed by sheer terror during a Japanese 120 plane strike.

More than 100 Flotilla Five amphibious veterans were interviewed for this volume—check the all-star line-up under "Bibliography." Net result: many humorous and/or heroic stories provide an entertaining change of pace from the recounting of historic events. Some examples:

Jack Johnson's LCT-182 crew loaded a 20-mm shell magazine with nothing but tracers and fired them over the San Francisco-Oakland Bay Bridge one night while tied up at a pier on the waterfront. It resulted in a quick exit as the first fully assembled LCT to be hoisted aboard an LST headed for the South Pacific.

Rogers Aston, LST-446 gunnery officer, recalled the big 7 April 1943 Guadalcanal-Tulagi air raid, consisting of an unheard of 110 Zeros covering 67 Val dive bombers. Two 500-pound bombs struck *Kanawah*—a World War I veteran oiler—leaving her burning, and dead in the water. Aston's rescue party found two injured men in the engine room and transferred them to the 446 for medical care.

Bill Bertsch, LCI-64 radioman, remembers a practical joke played on one of their crew replacements while tied up at the Amphib repair base in Carter City on Florida Island. Bertsch and his pals told the new guy about a Quonset hut with a bar and gorgeous native girls that really liked to take care of LCI crewmen. When the unsuspecting victim found that he had won the daily liberty lottery, he dressed up in whites to go ashore. He was plenty mad when he got back, but they all became good buddies later on.

The Appendix includes handy reader-friendly sections on "Amphibious Force Ships and Craft" and "Abbreviations and Acronyms plus Ship and Aircraft Designations."

THE AMPHIBIANS
ARE COMING!

VOLUME ONE

AMPHIBIOUS OPERATIONS IN THE SOUTH PACIFIC IN WORLD WAR II

When I'm buried, my coffin should be in the shape of a landing craft, as they are practically killing me with worry.

—General Dwight D. Eisenhower, USA

Evolution of American
Amphibious Operations
1775-1942

I have drawn on two primary reference sources for this first chapter. Vice Admiral George C. Dyer's work tracks WWII amphibious operations in the Pacific—from Guadalcanal to Okinawa—led by Admiral Richmond Kelly Turner.[1] Historian John Lorelli's book covers the development of amphibious operations in all theaters of operation preceding and during WWII.[2]

Revolutionary War, 1775-1783 Continental forces mounted an abortive amphibious assault against the British in Maine that ended in disaster. However, American marines scored an early success when they landed in the Bahamas to seize a British fort.

Mexican-American War, 1846-1848 The U.S. Navy first dealt with the challenge of delivering a huge number of troops to the hostile shores of Vera Cruz.

Civil War, 1861-1865 Federal forces conducted intensive amphibious operations including a blockade that deprived the Confederacy of foreign trade, including arms.

Spanish-American War, 1898 In June, a battalion of American Marines landed at Guantanamo Bay and 16,000 U.S. soldiers landed near Santiago—both assaults were unopposed. Another 13,400 U.S. troops landed in the Philippines and in Puerto Rico. America was now a colonial power with overseas possessions to defend.

World War I, 1914-1918 U.S. Marines were brigaded with soldiers in trench warfare. However, the British landing at Gallipoli, Turkey and subsequent forced withdrawal after severe losses, made significant impact on future amphibious operations.

The 1930s Despite competing claims on scarce military resources, a committee of marine and navy officers reduced the accumulated amphibious experience to writing. Entitled "Marine Corps Landing Operations," it was the first American military publication devoted solely to amphibious operations. In Lorelli's words:

> The crystalline moment for the modern Marine Corps arrived in January 1933, when the Joint Board issued a general doctrine covering the conduct of joint Army-Navy overseas operations. Among other things, 'Joint Overseas Expeditions' addressed the problems of amphibious operations, the primary responsibility for which had been previously assigned to the Marine Corps.[3]

LtCol Earl "Pete" Ellis, USMC, who had put forth his ideas in writing as early as 1921 in "Advanced Base Operations in Micronesia," MajGen John Lejeune, Commandant of the Corps and LtGen Holland M. Smith were quick to seize the moment by proposing the formation of a standing body of marines trained and equipped for expeditionary operations in support of the fleet.

In December 1933, Navy Department General Order 241 created the Fleet Marine Force, replacing the former Marine Corps Expeditionary Force. Even while this organizational change was taking place, the doctrine that would guide it was being formalized.

The Marine Corps promptly produced a document issued in January 1934 as the *Tentative Manual for Landing Operation*.

John Lorelli:

> That its creators got it mostly right in what has been called a 'remarkable document' is demonstrated by what the original manual spawned: After one metamorphosis as the Tentative Landing Operations Manual in 1935, it became the Navy's Fleet Training Publication 167, Landing Operations Doctrine, U.S. Navy in 1938. Further proof of its influence is found in the manual's almost verbatim adoption by the Army as the basis for its own field manual on amphibious operations... In only a few months, a handful of dedicated officers had created the operational guidelines for the most complex and far-ranging amphibious operations the world would ever see.[4]

Even after three revisions in May 1941, August 1942, and August 1943, the tenets of the original manual remained operative throughout World War II. The new manual and its revisions addressed the key components of an amphibious operation with specific answers. John Lorelli:

The naval commander had authority over all parts of the task force, amphibious and support ships alike as well as all embarked personnel. Experience would cause some changes, but the age-old problem of who commanded what in a joint expedition seemed to have been answered.

The manual then asserted that despite the known limitations on capability and control of naval gunfire, such support was essential for any landing to succeed. More effective ammunition and methods of fire control would have to be developed to overcome deficiencies and existing capabilities would have to be maximized. Naval officers would be assigned to shore fire-control parties to direct ship gunfire.

Air support was recognized as an important component of a successful assault. Naval and marine airmen would range ahead of the assault force on scouting and softening-up missions. The manual writers believed what was lost in surprise by aerial assaults would be more than made up by increased offensive punch.

Once the invasion began, the airmen would prevent enemy air power from intervening, spot for ship gunfire, and disrupt defender reinforcements. There was considerable discussion and some argument about the role of air power, but the framework was in place for what eventually evolved as doctrine.

The new manuals envisioned ship-to-shore movement in a much more coordinated and powerful attack than ever before. The basic assault unit was a marine infantry battalion integrated with supporting arms and all necessary equipment embarked. Transports carrying the assault force would anchor opposite the landing beach and disembark troops into assault craft carried to the scene by the transports.

The assault craft would proceed in a group to the line of departure and from there to the beach in line-abreast formation. Landing boats would be armed and capable of putting down enough fire to keep the beach defenders' heads down. Artillery and light tanks were to be included in the earliest possible phase of the landing.

Once the first-wave troops were ashore, follow-up waves of infantry and support elements were to be coordinated and directed by a naval beach party and a shore party made up of army or marine personnel.

Specific directions described combat loading of the transports. Supplies that would be used first were loaded at the top of the hold in the order needed. Less essential items were loaded farther down with the least essential at the bottom. Tables were worked up listing cubic dimensions of all equipment; quartermaster officers used these tables and plans of ship holds to figure loading schemes for each transport.

If the *Tentative Manual* missed anything, it was adequate emphasis on logistics. It did not mention follow-up supply efforts and no provision was made for permanent shore parties. This oversight was corrected in *FTP 167*. Even with thirty-two pages of instructions, logistics would long remain the stepchild of amphibious operations.

Obviously, there is a difference between laying instructions out on paper and putting them into action. *The Fleet Landing Exercises*— annual events conducted from 1935 through 1941—subjected every section of the manuals to the rigors of operational testing.

Various targets and gunfire missions called for specific types of ships. Destroyers seemed best for close-support fire missions like beach defenses and coastal artillery batteries. Cruisers and battleships got the jobs of deep support and long-range missions associated with neutralizing an enemy's artillery positions, harassing reserve areas and supply lines, and disrupting communications. To aid shipboard observers and the shore fire-control parties, aviators got considerable practice in spotting for naval gunfire, a task made a lot simpler by development of the gridded map. Aviators also devoted considerable effort to learning the fundamentals of effective ground support. The need for specialized landing craft was reconfirmed, as ordinary ship's boats remained unsuitable for rapid landing and deployment of large numbers of assault troops.[5]

In 1937, Lt Victor Krulak, while serving with the 4th Marines in China, saw what he immediately recognized as the answer to the problem—a sturdy Japanese-made boat with a bow ramp capable of transporting heavy vehicles and depositing them directly on the beach. He realized immediately that the Japanese were light-years ahead of us in landing craft design and construction.

Two years later, when Lt Krulak returned to the States, he was chagrined to read a marginal comment from some Navy Bureau of Ships skeptic, that his report was the work of "some nut out in China."

Krulak's experience was typical of the time: While he watched the Japanese employ a variety of mission-built landing craft, the Marines were able to convince the Navy to purchase only a single design from a New Orleans-based boatbuilder named Andrew Higgins. However, that one-boat buy was the beginning of a relationship between the Marine Corps and Higgins that would have important consequences for the development of amphibious warfare.

The Navy wasn't completely asleep at the switch. In 1937, the Secretary of the Navy created the Continuing Board for the Development of Landing Craft. Funds remained scarce, but at least a mechanism was in place dedicated to solving this problem. One result was that several experiments begun under the "Special Boat Plan" of 1938 would, over the next three years, put some extremely useful landing craft into the hands of the Navy and Marines.

Amphibious Terminology

Let's agree on several frequently used terms in this book:[6]

Amphibious operation Attack launched from the sea by naval and landing forces embarked in ships or craft.

Amphibious force Naval force and landing force, together with supporting forces who are trained, organized, and equipped for amphibious operations.

Landing force The troops organized for an amphibious assault. Also, a portion of a ship's crew detailed to go ashore in an organized unit for any military operation.

Landing ship An assault ship designed for long sea voyages and rapid unloading over and onto a beach.

Landing craft Craft employed in amphibious operations, specifically designed for carrying troops and equipment and for beaching, unloading, and retracting. (Also used for logistic cargo resupply operations.)

It should be noted that someone in the Navy's Bureau of Ships arbitrarily decided that the dividing line between a landing ship and craft would be 200 feet in length, hence the 158-foot LCI, very much a sea-going vessel, was designated a craft.

Two other terms frequently need clarification—commercial vs. combat loading of transports and cargo ships:[7]

Combat loading Essential equipment, vehicles and supplies must be loaded in the same ship with the assault troops that are to use them, and stowed in such manner that all may be unloaded in the order that it is likely to be wanted to meet tactical situations immediately upon landing. Special davits have to be fitted for handling the landing craft, rope ladders or cargo nets for debarking troops, and the crew has to be trained to unload in complete darkness.

Commercial loading   In ordinary transport loading, as much cargo and as many troops as the ship will carry are placed on board in the expectation of disembarking on a friendly dock or shore where everything can be sorted out.

Early 1940s Amphibious Developments

Thanks to Admiral Ernest J. King, Commander in Chief Atlanta Fleet, and Major General Holland M. "Howling Mad" Smith, 1st Marine Division, the drive to get America's amphibious forces ready for war was accentuated in early 1941.

Admiral King's reputation was as an acerbic, intolerant, but brilliant and highly competent man. His uncompromising demand for excellence was felt throughout the Fleet. MajGen Smith was an outspoken perfectionist and early adherent to the gospel of amphibious warfare.

In June 1941, Smith began amphibious planning for the Atlantic Fleet and for Army divisions. (A year later he would take command of the Pacific Fleet's amphibious force to organize and train Marines for the Pacific War.)

The U.S. Army's role had been slowly evolving in parallel with that of the Marines although there were doctrinal differences about command and tactics that stemmed from their unique perceptions of the amphibious problem. Historian Lorelli described the differing perceptions:

> Marine focus was primarily on assaulting defended islands in the Pacific, an operation that presented a quite different military problem from forcing entry onto a continental land mass to open a large-scale campaign.

> Despite their different perceptions of the problem, Army commanders were impressed enough with what the Navy and Marines had accomplished to initiate the process that eventually saw FTP

167 adopted almost unchanged in June 1941 as the Army's Field Manual 31-5, *Landing Operations on Hostile Shores.*

That the Army adopted a Navy manual did not eradicate some profound differences in perception about the nature of amphibious warfare: there would be some vicious bureaucratic battles over division of labor and the manner in which soldiers were to be landed on a hostile shore. Nonetheless, the progress represented by FM 31-5 was well timed. Europe was again engulfed in an all-out war and the Japanese were threatening to export their war with China to the rest of Asia.[8]

General Smith, as Commander of the 1st Marine Division, recognized the need for purpose-built landing craft. Smith also became a strong backer of Andrew Higgins during the battles over design and procurement of landing craft during this period.

Here's how John Lorelli summarized amphibious developments during the 1940-42 period:

An important event was the 6 June 1941 creation of the First Joint Training Force and the appointment of Holland Smith as its commander. A like command was set up on the Pacific coast under MajGen Clayton Vogel. Smith used the time remaining before the United States entered the war to push his amphibious corps, which consisted of the 1st Marine Division and the Army's 1st Infantry Division, to a higher state of readiness.

The "Special Boat Plan" of 1938 began to bear fruit: orders were placed for an armored, machine-gun-armed support craft (LCS) to accompany the landing boats. The first models of the new bow-ramped landing boat (LCP(R)), were successfully tested as was its new, larger cousin, the landing craft, mechanized (LCM). Andrew Higgins built both of the latter boats. The LCM was available only because Holland Smith and other Marines waged a long battle with the entrenched bureaucracy of the Navy's Bureau of Ships.[9]

We'll profile the amazing accomplishments of Andrew Jackson Higgins a bit later. In the meantime, to give you some idea of the urgent need for landing craft production as the war clouds gathered, consider the following:

- On 1 October 1939, when World War II was getting underway in Europe, the Navy had only two large transports (APs) in commission. They operated directly under the Chief of Naval Operations in logistic support of overseas commands, largely in the personnel area.

By 15 October 1940, there were two additional large amphibious transports (APs) in commission in the Fleet, and four fast destroyer-type transports (APDs).

- On 24 February 1940, there were only 35 personnel landing boats in the whole Navy built for that purpose. On this same date, there were 5 tank lighters and 6 artillery lighters. By 30 September 1941, the 36-foot personnel landing craft had been adopted as standard, but their availability had not caught up with demand.
- By 23 October 1941, there were 30 large APs, needing 816 landing boats, and 11 AKs needing 80 landing boats in commission, being procured, or converted.[10]

On 18 April 1942, the commanders of the newly established Amphibious Force of the Atlantic Fleet (RAdm R. M. Brainard) and Pacific Fleet (VAdm Wilson Brown) attended a conference at Admiral King's headquarters and came up with a number of agreed-upon principles relating to amphibious organization and training, and made a number of recommendations. Bottom line: More of everything was needed.

In giving Admiral King his generally favorable endorsement to these principles and recommendations, Rear Admiral Turner, strategic planner on King's staff at the time, added a new and strong recommendation that:

A Joint Army, Navy and Marine section under a Flag Officer, be established in COMinCH Headquarters with specific responsibility to develop materiel and methods for amphibious forces. These matters are handled by a number of agencies throughout the Department and should be coordinated under one head. This is a large project and requires specialized handling here, as well as in the field. Until such action is taken, it is not believed that we will make satisfactory progress.[11]

Rear Admiral Richard S. Edwards, Deputy Chief of Staff, in forwarding Rear Admiral Turner's memorandum wrote: "The amphibious problem is assuming large proportions. Control is badly scattered in the Department. It should be centralized as Turner suggests...I concur that an Assistant Chief of Staff be appointed for this purpose."

It evidently took weeks to get General Marshall's concurrence, for the special section [F-26] to handle Amphibious Warfare was not established until 4 June 1942, and then with a complement of only six officers.

In the immediate pre-December 7, 1941, Navy amphibious ships were organized administratively into divisions and/or squadrons and assigned to the "lowly" Train Squadrons, whose primary mission was logistical support of the Atlantic and Pacific Fleets. As the number of amphibious ships and landing craft mushroomed, and as the number of prospective tasks for them multiplied, it was obvious that the amphibious ships should be placed in a separate "Type" command within the major fleets, such as had long existed for the aircraft carriers, battleships, cruisers, destroyers, submarines and other ships of a particular character or classification. The Type commander handled matters dealing with personnel, materiel, and basic training.

On 14 March 1942 and 10 April 1942 respectively, the Amphibious Forces of the Atlantic and Pacific Fleets were created in accordance with instructions from COMinCH, and in due time all amphibious units within the two Fleets were assigned to them.

Organizational rosters issued close to these dates show that there were 12 **APs**, 4 **AKs** and 2 **APDs** in the Atlantic Fleet and 6 **APs**, 2 **AKs** and 3 **APDs** in the Pacific Fleet, when the Amphibious Forces were established as separate entities. And this was only four to five months before Guadalcanal.

VAdm Dyer sheds some light on ship designations in his book with these words:

> The designation of the major amphibious types such as **APs**, **AKs**, and **APDs** warrants a word of explanation. In the 'Dark Ages,' when the standard nomenclature for the classification of naval ships was first promulgated by the Secretary of the Navy, the Navy had numerous colliers and tugs but few cargo ships and no transports. So the basic letter **C** was assigned to colliers and **T** to tugs. Later, such other obvious assignments as **D** to destroyer, **H** to hospital ship, **N** to net layer and **R** for repair ship were made. With the obvious coincident letters all assigned, transports drew **P** and cargo ships **K** from the remaining available letters of the alphabet.

> At the time of designating letter assignments, transports and cargo ships were auxiliaries to combatant ships of the fleets and so carried the basic **A** for auxiliary in front of their class-type designation. Thus, an **AP** was a naval auxiliary and a transport and **AK** was a naval auxiliary and a cargo ship.

Since it became apparent in 1942 that transports and cargo ships of the Amphibious Forces were anything but auxiliary in carrying the war to the enemy, the **A** in their designation galled those who served in these ships. The hurt was only partially relieved when early in 1943, their designations were changed to **APA** and **AKA** and they became Attack Transports and Attack Cargo ships.[12]

Many a commander, including CinCPAC, continued to refer to **APAs** and **AKAs** as auxiliaries long after the designation changes based on numerous reports reviewed by the author. The Bureau of Naval Personnel rated command duty in large combatant ships— carriers, battleships, cruisers—and the command of multiple units such as destroyer squadrons, as requiring the service of the "best fitted" officers in the senior grades. For many years, auxiliary ships and other lessor commands had been rated less desirable than large combatant commands.

As converted merchantmen (ocean liners and cargo ships) came into commission in the Navy in 1941 and 1942, many of their COs reportedly felt like they were being shanghaied to a second-class navy. (Supposedly, they had lost station on their Naval Academy classmates as they battled for promotions before the selection boards.) According to VAdm Dyer:

> The prime billets for the BUPERS 'hot shots' were the big carriers, and the new battleships, and Rear Admiral Turner's efforts to draft some of these 'hot shot' officers into the amphibious ship commands were futile, even after he had acquired three stars on his shoulders. He was forever grateful to those officers in our Navy who had acquired less than an ultra plus ultra rating in the peacetime Navy, but who turned in a superb and winning performance in battling through to the beaches with their troops and long tons of logistic support.[13]

Inter-Service Rivalry and Responsibilities

It is important to remember that in pre-World War II days and for many months after 7 December 1941, both the U.S. Army and the U.S. Navy had overlapping functions in both the overseas movement and assault phases of Joint Overseas Expeditions. Joint Overseas Expeditions included (1) joint overseas movements and (2) landing attacks against shore objectives. These functions which bore the approval of the Secretary of War (Army) and the Secretary of the

Navy were set forth in *Joint Action of the Army and the Navy* prepared by the Joint Board in 1927 and revised in 1935.[14]

VAdm Dyer described these complicated and frequently controversial relationships:

The general principle which frequently overrode the detailed assignment of tasks was known to all. It read: 'Neither Service will attempt to restrict in any way the means and weapons used by the other Service in carrying out its functions.

The Army was specifically charged, in connection with Joint overseas movements: 'To provide and operate all vessels for the Army, except when Naval opposition by the enemy is to be expected, in which case they are provided and operated by the Navy.'

In October 1940, the Army Transportation Service had fifteen ocean-going vessels, including eight combination troop transports which carried some cargo, and seven freighters. In mid-December 1940, the War Department received authority to acquire seventeen additional vessels. This addition made the Army's Transport fleet larger than the Navy's Amphibious Force which numbered only 14 transports and eight cargo ships on 18 January 1941 and in late April 1942 had but 18 regular transports attached to the fleets, 13 working up to join, and seven more projected.

Under War Plan 'Rainbow Five,' the Navy was assigned responsibility to: 'Provide sea transportation for the initial movement and continued support of Army and Navy forces overseas. Man and operate the Army Transportation Service.'

The Navy plans and projects underway in 1941 hopefully provided the first installment of personnel and ships for its assigned tasks in joint overseas movements, but it had no personnel earmarked or available for the very considerable chore of 'Man and operate the Army Transportation Service.' Nor, as long as Army troops moved overseas in Army transports, were there naval personnel available or trained to perform the duty set forth in connection with 'landing attacks against shore objectives,' where the Army was given the task of: 'Deployment into boats used for landing, these boats being operated by the Navy.'

The Navy failed either to adequately plan for or, on the outbreak of war, to adequately undertake these two responsibilities despite the fact that in 1941 'Admiral Turner, Director of War Plans, advocated making the Naval Transportation Service a going concern' ready and able to take over the logistic and amphibious duties of the Army Transportation Service.'

Consequently, the Navy was in no position to criticize the Army in the early days of the war for moving ahead rapidly in expanding its amphibious capabilities, because it appeared that the Army would not only have to provide the amphibious transports by which it might journey to foreign shores, but the boats and boat crews needed to make the actual landings during European amphibious operations.

The Army and the Navy proceeded as they did because each had primary authority and responsibility in certain areas relating to amphibious operations. However, coordination and standardization of procedures in training for amphibious warfare in the United States was provided for and effected by the Commanders of the Amphibious Forces, Atlantic and Pacific Fleets, and in overseas areas by the Theater Commanders.

This situation promoted competition, basically friendly though knife-edge keen between the two services. It resulted in rapid progress, some wasteful duplication of effort and spending of money, and tremendous confusion at the soldier and sailor level, who could not understand, for example, the why of Engineer Amphibian Commands which trained Army boat regiments and soldier 'coxswains'.[15]

Admiral King, who as Commander in Chief of the Atlantic Fleet was bossman for Fleet Landing Exercise Seven in February 1941, reported on one aspect of this rivalry as follows:

Two combat teams of the First Division, United States Army, commanded by Brigadier General J. G. Ord, USA, arrived in the Army Transports *Hunter Liggett* and *Chateau Thierry* to take part in the exercise. I soon discovered that they [three Army General Staff Officers] regarded themselves as in a position to criticize the amphibious techniques of the far more experienced Marines. Creeping and walking normally precede an ability to run, and as it seemed to me, that so far as amphibious landings were concerned, the Marines had learned to walk and were beginning to get up speed, while the Army still had to master the art of creeping, was both amused and annoyed by the attitude of these observers.[16]

Despite this indication of a strong belief that the Marines would function better than the Army in the amphibious arena, Admiral King kept a painfully tight rein upon expansion of the personnel of the

Navy. (King was also the one who restrained the amphibious Navy in the early days of 1942, making it impracticable to man the needed transports, cargo ships and amphibious ships and craft.)

Transports with their boat crews were expensive in personnel. Many officers had no great desire to see men who were desperately needed in the explosive expansion of patrol craft and destroyers fighting a seemingly losing battle against the German submarine, diverted into the amphibious arena. Many naval officers believed it would best serve the Navy's war capabilities to let the 'expansion-minded Army' take over certain amphibious duties and suffer the pains and penalties of the expansion.

When the question of 'who should be prepared to do what' in amphibious warfare was raised in the early months of 1942, the Navy's official position was that amphibious operations in island warfare should be a function of the Navy, and that amphibious operations against a continent should be a function of the Army.

The assigned reasons: In the first case landings would be repeated many times, and continuous Naval support is essential; whereas, in the second case, after the initial landing, the Navy's chief interest would be protection of the line of sea communications.

As late as 29 April 1942, the Army was still proposing that it should be responsible for all amphibious operations in the Atlantic area and the Marines in the Pacific area of operations. It was not until early February 1943 that the Navy agreed to undertake the amphibious training of boat operating and maintenance personnel to meet future Army requirements and, based on this promise, the Army agreed to discontinue all amphibious training activities in the United States. The control and assignment of amphibian units and amphibious training activities in overseas theaters were left to theater commanders to determine. This represented a major advance toward assuring that all amphibious troops and all amphibious craft would have the same fundamental indoctrination in amphibious operations.

Amphibious Force Command Relations

Here's how historian Dyer described another extremely controversial subject:

When on 29 April 1942, Admiral King issued his LONE WOLF Plan for the establishment of the South Pacific Amphibious Force, he laid the ground work for a lot of later Marine Corps abuse of RAdm Richmond Kelly Turner. This extremely terse and stimulating order, which made possible the successful WATCHTOWER Operation [Guadalcanal] had this important paragraph:

IX. Coordination of Command

a.   Under the Commander, South Pacific Force, the Commander of the South Pacific Amphibious Force will be in command of the naval, ground and air units assigned to the amphibious forces in the South Pacific area.

b.   The New Zealand Chiefs of Staff are in command of any United Nations units assigned to New Zealand specifically for the land defense of the Commonwealth of New Zealand.

The Commanding General, First Marine Division (Major General Alexander A. Vandegrift, USMC) received registered copy No. 35 of the order. The Commandant of the Marine Corps received five copies.[17]

Once the COMINCH order had been issued, the responsibility for exercising the command lay with Commander Amphibious Force, South Pacific. Rear Admiral Turner exercised command of the Marines during the early months of the WATCHTOWER Operations because the Commander in Chief directed him to do so. There was nothing in either the then current version of the Landing Operations Doctrine, 1938 Revised Fleet Training Publication 167, or in the operations orders or instructions issued by any senior in the chain of command for the WATCHTOWER Operation which watered down the COMINCH directive. This directive was reaffirmed by the Joint Chiefs of Staff on 2 July 1942.[18]

In October 1942, when Marine Commandant LtGen Thomas Holcomb visited Amphibious Force, South Pacific, he suggested the following changes in organization and command relationships to Adm Turner:

a.   Detached the First Marine Corps from the Amphibious Force, SOPAC, and established the Corps Commander on the same echelon of command as Commander Amphibious Force, SOPAC.

b.   Provided that joint planning in the future by COMGENPHIBCORPS and COMPHIBFORSOPAC would be conducted under the control of COMSOPAC.

c.   Provided that after conclusion of the landing phase of an operation, during which Marine units from the Amphibious Force command landed, a task organization for the shore phase of the operation would be established, or the Marine Corps units would revert to Corps command, when and as directed by Commander South Pacific.[19]

For the most part, these changes were implemented. This established a pattern carried out with minor modifications, throughout the Pacific phase of WWII.

Early World War II Lessons Learned

Many valuable lessons were learned from America's first two amphibious operations in WWII. They were totally different operations in many ways. Guadalcanal was a hot, steamy, mosquito-infested island in the Pacific. French Morocco was part of a huge continent. Together, the two operations proved conclusively that amphibious training in all services got a very late start.

Guadalcanal, 7 August 1942

The American invasion of Guadalcanal, code-named WATCH-TOWER, which opened the first U.S. offensive of World War II, was also the first amphibious operation undertaken by the U.S. since 1898. The Marine landings on neighboring Florida and Tulagi Islands faced much more opposition than the Marines who walked ashore at Guadalcanal. In retrospect, the operation started fairly

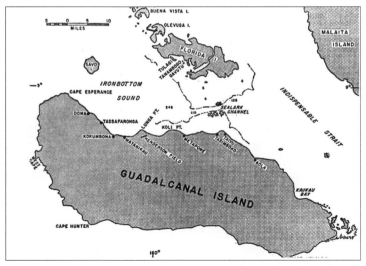

Guadalcanal and Florida Islands. Courtesy of Naval Historical Center.

Guadalcanal Invasion. Amphibious forces off Guadalcanal on D-day, 7 August 1942. Four transports (AP) and a large number of small landing craft are present. Courtesy of National Archives.

smoothly because the daytime landings were a complete surprise to the Japanese, whose scouting aircraft had been grounded by bad weather.

Actually, WATCHTOWER was a desperate gamble. The Navy did not control the sea, making communications anything but secure, and American combat power was stretched thin. Planning was hastily done, there was little intelligence, and logistical support was more idea than reality. It has frequently been described as an 'offensive-defensive action' because it was designed to stop the southward-rolling Japanese.

Bottom-line: It would take 26 weeks of hard fighting to secure what had been occupied in little more than that number of hours because the Japanese, through actions at sea, were able to pour reinforcements onto the island, unopposed for the most part, with night landings.

Tactically: In the sense of coming to grips with the enemy— Guadalcanal was a profitable lesson book. The recommendations of Guadalcanal commanders became doctrine for Allied fighting men the world over. And it was the veteran from the 'Canal who went back to man the new ship or to form the nucleus for a new regiment.

Strategically: Guadalcanal was worth every ship, plane, and life that it cost. The enemy was stopped in his tracks. Task one in the arduous climb to Rabaul was neatly if tardily achieved.

Historian John Lorelli describes an operation order from Admiral Turner to a reinforcement convoy headed for the 'Canal in November 1942 to illustrate the implementation of lessons learned during the first three months of WATCHTOWER:

> Point by point, Turner told his men what he expected: each ship was to hold four rehearsals before reaching the transport area; as many cargo nets as possible were to be loaded beforehand; shore parties were to be the first men on the beach; each transport was to provide a salvage boat; each ship's beach party was to clearly mark its designated section of beach with an 8x6-ft. sign; cargo was to start ashore 'at the earliest possible moment and move as fast as possible'; every ship was to be kept in use continuously and all cargo nets were to be employed. Turner made sure all hands were aware of the stakes. 'It must again be stated, in the most emphatic terms that the safety of our [Guadalcanal] position, our ships, our troops and crews, depends directly on the speed of unloading.' He further emphasized his concern to his captains by encouraging them to 'Give wide publicity to...this plan, and to the expectancy of battle. Drill thoroughly in all measures of preparation.'[20]

VAdm Dyer summed up the lessons learned at Guadalcanal in his book. Here are some paraphrased highlights:

Transports: By and large, the 19 large transports and cargo ships of Task Force 62 that arrived at Guadalcanal/Tulagi on 7 August did not have near enough officers and men to continuously unload over a 72-hour period. It was both good and bad fortune that the Japanese made three air raids and threatened another during the first 48 hours of unloading. For these gave many of the boat crews a breathing spell, and also supplied an urgency to the need to get the unloading job done. So, the first lesson learned at the 'Canal by amphibians was that they just had to have more people in their ships and craft.

The shortage of transport personnel was summarized in the USS *Neville* report this way: 'Due to the physical exhaustive nature of the work on transports during unloading it is essential that transports be fully manned for an operation of this kind.'[21]

Beach Troubles: The second lesson the amphibians learned at

First Division Marines storm ashore across Guadalcanal's beaches on D-Day, 7 August 1942, from the attack transport Barnett (AP-11) and attack cargo ship Formalhaut (AK-22). The invaders were surprised at the lack of enemy opposition. Courtesy of National Archives.

Coast Guardsman directs traffic on beach at Guadalcanal as landing craft unload supplies and equipment from AKs. Courtesy of U.S. Coast Guard.

Guadalcanal was that the logistic support of the troops over the beaches in the first 24 hours had to be both beefed up and stream-lined.

In WATCHTOWER, the Marine plans provided that about half the 1st Pioneer Battalion which totaled about 660 men would be diverted to the Support Group which was assigned the task of close-in ground defense of the beachhead area at Red Beach at Guadalcanal. One platoon of 52 men went to Tulagi. The rest of the battalion had been parceled out to various regiments as reinforcing elements.

With this disposition of Marine labor resources— specially trained and needed for the unloading of logistic support from ship's boats— it is not surprising that logistic chaos took over at the beachhead.

Marines unloading supplies on Guadalcanal Beach, 1942. National Archives.

This was only partially alleviated when Captain Reifsnider ordered each transport and cargo ship to land 15 sailors to assist in handling supplies at the beachhead.[22]

Commander Transports summarized one aspect of the problem: "The statement of the Assistant Beachmaster from the *George F. Elliott* that literally hundreds of Marines were sitting on the beach watching the confusion mount, while hundreds of others were roaming through the coconut groves, etc., is confirmed by reports of officers sent ashore by me to investigate."[23]

The Boat Group Commander, USS *Barnett* wrote: "There were approximately fifteen or twenty men unloading boats and about fifty others in swimming. I beached my boat and started looking for the Beachmaster who could not be found. While looking for the Beachmaster, I saw about one hundred men lounging around under the palm trees eating coconuts, lying down shooting coconuts from the trees; also playing around and paddling about in rubber boats. All of these men were Marines that should have been unloading boats."[24]

The Captain of the *Hunter Liggett* reported: "After dark, conditions reached a complete impasse. It is estimated that nearly one hundred boats lay gunwale to gunwale on the beach, while another fifty boats waited, some of these up to six hours for a chance to land.

No small share of the blame for this delay, which prolonged by nearly twenty-four hours the period when the ships lay in these dangerous waters, would seem to rest with the Marine Corps personnel and organization. The Marine Corps Pioneers, whose function it was to unload the boats and keep the beach clear, were far too few in numbers. As a result much of this work was accomplished by boat crews, and stores which they landed at low water were frequently damaged or destroyed by the rising tide before the Pioneers removed them to safety."[25]

Commander Transport Group XRAY, discussing the delays in unloading caused by the Japanese air attacks, stated: "Notwithstanding the foregoing interruptions, supplies were piling up on the beach faster than could be moved, and by dark there were about 100 loaded boats at the beach and 50 more lying off waiting. It finally became necessary to discontinue unloading for the remainder of the night."[26]

The Captain of the cargo ship *Formalhaut* stated: "Discharging cargo on 24-hour basis—but very slow procedure due to shortage of transportation...unable to have boats unloaded at beach due to working parties there being engaged in repelling enemy snipers."[27]

Over at Tulagi, according to the transport *Neville's* War Diary: "It was not until about midnight that the first word had been received to send the important food rations and ammunition ashore and from then till daylight it went slowly due to insufficient personnel to unload and conflicting orders as to where to land the stores."[28]

Not all the beach trouble was caused by inadequate Pioneer parties. Often the transports and cargo ships overloaded the landing craft: "A considerable number of landing boats, chiefly ramp lighters, were stranded on the beach, adding to the confusion. These boats had been loaded too deeply by the head, and could not be driven far enough up on their particular beach to keep from filling and drowning the engine when the ramp was lowered."[29]

After the landing RAdm Turner wrote: "There were two primary reasons for failure to completely unload. First, the vast amount of unnecessary impediments taken, and second, a failure on the part of the 1st Division to provide adequate and well organized unloading details at the beach. The Marine officers on my staff feel very strongly on these matters—as strongly as I do."[30]

Guadalcanal 1942 Transport President Jackson (AP-37) and Cruiser San Francisco (CA-38) underway during air attack. Naval Historical Center.

In spite of the above, the amphibians unloaded a large percentage of the Marines' logistic support in 26 hours, even though they were interrupted by three Japanese air raids, one of 45 planes, and another of 43, and rumors of other raids which had caused the amphibians to stop unloading and get underway. But the transports and cargo ships did not get 100 percent of the logistic support ashore and that was the least they could do to accomplish their mission and satisfy the Marines.

Intelligence: Our naval intelligence in regard to the Solomons was practically non-existent in 1942. There was little or no knowledge of enemy troop strength. Scant information was available about the topography of the island or the nature of Japanese defenses. Only outdated maps were available. An Army Air Force B-17 carrying two Marine officers flew a reconnaissance mission over Guadalcanal and Tulagi, and photos taken during this mission were used to produce a map of the planned landing area.

Troops: MajGen Alexander Vandegrift only had six weeks to train his 1st Marine Division when he arrived in New Zealand on 12 June 1942—he had expected six months. Despite Vandegrift's concerns, 11,000 Marines landed on Guadalcanal without hindrance from the surprised Japanese. Across Sealark Channel, resistance to the landings on Tulagi and Gavutu varied from isolated shots by snipers to an assault under a hail of machine-gun fire. That the Japanese soldiers and naval landing troops of 1942 were true inheritors of the samurai code of Bushido was made bloody evident.

General Vandegrift later wrote of the "astonishing" tenacity of the Japanese and their willingness to die rather than surrender. Because the Japanese fought under a completely different set of rules, their behavior was incomprehensible to Americans. Every Japanese serviceman knew by heart the Imperial Rescript for Soldiers and Sailors: "Be resolved that honor is heavier then a mountain and death lighter than a feather." One lesson learned the hard way.

Gunfire Support: Unfortunately, all three of the 8-inch gun ships which had specific heavy gunfire support tasks were sunk within 48 hours of the landings, so the marriage of gunfire support duties with the control of boat waves by destroyers had been short and generally unhappy.

Close Air Support: The most important lesson learned in the first two days of Operation WATCHTOWER was that shipboard air controllers had to remain within radio range of both aircraft and the ground units. The *McCawley* had not been specifically built as an amphibious flagship. The demands of providing communications, including the need of the air controllers to coordinate air support, overwhelmed her inadequate radio facilities. None of the units ashore had any direct contact with the aircraft orbiting overhead. Any request for support against a specific target had to be relayed to the *McCawley,* then to the senior air group commander circling overhead, and thence to the attacking aircraft. Trouble with the *McCawley's* radio equipment limited her range to only 8 miles, requiring a destroyer as a relay ship.

APD High-Speed Transports: The 4 converted four-piper World War I Wickes Class destroyers of Transdiv 12, *Colhoun, Gregory, Little* and *McKean,* filled the Marine's need for a rapid ship-to-shore troop delivery system. (Unfortunately all four were lost during the Solomons Operations in 1942-43.) For this reason the "Green Dragon" story is featured in the next chapter as a continuation of "Early WWII Lessons Learned." Keep in mind, the revolutionary new shore-to-shore landing ships and craft would not be available until 1943.

Invasion convoy en route to North Africa carrying troops, materiel and munitions for Operation TORCH. Courtesy of U.S. Navy.

North Africa, 8 November 1942

The North Africa Campaign, code-named Operation TORCH, began on 8 November 1942 when U.S. and British troops under the command of Gen Eisenhower, landed in Casablanca, Morocco and Algiers, and Oran, in Algeria.

The invasion fleet—the largest concentration of Allied naval forces yet assembled—was fortunate not to be intercepted by German reconnaissance aircraft or U-boats, and the German high command, believing that the shipping was en route to besieged Malta, was taken by surprise.

Algiers quickly surrendered, but French troops at Oran and Morocco surprised the invaders by holding out. (The Allies were invading what was a part of the technically neutral country of Vichy France, with which the United States still had diplomatic relations.)

Casablanca was an all-American landing. Anglo-American troops went ashore at Oran and Algiers—with Americans in the first waves in an attempt to reduce French opposition. Admiral Jean Darlau, commander of the Vichy French defending forces, at first agreed to order a cease-fire but his superiors refused. (Darlau would sign a cease-fire agreement with Eisenhower five days later.)

There were many differences between the Guadalcanal and North Africa Campaigns. For starters, the North Africa landings were night

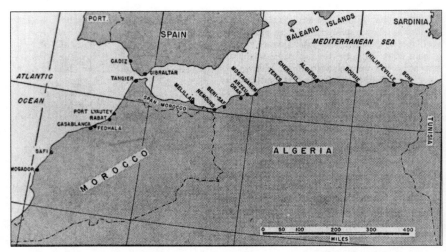

North Africa Operation TORCH Invasion shores. Naval Historical Center.

operations. Second, the French Colonies of Morocco, Algeria, and Tunisia were far to the west of the combat zone, behind the German's Afrika Korps. Third, there were modern ports at Casablanca and Algiers through which the Allied forces could be supported for the drive against the German rear.

The combined Operation TORCH planning staff had faced two serious problems. First was the severe shortage of shipping needed to support all of the proposed landings. A compromise was eventually worked out whereby the U.S. Navy would have responsibility for the three landings on the Moroccan coast and the Royal Navy would be responsible for the two landings on the Mediterranean coast of Algeria.

The second concern was both a political and military question: Would the landings be opposed? Morocco and Algeria were under the control of the collaborationist Vichy French government and no one was sure what they would do.

U.S. Amphibious Forces learned some new lessons in North Africa—mainly the challenges of invading a large continent as opposed to assaulting an island. Unfortunately our Army troops had to experience many of the same lessons learned the hard way by the Marines at Guadalcanal a scant three months earlier.

Many of the 'Canal problems plagued the Navy attack force here

U.S.–U.K. convoy unloads on African beach at St. Leu, Department of Oran. Courtesy of U.S. Army.

too. They could be summed up in six words: shipping, landing parties, and beach troubles.

For starters, the crews of the fleet supply train—mainly large troop transports and cargo ships—were still totally lacking in the small boat seamanship and cargo handling skills needed for amphibious warfare.

Loading of landing craft was excruciatingly slow. Two strong imperatives drive the unloading of an amphibious task force: the first is the pressing need forces ashore have for reinforcements, vehicles, and supplies to sustain the momentum of their assault. The second is that a fleet of transports tied to a single geographical location is too tempting a target to be ignored for long. The defenders know that if the transports can be destroyed or forced to withdraw, the landing must fail.

While the soldiers prepared to continue the battle, unloading the transports continued despite the growing fatigue of the overworked boat crews. Less than two percent of the cargo had been brought ashore on the first day, creating a crying demand for rations, ammunition, and communications gear.

The captain of the transport *Charles Carroll* had this to say on the subject:

> The most glaring deficiency of Operation TORCH was the lack of discipline in boat crews. It is believed that this inadequacy will have to be shared by all those in the chain of command...through the commanding officers of transports to those in higher authority who placed a Herculean responsibility on such immaturely trained men. They were unskilled in handling their boats, they were unlearned in even the simplest elements of seamanship. The supreme test of their training was made under conditions where only experts could hope to succeed part of the time.[31]

Historian John Lorelli described the lack of cargo landing and boat loading skills:

"The Army believed the delay in loading stemmed from poor positioning of the transports and a general lack of trained boat coxswains. The Navy countered that the pooling of boats needed to accommodate the Army's excessive demands for men on the beach was the main problem. The Navy also argued that the soldiers were far too 'sluggish' in embarking in the boats."

The skipper of the *Harris* wrote: "It must in fairness be said...that many of the troops had practically no training and they carried a tremendous amount of equipment on their backs. Much too much and too heavy."

The *Harris'* executive officer also noted that improper stowage of cargo greatly delayed unloading. In several instances, material needed in the first wave was stowed as deep as the fourth deck instead of the first where it should have been.

There is a kernel of truth in the arguments of either side, but the real crux of the matter is that both services were still new to the business of amphibious warfare.

Another frequent problem was boat crews lowering the bow ramp too soon, flooding the boat. These difficulties would be addressed with more intensive training, the formation of boat salvage groups, and the fitting out of a designated repair and salvage ship. On its part, the Army would make salvage part of the training syllabus for engineer units assigned to beach duty.

Landing Craft

Several small landing craft were used in the Guadalcanal and North African campaigns:

1. **Landing Craft Personnel/Large, LCP(L)** The original Higgins boat, a 36-foot assault boat built of plywood with a low, square bow propelled by gasoline or diesel engines. *Capacity:* 30-36 troops or 6,700-8,100 lb. cargo depending on fuel load. *Crew:* 3. *Speed:* 8 knots fully loaded. *Armament:* Two .30 cal. machine guns in Gunner's Cockpits.

2. **Landing Craft Personnel, Ramped, LCP(R)** The 36-foot Landing Craft, Personnel/Ramp, differed from the LCP(L) by the addition of a small bow ramp. Statistics similar to LCP(L). Also can be carried on APD, AKA and APA davits from which they may be lowered when fully loaded.

3. **Landing Craft, Vehicle, LCV** The 36-foot Landing Craft, Vehicle, fitted with a larger bow ramp so that it could land a truck or other vehicle transported on deck, in hold, or on single-or three-tiered davits. Not designed to be lowered when loaded. *Capacity:* One 1-ton truck, or 36 troops, or 10,000 lb. cargo. *Crew:* 3. *Speed:* 9 knots (loaded).

4. **Landing Craft, Mechanized, LCM** The earliest models of the 50-foot Landing Craft, Mechanized, built of steel, diesel-powered and—depending on model— capable of carrying a single tank weighing from 13 1/2-to 30-tons. *Crew:* 4-6. *Speed:* 7 1/2 knots (loaded). *Armament:* Two Lewis or .50-cal. machine guns.

5. **Landing Craft, Vehicle/Personnel, LCVP** Essentially an improved LCV with steering and gunner's cockpits in the hold. Design was soon standard for all ships and superseded LCV in production. *Capacity:* 36 troops, or 6,000 lb. vehicle or 8,100 lb. general cargo. Can be lowered when loaded from davits. *Crew:* 3. *Speed:* 9 knots. *Armament:* Two .30-cal. machine guns.

Author's Note: Appendix "A" to this book provides the reader with a brief overview of the many amphibious force vessels used by the United States during World War II ranging from large cargo ships and troop transports—with their small ship-to-shore landing craft—to the larger shore-to-shore landing ships and craft.

LCP(L) shown beaching its troops (Was soon superseded by the LCP(R) and LCVP.) Courtesy of U.S. Navy.

LCP(R) Personnel assault boat similar to the LCP(L), with a ramp added to decrease debarkation time. Soon superseded by the LCVP. Courtesy U.S. Navy.

LCV Small vehicle carrier for initial and subsequent landing waves. Also used as personnel and cargo carrier. Was superseded in production by the LCVP. Courtesy of U.S. Navy.

LCM(2) Capable of landing a single tank or motor vehicle on beach. Cargo and personnel carrying are secondary functions. Early U.S. model was generally superseded by LCM(3). Courtesy of U.S. Navy.

LCVP Capacity for 36 troops or 6,000 lb. vehicle or 8,100 lb. cargo can be lowered when loaded from ship davits. Courtesy of U.S. Navy.

Beaching Problems The lack of seamanship training coupled with deficiencies in organization made for a supply officer's nightmare. John Lorelli:

The lack of training in basic boat handling skills, the extreme difficulties inherent in coordinating boat movements at night, and the unfamiliarity of the soldiers with debarking quickly proved it was going to take far longer than expected to get the troops into the boats. First came the problem of forming boat pools. The number of soldiers assigned to the first wave far exceeded the boat capacity of any given transport.

The landings across the various beaches were generally successful, but each had its share of difficulties. There were expected
failures in execution: some scout boats were out of position, landing craft missed their rendezvous points, and other boats landed
hundreds of yards, even miles, from their assigned beaches. There
were collisions, engine failures, faulty compasses, and boats holed
by rocks.

Surf conditions varied from excellent to moderate but the inex-
perience of most coxswains immediately began to take a toll on
the landing craft. One ship lost eighteen of twenty-five boats employed in the first wave and of the remaining seven, five were lost
when the second wave came ashore. Except for two ships manned
by the Coast Guard with a more solid core of experienced boat
handlers, the other transports suffered disproportionately high
losses of landing craft. Besides the normal difficulties of beaching
a landing craft, the large number of inexperienced coxswains had
been asked to beach on an ebbing tide, a problem of seamanship
that was beyond most of their capabilities.

The continuing problem of excessive wastage of landing craft
led the commanding general of the 34th Infantry Division to suggest that the Army should take charge once the troops got into the
landing craft. General Eisenhower's response was in keeping with
his desire to keep efforts focused on the real enemy: he reminded
his subordinate that the Navy has control until the troops are ashore,
then the Army takes over. [32]

Once the troops were ashore, the now familiar litany of problems
associated with managing the flow of supplies was present at all
landings. Historian Lorelli described the confusion on the beaches
at Fedhala and Safi in French Morocco the first day:

Sufficient troops were ashore at Fedhala but the scene at the
beach was one of men working desperately to avoid chaos. Cargo
handlers worked through the night of 8-9 November; a situation
reminiscent of Guadalcanal resulted. What was coming ashore was
not getting off the beaches or piers either quickly or in an organized way. Army shore parties had been established, but as with
the Marine Pioneer battalions in the Pacific, their numbers were
too few and their organization flawed.

Naval working parties from the transports joined the Army men,
but the work lagged. The Op-Plan gave no single officer sufficient
authority to exert proper control over the combined effort. Com-

munication between beaches was also a problem as the Navy radios proved completely unsuitable for the rough treatment they received.

Among post-invasion recommendations were that the beach parties should be provided and commanded by the Army and that any naval shore parties be equipped with Army radios. A good deal of the congestion was caused by too few bulldozers to free bogged-down wheeled vehicles, and a shortage of trucks to move the supplies to dumps; 90 percent of the assault troops were landed on the first day, but only 16 percent of the vehicles. Though local labor was belatedly recruited into service, there would be little respite for the hard-pressed working parties until the transports finished unloading.

The Army response to its experience in North Africa was to beef up the number of men and increase the handling equipment assigned to shore parties.

The logistics problem was also present at Safi, though not to the same extent. Space in the harbor was limited, but most of the unloading was accomplished at pier side rather than across beaches. The same problem of insufficient motor transport plagued efforts at Safi and resulted in a jumbled mountain of supplies piling up open to pilferage and exposed to enemy action.[33]

Construction Priority Milestones

Thanks to the vision and commitment of career Marines like LtCol Ellis, Lt Krulack and a handful of brass like Gen Smith and RAdm Turner and with the support of President Roosevelt—with some well deserved prodding by Winston Churchill and the Royal Navy—we had some much needed small landing craft under construction when the Japanese made their sneak attack on Pearl Harbor on 7 Dec. 1941.

> *Let there be built great ships which can cast upon a beach, in any weather, large numbers of the heaviest tanks.*
>
> —Winston Churchill

January 1942 Landing craft construction was still relatively low on the Navy's shipbuilding priority list for three primary reasons:
- The Navy's lack of experience in amphibious warfare
- The pressing need for more combatant vessels
- Amphibious ships were still considered auxiliaries and second-rate duty to Navy career men.

March 1942 A Joint Planning Committee concluded that the shortage of landing ships and craft justified higher shipyard priorities to meet the projected needs of planners, e.g., 4,000 craft for the Pacific theater alone.

April 1942 President Roosevelt, as Commander-in-Chief, ordered an even higher priority for landing craft.

July 1942 The projected need for some 12,000 landing craft convinced Adm King to put landing craft on a par with combatants.

August 1942 Roosevelt, in his roundabout way, gave his "approval" to interfere with other shipbuilding when/if necessary. From that point forward, landing craft construction was top dog on the priority totem pole.

Higgins Landing Craft

The Higgins boat was a pivotal factor in the outcome of World War II. No other landing craft transported so many men and cargo during the war.

Higgins based his boat's design on a shallow-draft speedboat he invented in the 1930s to operate in 18 inches of water. It would land without a dock, while running over bogs and debris in Louisiana's murky waterways, to satisfy the needs of fur trappers and oil company drilling operators. Responding to these needs, Higgins developed the spoonbill-bow Eureka, the direct ancestor of the famous Higgins boats.

Andrew Jackson Higgins, the founder of Higgins Industries, had a running fight with Washington bureaucracy during the late 1930s and early 1940s. The Navy's Bureau of Ships—which had taken over the combined functions of the Bureau of Constructiona and Repair, and the Bureau of Engineering—considered Higgins an arrogant small boat builder and a pain in its side, until the spring of 1941, when some Marine Corps brass, including then Captain Victor H.

Krulak, met with Higgins to discuss the Corps' needs. Out of this meeting came the Eureka, with a ramp to replace the rounded bow, and the preliminary designs for a tank lighter which evolved rapidly into a 45-foot tank landing craft.

Tests were completed on the 36-foot ramped Eureka and 45-foot tank lighters in late May and early June of 1941, and Higgins soon became the nation's number one assault boat builder. His work force had grown from 691 in December of 1940, to more than 1,600 in June 1941. He had proven that with his LCP, LCVP, and now his LCM, that his company could design and produce the type of boats that the amphibious forces required.

Higgins soon expanded into eight separate Louisiana plants, employing over twenty thousand workers. At the peak of production, the combined output of his plants exceeded 700 boats a month. His total output for the Allies during World War II was 20,094 boats, a production record for which Higgins Industries several times received the Army-Navy "E" (for Excellence), the highest award that the armed forces could bestow upon a company.

Higgins Operators School

As a result of his interaction with the military, Higgins realized that proper design and high-quality construction were not enough to guarantee his boats' success. He had to be certain the military knew how to use them. The natural tendency of a boat operator is to reduce speed when a boat runs aground on a sandbar. A landing craft operates full throttle and continues to do so until it clears the bar. Even when troops are debarking on the beach, the engines continue running wide open. This procedure is extremely difficult to teach a coxswain to accept if in civilian life he had been trained to do the reverse. Therefore, Higgins knew that if his boats were to be successful, his personnel would have to teach the enlisted men and officers the proper techniques. The military agreed fully.

In July 1941, Higgins established the Higgins Boat Operators and Marine Engine Maintenance School at the request of Admiral Randall Jacobs, Captain Robert Emmett, Commander Red Jamieson, and General Holland Smith. As the Higgins school increased its enrollment, it also expanded its facilities and curriculum.

Higgins estimated that his company had trained more than thirty thousand men in amphibious operations and the care and maintenance of landing craft by the end of the war, at no cost to the government. An additional four thousand men were trained in celestial navigation. He stated, "I personally entertained at my home every member of the amphibious schools, and all the PT squadrons, both officers and men, and I gave the privates and the gobs the same kind of liquor I gave the officers—and I drank some of it myself." [34]

Amphibious Training Bases

As mentioned earlier, the construction of landing ships and craft in early 1942 created an obvious need for special training in amphibious operations, which, in turn, resulted in the establishment of Amphibious Training Bases (ATBs). The first of these bases was established in the summer of 1942 at Solomons, Maryland. Here's a U.S. Navy Bureau of Yards and Docks (BuDocks) summary of stateside amphibious base construction during WWII.[35]

Early in February 1942 the Commander in Chief of the Atlantic Fleet recommended that a training center for landing exercises be established in the Chesapeake Bay area. The letter of intent authorizing the contractor to proceed with the building was issued 23 June 1942, and field work was begun less than a week later.

Solomons, Maryland The contract called for the construction, at the mouth of the Patuxent River, of a complete base for a complement of 200 officers and 2,000 men. Subsequent construction enlarged the facilities to care for 940 officers and 6,650 men. With the African invasion imminent, the base was rushed to "usable completion" by the end of August.

Little Creek, Virgina Work was barely under way at Solomons before similar facilities in another Chesapeake Bay area—at Little Creek and on Willoughby Spit, both areas in close proximity to the naval operating base at Norfolk—were begun on 18 July 1942 under the same pressure as the Solomons base to meet the North African deadline. Little Creek was "usable complete" within a month, and the base was commissioned on the first of September. The Little Creek base ultimately included Camp Bradford, which was added in November 1942, and additional adjacent areas, becoming the largest of

Guadalcanal and North Africa landings called for intensive practice.
Landing Craft swarm to beach in invasion maneuvers in the peaceful waters
of Chesapeake Bay. Courtesy of U.S. Navy.

the amphibious training bases, with approximately 1,400 buildings affording facilities for 25,000 officers and men.

Fort Pierce, Florida By the beginning of 1943, a third large training center had been constructed at Fort Pierce on the Atlantic Coast, about midway between Miami and Daytona Beach, on 9,000 acres of leased land.

Coronado, California In July 1943, work was begun at Coronado in the San Diego area on a base to service amphibious operations in the Pacific. It was commissioned January 15, 1944. In August of that year, an addition to the base was established at Fort Emory, about 4 miles south of Coronado, on land taken over from the Army. The combined stations eventually had a capacity in excess of 16,000 officers and men.

Smaller bases were also built at Ocracoke, North Carolina; Panama City, Florida; Galveston, Texas; and Morro Bay, California.

Luck can be attributed to a well-conceived plan carried out by a well-trained and indoctrinated task group.

—Fleet Admiral Chester Nimitz

CHAPTER 2

APD Destroyer Transports

APD History

The APD evolved during the late 1930s and pre-war '40s to fill a projected need of the Marines for a rapid troop delivery system on hostile shores.[1] According to Marine historian Major Jon T. Hoffman, the first mention of destroyer transports came in a 1st Marine Brigade report on Fleet Landing Exercises 3 (FLEX 3). Brigadier General James J. Meade suggested in that February 1937 document that destroyers might solve the dual problem of a shortage of amphibious transports and fire support. With such ships, troops could move quickly close into shore and disembark under protection of the ships' guns.

Hoffman described the transition of the first experimental four-piper into an APD:

The Navy agreed to experiment with one of its flush-deck, four-stack destroyers. It had built a large number of these during World War I and most were now in mothballs.

In November 1938, the Navy reclassified the USS *Manley* (DD - 74) as a miscellaneous auxiliary (AG-28). After a few weeks of hasty work in the New York Navy Yard, the ship served as a transport for Marine units in the Caribbean. In the fall of 1939, *Manley* went back into the yards for a more extensive conversion. Workers removed all torpedo tubes, one gun, two boilers, and their stacks. That created a hold amidships for cargo and troops. The Chief of Naval Operations made it a rush job so the ship would be available for FLEX 6 in early 1940.

Company A, 1st Battalion, 5th Marines, was the first unit to use the revamped *Manley*. It used rubber boats to execute its 23 February 1940 assault landing against Culebra in the Caribbean.

Satisfied by the utility of the destroyer transport, the Navy redesignated *Manley* yet again, this time as the lead ship of a new class, APD-1. The APD designation denoted a high-speed transport.[2]

By the end of 1940, the Navy yards had reactivated five of *Manley's* sister ships and converted them in the same fashion.

These original six APDs would be the only ones available until the Navy rushed to complete more in the aftermath of Pearl Harbor.[3]

Keep in mind, the new landing ships and craft (LCTs, LCIs, and LSTs) were not even under construction at this point. More than a year would pass before their arrival in the South Pacific. Marine historian Hoffman completed his profile on the APDs with these words:

As the two raider battalions moved out into the Pacific, so did the APDs. All six ships [*Manley, Colhoun, Gregory, Little, McKean,* and *Stringham*] saw service in the Solomons campaign, but only *Manley* (APD-1) and *Stringham* (APD-6) survived.

Japanese bombers sank *Colhoun* (APD-2) on 30 August 1942, just after it had transferred a company of the 1st Raiders from Tulagi to Guadalcanal.

Enemy destroyers sank *Gregory* (APD-3) and *Little* (APD-4) in the early morning hours of 5 September 1942 after the two transports had participated with the 1st Raiders in a reconnaissance of Savo Island.

A torpedo bomber would end the existence of *McKean* (APD-5) on 17 November 1943 as she ferried troops to Bougainville.

Marine Raider Battalions Organized

"Howling Mad" Smith (then Brigadier General Holland M. Smith, USMC), commanded the 1st Marine Brigade during the FLEX 6 and 7 exercises in the Caribbean. By 1 February 1941, the 1st Marine Brigade—the largest Marine unit at the time—was redesignated the 1st Marine Division.

Smith was a pioneer in developing U.S. amphibious landing concepts. In June 1941, he commanded the Amphibious Force Atlantic Fleet (AFAF), which consisted of the 1st Marine Division and the Army's 1st Infantry Division. During maneuvers in North Carolina, he embarked the 1st Battalion, 5th Marines in the first six APDs and made it an independent command reporting directly to his headquarters.

The AFAF commander had not randomly selected the 1st Battalion, 5th Marines, for this role. In June 1941 he personally had picked LtCol Merritt A. "Red Mike" Edson to command that battalion, and had designated it to serve permanently with the Navy's APD squadron. General Smith began to refer to Edson's outfit as the "light battalion" or the "APD battalion."

By mid-February 1942, with the United States now at war, the Marine's MajGen Commandant designated two organizations as Marine Raider Battalions. MajGen Merritt A. Edson's group became the 1st Raiders on 16 February; BGen Evans F. Carlson's outfit was designated the 2nd Raiders three days later.

In June 1942, General Smith went to the West Coast to take command of the Pacific Fleet's amphibious force, and to organize and train Marines for the Pacific War. (In 1943-44 he would direct the Marine-Army landings in the Marshalls and Marianas.)

Four-Piper Conversions

The main conversion objectives were accommodations for assault troops and the means to efficiently embark and disembark them.

Accommodations were provided by removing the two boilers from fireroom No.1 and fitting the space with pipe-frame bunks and sanitary facilities. The new two-level troop space could sleep 3 officers and 144 enlisted men. As many as 200 troops could be carried for short trips.

The USS Ward (DD-139) was a flush-decker, and a four-piper, and in dazzle camouflage looked exactly like dozens of others, except for her hull number painted under the bridge at the break of the well deck. Courtesy of First Shot Naval Vets.

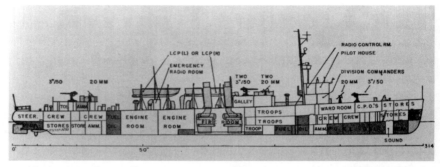

Early APD High-Speed Destroyer Transports were converted WWI flush-deck destroyers designed to land Marine raiding parties on hostile shores. ONI/226.

APD Destroyer Transport after conversion. Note LCP(R) Higgins boats on davits. ONI/226.

New diesel oil fuel tanks were installed under the troop space for use by the new landing boats. The portholes below the main deck were eliminated, and all excess paint was chipped away to reduce fire hazard and topside weight.

Embarkation Objectives were achieved by removing the mainmast and the four triple torpedo tube mounts, and installing heavy gravity-type davits between the shelter deck amidships and the after deckhouse. The davits could accommodate the new LCP(R) assault boats capable of carrying 36 troops, one small vehicle, or up to 5 tons of cargo.

Armament changes were significant. Four 3"/50 dual purpose rifles replaced the WWI-vintage 4"/50 surface guns and seven 20-mm antiaircraft guns took the place of two .50-cal. machine guns.

The USS Dent (APD-9) steams close aboard the Ward (APD-16) to exchange messages. Courtesy Four Stack Naval Vets.

Of course, not all APDs were armed the same way. Later on, a few lucky APDs received 40-mm singlemounts.

The main change in outward appearance was the loss of the two forward stacks, the cluster of landing craft amidships, and the mottled green and brown camouflage coat to better hide along jungle coasts. The Marine Raiders lost no time dubbing the APDs "Green Dragons."

Specification Notes: Full load displacement went from 1,247 to 1,600 tons; full load draft from 9'8" to 11'4"; speed from 34 knots to about 28; and ships complement from 131 to 116 officers and enlisted men. Troop capacity for the new APDs: 3 officers and 144 enlisted men.[4]

Curtis G. Clark, CWO3, USN (Ret.) and Secretary/Treasurer of Four Stack APD Veterans, recalled the noise aboard the *Talbot* (APD-7): "Underway the noise level increased in all areas, especially in the engine room and fireroom and the noise from these areas carried into some of the living spaces as well.

"Combat was a different story, depending on what we were doing. In amphibious operations, boats were being lowered, troops embarked, boats hoisted etc., with or without gunfire. Underway and during air attacks or shelling beach areas, the noise was unbearable anywhere on the ship. The ship was too small to cover up any of these sounds."

A total of 273 flush-deckers were built between 1918-1922 including the 50 lend-lease destroyers that went to England in 1940. They were built by eleven shipyards—eight on the East Coast and three on the West Coast.[5]

The U.S. Navy—with some prodding by the Marines—ordered 26 more flush-decker conversions shortly after Pearl Harbor. Six more APDs were commissioned in 1942, fourteen in 1943, and seven in 1944. In addition, the Navy ordered 95 Destroyer Escorts converted to the APD configuration of which 40 were commissioned in 1944 and 55 in 1945.[6]

The Amphibious Task Ahead

Consider this: On 1 October 1939, when World War II was getting underway in Europe, the Navy had only two large transports (APs) in commission. They operated directly under the Chief of Naval Operations in logistic support of overseas commands, largely in the personnel area. There were no amphibious forces. By 15 October 1940 there were two additional large amphibious transports (APs) in commission in the Fleet, the *Barnett* (AP-11) and the *McCawley* (AP-10), and five destroyer-type transports: *Manley, Colhoun, Gregory, Little* and *McKean.*

By September 1941, the 36-foot assault landing boats had been adopted as standard, but their availability had not caught up with the demand.

By 23 October 1941, there were 30 large transports (needing 816 landing boats) and 11 AKs (needing 80 landing boats) in commission, being procured or converted.[7] But the Navy had only 16 APs, all in the Atlantic Fleet. In addition there were five large amphibious cargo ships (AKs) and six destroyer hull transports (APDs) in the Atlantic Fleet, but only two AKs in the Pacific Fleet, making a total of 29 amphibious ships.[8] But still no Amphibious Force!

On 14 March 1942, and 10 April 1942 respectively, the Amphibious Forces of the Atlantic and Pacific Fleets were finally created in accordance with instructions from Adm Ernest King, COMINCH, and in due time all amphibious units within the two Fleets were assigned to them.

Organizational rosters issued close to these dates show that there were twelve APs, four AKs and two APDs in the Atlantic Fleet and six APs, two AKs and three APDs in the Pacific Fleet, when the Amphibious Forces were established as separate entities. And this was only four to five months before Guadalcanal! Any wonder the Guadalcanal campaign was dubbed a "shoestring operation"?

Thanks to the foresight of Marine Corps planners and strategists like Marine Corps Generals James Meade and Holland Smith, we had just enough amphibious resources to launch a shoestring operation in mid-1942.

Looking back with the benefit of hindsight, the Corps had the support of very few naval officers in the 1930s in its quest for improved landing craft. For example, the Fleet Landing Exercises at the time still featured landings made using standard ship's boats. These were not designed for heavy surf conditions or for crossing coral reefs. Most restrictive was their size—each could hold only a few troops. The Marines argued that using these boats made it impossible to put enough men on shore to establish and hold a beachhead. A behind-the-scenes struggle over the design of better landing craft ensued.

Some Marine Corps officers had been working with Andrew Higgins since 1934 on a small, shallow-draft boat that could easily carry a complement of men up to a presumably hostile beach. Higgins—a major story in himself—had developed such a craft in 1927 for use by oil-men in the Louisiana bayous.

By 1939 these landing craft were fitted with bow ramps that expedited the unloading of troops and materiel. This early design became the model for a whole series of landing craft developed during World War II. However, there were few available when the war began, and as late as the Guadalcanal landings, many Marines were still being ferried ashore in ship's boats.

To support their special operations, the US Marines requested a fast sea-borne transport from the Navy. The USS *Manley* (DD-74) was reclassified as AG-2 on 28 November 1938 and became the first of the future APDs.

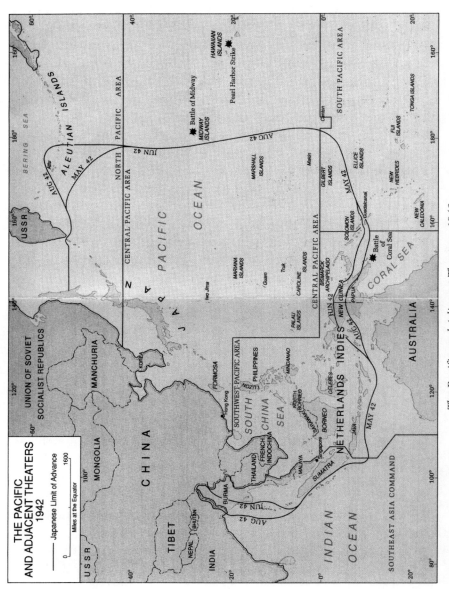

The Pacific and Adjacent Theaters, 1942.

Guadalcanal-Tulagi Operation

The Guadalcanal campaign was unique among amphibious operations conducted in the Pacific during World War II. Neither the United States nor Japan enjoyed an overwhelming naval superiority that, in almost every other case, ensured victory for the greater force. Relative equality made the naval forces of each side a constant threat to the supply lines of the other. Consequently, both sides relied upon the high-speed transport, converted destroyers that were well armed and fast enough to evade more powerfully armed warships.[9]

APD Action Highlights

The big APA transports off-loaded the 5th Marines as planned, and at 0909 on 7 August the first assault boats ground to a halt on Red Beach. Soon after, the three battalions of Cate's 1st Marine Regiment landed and began to advance southwest toward Mount Austen. Meeting no resistance, they cautiously moved toward their day's objective: Alligator Creek, two miles west of the landing beach.

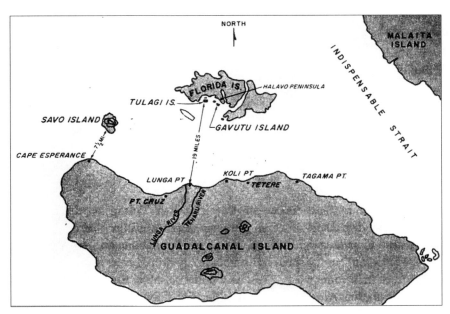

Guadalcanal and Tulagi. Courtesy U.S. Navy.

Meanwhile, Marine units commanded by the assistant division commander, BGen Rupertus, hit Florida and Tulagi islands as well as the smaller islands of Gavutu and Tanambogo. The 1st Battalion, 2nd Marines landed on the tip of Florida Island and met no resistance. This was not the case with the 1st Raider Battalion assaulting Tulagi or the 1st Parachute Battalion at Gavutu. These landings were made on 7 August by *Colhoun* (APD-2), *Gregory* (APD-3), *Little* (APD-4) and *McKean* (APD-5). The Raiders, after securing their beachhead and advancing into the town, were hit with heavy mortar and machine-gun fire. During the night of 8 August, they beat back four major frontal attacks, then systematically cleared most of the caves of surviving Japanese the next day. After Tulagi was cleared, most of the Marines were moved to Guadalcanal.

The APDs provided the first of many, many contingents of men and supply support the early evening of 15 August—only six days after TF 62 had left—using four destroyer transports, carrying a total of 120 tons of aviation gasoline, lubricating oil, bombs, spare parts, and 120 aviation ground personnel mostly from CUB One.[10]

Invasion operations for the Marines always included debarking down the nets with full packs and combat gear. Those not going manned the rails. Courtesy of First Shot Naval Vets.

Manley (APD-1) reached Espiritu Santo, New Hebrides Islands on 14 August 1942. She immediately loaded special cargo for Guadalcanal. Loaded with bombs, ammunition, and gasoline, she and *Stringham* (APD-6) got underway on 16 August. At the destination, they exchanged their cargo for wounded Marines and were back at Espiritu Santo on the 19th.

Broad scale but irregular logistic support for the Marines commenced when store ships *Alhena* (AK-26), *Formalhaut* (AK-22), and the *McFarland* (AVD-14) loaded with aviation gasoline drums, plus six APDs loaded with rations arrived at Guadalcanal on 21-22 August 1942. They landed over 2,000 tons of logistic support including 200 tons of rations, some personnel of the 2nd Marine Regiment, plus equipment and supplies.[11]

At 1400, 30 August 1942, when *Colhoun* was on patrol off Guadalcanal, she was hit by a Japanese bomber. The first bombs wrecked the ship's boats and after davits, and started a diesel fire in the boat wreckage. In a second attack, a succession of hits on the starboard side brought down the foremast, blew two 20mm guns and one 4-inch gun off the ship, and damaged the engineering spaces. Two more direct hits killed all the men in the after deck house. Tank lighters from Guadalcanal rescued the survivors before *Colhoun* sank. Fifty-one men were killed and 18 wounded in this last fight of the *Colhoun*. As she discharged stores on the beach that afternoon, *Little* witnessed the awful destruction of her sister ship.

USS Colhoun (APD-2) was sunk by Japanese bombers on 30 August 1942, just after she had transferred a company of the 1st Raiders fram Tulagi to Guadalcanal. Courtesy USMC.

The three remaining APDs in the area, *Little, Gregory,* and *McKean* continued to support and help supply the Marines.

As dusk fell every evening, control of the disputed waters of Iron Bottom Sound passed to the Japanese transport destroyers of the *Tokyo Express* which sped down the Slot to carry on their troop build-up. The question of who dominated the black night-time waters of the Sound was settled—at least temporarily.

On 3 September, General Geiger arrived to assume command of the 1st Marine Aircraft Wing. His task was to see that the U.S. Navy retained control of the approaches to the island in the daylight hours so that supplies, ammunition, and the vital gasoline could be brought in by the APDs and the occasional freighter.

On 4 September 1942, APDs *Gregory* and *Little* were returning to their anchorage at Tulagi after transferring a Marine Raider Battalion to Savo Island. The night was so inky black, with a low haze obscuring all landmarks, that the ships decided to remain on patrol rather than risk threading their way through the dangerous channel. As they steamed between Guadalcanal and Savo island at ten knots, three Japanese destroyers (*Yadachi, Hatsuyuki* and *Murakumo*) entered the Slot undetected to bombard American shore positions.

At 0056 on the morning of 5 September, *Gregory* and *Little* saw dashes of gunfire which they assumed came from a Japanese submarine until radar showed four targets. Apparently a cruiser had joined the three destroyers. While the two out-gunned but gallant ships were debating whether to close for action or depart quietly and undetected, the decision was taken out of their hands. A Navy pilot had also seen the gunfire and, assuming it came from a Japanese submarine, dropped a string of five flares almost on top of the two APDs.

Gregory and *Little,* silhouetted against the blackness were spotted immediately by the Japanese destroyers who opened fire at 0100. *Gregory* brought all her guns to bear, but was desperately overmatched. Less than three minutes after the fatal flares had been dropped, she was dead in the water and beginning to sink. Two boilers had burst and her decks were a mass of flames. Her Skipper, LCmdr H.F. Bauer, himself seriously wounded, gave the word to aban-

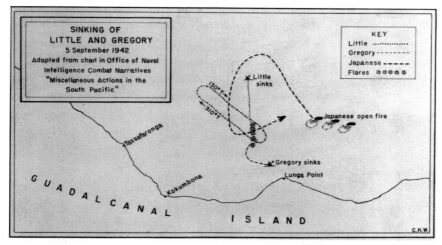

Sinking of Little (APD-4) and Gregory (APD-3) 5 September 1942 off Lunga Point, Guadalcanal. Courtesy Samuel L. Morison.

don ship and *Gregory's* crew reluctantly took to the water. Bauer ordered two companions to aid another crewman yelling for help, and was never seen again. For his brave and gallant conduct, LCmdr Bauer posthumously received the Silver Star.

Little opened fire on the enemy destroyers, but took direct hits from salvos that left her helpless and ablaze by 0115. At 0123, with all of *Gregory's* and most of *Little's* crew in the water, the Japanese ships began shelling again—aiming not at the crippled ships, but at their helpless crews in the water. All but 22 of *Gregory's* crew survived, six of them swimming through the night all the way to Guadalcanal. *Gregory* sank stern first some forty minutes after the firing had begun and was followed two hours later by *Little*.[12]

Fleet Admiral Nimitz praised the courageous ships after their loss: "Both of these small vessels fought as well as possible against overwhelming odds. With little means, they performed duties vital to the success of the campaign."

On 8 September 1942, *Manley* took part in a surprise landing by the First Raider Battalion on Taivu Point, Guadalcanal. The Marines were put ashore at 0500 and were reinforced by paratroopers at 1130. *Manley* took the opportunity to bombard Tasimbobo village. The raid was a big success. Enemy stores, ammunition, and equipment were destroyed and many 75-mm guns were pulled off into deep water by Higgins boats. Larger guns were dynamited and their ammunition sunk. Reembarkation was completed by 1830 and *Manley* returned to Lunga Point to put the Raiders ashore. As *Manley* was unloading, the shore station ordered her to clear out at highest speed since a raid by Japanese heavy units was expected momentarily. With 200 Marines, including wounded and dead on board, she remained in the area until 2110 when she hoisted all boats and headed out Lengo Channel with *McKean.*

Supplies were desperately needed for the troops on Guadalcanal, and as soon as the remaining ships could refuel and load, they were sent out again. Various combat situations occurred during these supply convoys. During the approach to Tulagi, supply ship *McFarland* joined the formation and, on the afternoon of September 21, became the target for a single torpedo from an enemy submarine which missed astern.

On the morning of 23 September 1942, *Manley* received orders to take torpedoed destroyer *Blue* in tow and made repeated attempts to do so until destroyer *Henley* arrived to take over the job. It was impossible to get *Blue* into harbor before nightfall, and with a Japanese surface force approaching the area, it became necessary to scuttle her. Ninety-nine men were taken aboard *Manley* who was then detailed to screen supply ship *Fomalhaut.* Only two hours of fuel remained by the time she arrived back at Espiritu Santo.

During the latter part of 1942 and early 1943, the land, sea, and air struggle for Guadalcanal continued. In late January 1943, the remaining enemy soldiers on Guadalcanal had withdrawn to Cape Esperance and were taken off by destroyers in early February. Except for mopping up, the battle for Guadalcanal Island was over.

On 29 January 1943, rookie *Sands* (APD-13) was detached from duties at Tulagi and ordered to accompany the tug *Navaho* (AT-64) to Rennel Island to assist the cruiser *Chicago* (CA-29). The next morning, the tug took the damaged cruiser in tow and *Sands* joined the five escorting destroyers in a circular screen. The eight ships began making their way to Tulagi. At 1620, the formation was attacked by Japanese torpedo planes. Anti-aircraft guns on *Sands* and the destroyers fired on the intruders. *Chicago* took another torpedo

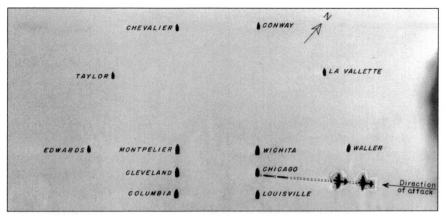

Torpedoing of Chicago *(CA-29) at 1945 on 29 January 1943 during the Battle of Rennell Island. Courtesy Samuel L. Morison.*

and 20 minutes later, sank. Six officers and 56 enlisted men went down with the ship. *Sands* picked up 300 survivors and took them to Espiritu Santo. Another 749 survivors were collected by *Navajo, Edwards* and *Waller.*

Numerous errors of judgment contributed to the loss of *Chicago.* One historian labeled the mismanaged affair "tactical ineptitude of the first order." We'll take a closer look at this tragic loss in my next volume on the Solomons Campaigns.

Guadalcanal Evacuated 1-9 February 1943

Unknown to the Americans, the enemy had chosen the night of 1-2 February to begin his big evacuation —Operation "KE." Consequently, General Alexander Patch, USA, proceeded to land a regimental combat team on the southwest coast of Guadalcanal to plug the enemy's Tokyo Express reinforcement channel near Cape Esperance. The troop lift: six "earlybird" LCTs (landing craft, tank) that had just arrived at Tulagi the previous month and guideship APD *Stringham* screened by DDs *Fletcher, Radford, Nicholas* and *DeHaven* and by Henderson Field fighter planes.

After the seven-hour trip around the Cape, the troops and their gear were barely deposited on Verahue beach when all hell broke out. RAdm Morison:

Destroyers *DeHaven* and *Nicholas,* escorting back to Ironbottom Sound three LCTs which had completed unloading, had reached a point about three miles south of Savo Island. *Radford* and *Fletcher* were still on the other side of Cape Esperance escorting the other landing craft and, by some unexplained mismanagement, they had all the fighter escort, leaving *DeHaven* and *Nicholas* bare. Enemy dive-bombers winged in over Florida Island at 1450 and turned toward Savo Island. Guadalcanal radio hastily broadcast a warning which put both destroyers and LCTs very much on the alert.

Within a few minutes the formation of 14 Vals appeared. On board *DeHaven* there was a delay in getting permission to shoot, and it was not until six of the enemy peeled off from a low altitude of 5,000 feet that the destroyer fought back. Three bombs hit *DeHaven* and a near-miss mined the hull. Commander Charles E. Tolman was killed by a direct hit on the bridge; the ship settled quickly by the bow and, within two minutes, was on her way down to the Ironbottom graveyard with 167 of her crew.

During this brief action the machine guns of LCT-63 and LCT-181 shot down a plane, and after it was over, the landing craft rescued 146 survivors including 38 wounded. Destroyer *Nicholas* (Lieutenant Commander Andrew J. Hill), which attracted the attention of eight Japanese planes, got out of it with only near-misses that damaged the steering gear and killed two men.[13]

In the next chapter, Ensign John McNeill, LCT-159 skipper describes the above action from his perspective.

At 1625, February 9, in a village on the Tenamba River, General Patch's 2nd Battalion of the 132nd Infantry coming from the west, met the 2nd Battalion of the 161st Infantry coming from the east. General Patch radioed Admiral Halsey: "Tokyo Express no longer has terminus on Guadalcanal."

The February-May 1943 period—dubbed "The Lull Between Storms"—was relatively quiet as the Allied forces prepared for the leap-frogging amphibious operations from Guadalcanal to Bougainville. But due to space limitations in this volume, that will be the subject of our next book. Rest assured that we will continue to chronicle the participation of the Green Dragons in these campaigns.

The following chart lists the campaigns and ultimate fate of the 13 APDs that served in the Solomons between August 1942 and December 1943. Five, or 38%, were sunk as a result of enemy action.

Now that's hazardous sea duty!

Curt Clark added this aside to the APD story: "As the battle for the Solomons progressed, the APD crews became adept at 'less than regulation' resupply and modification. 'Their Marines' learned they could depend on the Green Dragons for quick transportation, gunfire support, hot coffee, a hot meal, or a hot shower. Supply dumps

WWII BATTLE HISTORY OF APDs IN THE SOLOMONS*

APD/DD	NAME	CAMPAIGN	FATE
1/74	Manley	P9	Scrapped 1945
2/85	Colhoun	P8•P9	Sunk by aircraft Guadalcanal 1942
3/82	Gregory	P9	Sunk by aircraft Guadalcanal 1942
4/79	Little	P8•P9	Sunk by aircraft Guadalcanal 1942
5/90	McKean	P8•P9•P21•P24	Sunk by aircraft Bougainville 1943
6/83	Stringham	P8•P9•P21•P22•P24	Scrapped 1946
7/114	Talbot	P21•P22•P24	Scrapped 1946
8/115	Waters	P19•P21•P24	Scrapped 1946
9/116	Dent	P19•P21•P24	Scrapped 1946
14/103	Schley	P19•P21•P22	Scrapped 1946
15/137	Kilty	P21•P22•P24	Scrapped 1946
16/139	Ward	P19•P21•P22•P24	Sunk by Kamikaze Ormoc Bay 1944
17/164	Crosby	P21•P22•P24	Scrapped 1946

* **Sources**: a) Four Stack APD Veterans Association;   b) *History of U.S. Naval Operations in WWII,* Vol. XV, p. 93.
Campaign codes: P8-Guadalcanal-Tulagi; P9-Capture/Defense of Guadalcanal; P19-Consolidation of the Solomons; P21-New Georgia Group Operation; P-22-Bismarck Archipelago Operation; P-24-Treasury-Bougainville Operation.
Note: The above data do not include the 1944 operations in the Green Islands, New Britain and New Ireland.

USS Ward (APD-16) afire after a Kamikaze hit in Ormoc Bay, Leyte on 7 December 1944. Ward, then a destroyer, had fired the first shot of the Pacific War at Pearl Harbor exactly 3 years before. National Archives.

quickly learned that when a Green Dragon crew showed up, 'turn your back and let them have what they need.'"

Bob Witherspoon, a *Kilty* (APD-15) radarman who was later commissioned and retired a Commander, described some of the advantages of an APD this way. "The APDs could go in fast, get the troops ashore, then retire quickly out of firing range. They were built...for going behind the lines and letting the Marine Raiders off. The APDs did more than transport troops—they were very versatile. The ships had sonar, so they could detect submarines. They were destroyers, and so could escort a task force. They had medical facilities, so they could take wounded and transfer them to hospital ships. And they had the armament to bombard a beach."

Other APD Actions

A total of 26 WWI destroyers and 6 destroyer-type seaplane tenders (APDs 31-36) were converted into APDs for WWII action. While the 13 APDs in this story were participating in the Solomons operations, the *Kane* (APD-18) made the Aleutian landings in the North Pacific. Meanwhile APD TRANSDIV 13 composed of *Tattnall* (APD-19), *Roper* (APD-20), *Barry* (APD-29), *Osmond Ingram* (APD-35) and *Greene* (APD-36) were sent to the Mediterranean to land Free French and U.S. Commandos on islands off the coast of Italy and France before joining the "pack" in the Pacific in 1944.

As the war progressed across the Central and Southwest Pacific, APDs took on new responsibilities and challenges. Many had been out twenty or more months without overhauls. The crews were tired and the APDs were literally bursting at the seams. For this reason, 95 Destroyer Escorts (DEs) were also converted to APDs during 1944 and 1945.[14] (We'll call them "DE/APDs" to differentiate these from the original DD/APDs.)

Some APDs shifted from transporting Marines to Underwater Demolitions Team (UDT) duty and close-in support. Fifteen APDs were in on the Marianas campaigns, 18 served in the Philippines, and 22 were there for the final Okinawa push.

APD Scorecard

All 32 original APDs—considered "expendable" by some in high places—were manned by officers and men who never gave this a second thought, and were dedicated to keeping them on line to fulfill their mission.

Thirty-two APDs started out, 10 were lost, and 22—including the *Belknap,* damaged by enemy action in the Philippines—made it home only to be scrapped.[15] A total of 301 "Green Dragon" sailors were wounded and 269 were killed in action.

Collectively, the APD crews garnered 32 battle stars during 72 engagements plus various Presidential and Unit Citations as well as numerous Silver and Bronze Stars and Purple Hearts. Someday, it is hoped, historians will give them proper credit for their many achievements. This "salute" is a small step in that direction.

The following article epitomizes what the living conditions on an APD were like in World War II. It is reproduced here in hopes that it provides those who are unfamiliar with this aspect of naval service with a feel for the demands of "You called — We hauled" operations. Hopefully, it will also serve to refresh the long-forgotten memories of a few old salts who have been privileged to crew an APD.

Life Aboard a Four Stack Destroyer and a Two Stack APD

The following reflections by one crew member who served seven years in two "four stackers"—one an APD—should give the reader some insight into how these amphibian pioneers lived and worked. It may also help you understand the common bond they share, and why they formed the Four Stack APD Veterans Association, still going strong 55 years after V-J day.[16]

Each DD/APD was unique, in its own configuration, built and converted by various shipyards with plans, in many cases of their own configuration. Each, however, was 314 feet long by 31 feet wide and capable of doing 32-35 knots as a DD and 28-30 knots as an APD. They had a cruising range of 4,000-5,000 miles at 14 knots on 375 tons of oil. They had a draft of around 10 feet and a displacement of 1,200-1,300 tons as a DD and 1,700 tons as an APD. This is how I remember it.

Living Quarters, Mess Decks, and Heads

• **Wardroom** (*Officers' Country*) Located below the main deck between the forward fireroom and the Chiefs' Quarters. CO & XO had individual staterooms. The Engineering Officer had a small stateroom adjacent to the CO's stateroom entered off the "well deck." All other officer staterooms were off the ward room. The Communications Officer, if no Division Commander was aboard, used the "flag" cabin on the main deck outside the radioroom. All other junior officers were two to a stateroom. Mess Attendants were assigned to each room to keep them clean, make bunks and see that the officers' clothes were laundered/dry cleaned as necessary. Officer complement varied from 8-10 officers depending on ship's operations/assignment. All staterooms were small except CO's, and were cooled in summer by forced air vents and electric fans mounted on the bulkhead. In cold weather officers obtained small electric heaters, or wore extra clothes. Limited steam heat was available. The wardroom had its own head and shower facility. Each stateroom had a wash bowl and cabinet for toilet articles.

• **Chiefs' Quarters** Located in the bow, below the main deck, forward of *Officers' Country*. Two mess cooks were assigned to serve meals and keep compartments clean. Complement varied from 8-12 Chief Petty Officers. CPOs had the luxury of having an "upright" locker in which to hang their uniforms. All other items were kept in "foot lockers" under their bunks. The mess table was in the center of the quarters, away from the bunks, so the Chiefs could sit around the table without interfering with anyone in their bunks. Forced air ventilation and electric fans cooled the compartment, plus port holes that could be opened for cool air. The CPO quarters had its own head and shower, plus a wash room with two wash bowls and mirrors.

• **Enlisted Living Quarters** Two compartments forward. The forward Petty Officers Compartment [referred to as the forward Guinea Pullman], below the Chiefs' Quarters and the Forward Seaman Compartment, below the wardroom.

These, at best, were not too comfortable. You could sit at the mess table, or lie in your bunk. If you were sitting on your foot locker, your bunk had to be raised and locked in the "stowed" position. If you had an upper bunk, it might be possible for you to stay in your bunk while others were sitting at the table.

Unless you were a "watch stander" coming off a long mid-watch 0000-0400, your bunk had to be raised and locked in the stowed position. Reveille was at 0500 [5:00 a.m.], lights out at 2200 [10:00 p.m.] in port, and 2100 [9:00 p.m.] underway [or after the movie in both cases]. These compartments were cooled by forced air vents and electric fans. Heat was provided by steam, if it worked.

In the Aleutians when it was cold outside the bulkheads inside the ship would "sweat" and the water would run down into foot lockers. When it really got cold we would go to bed at night with both regular and winter underwear, clean dungarees and socks, with two blankets and our pea coat over us. You could lie in your bunk and scrape frost off the inside bulkheads with your fingers.

In the Tropics it was too hot to sleep. Many would take their mattress and find a cool spot topside at night. Others would just stay below and "sweat it out." Our clothes and shoes became affected with mildew and would turn rotten if they weren't dried or cleaned regularly.

Forward Petty Officers Compartment   One mess cook assigned to serve meals and clean compartment.

Forward Seamen Compartment   Two mess cooks assigned to serve meals and clean compartment.

After Fireman Compartment   Two mess cooks assigned to serve meals and clean compartment.

After Petty Officers Compartment   One mess cook assigned to serve meals and clean compartment.

Enlisted Head & Shower Room   All enlisted shared the same shower and head facilities on the fantail in the after deck house. It was a long walk in heavy weather from any forward compartment, bridge or radioroom.

Galley Area   This area was topside, known as the "galley deckhouse." Meals were cooked in and on an oil-fired range/oven and in large steam kettles. All considered, the food was pretty damn good in most cases. Fresh fruit, fresh vegetables, ice cream, and fresh milk were available only in port or when we managed to "con" some large ship when refueling at sea. Storage space was limited and conserved for canned food. We did have reefers for the storage of fresh meat, which was also limited.

Armament

As a Four Stack Destroyer: the usual consisted of four 4"/50 single purpose rifles, a variety of machine guns, twelve 21-inch torpedo tubes, a depth charge rack on the fantail and one "I" gun depth-charge rack port and one starboard.

As a Two Stack High Speed Transport: this varied, somewhat, from ship to ship. The 4-inch guns were usually replaced with 3"/50 dual purpose guns and/or twin 40-mm guns. Several 20 mm guns were added as well as several .50-caliber machine guns. The numbers depended on where and how they were procured. [Some by *"midnight small stores"*] and the deck space you had available. Many were installed by ships' company.

Engineering Spaces

As a Four Stack Destroyer:
(1) Forward Engine Room with access through the after engine room.
(2) After Engine Room with access from the main deck.
(3) Forward Fireroom consisting of two boilers.
(4) After Fireroom consisting of two boilers.

As a Two Stack Fast Transport: the forward and after engine rooms remain basically the same, except the hatch between the engine room was sealed off and entrance to the forward engine room was from the main deck.

Electronics Equipment

For the Four Stackers, communications were primitive until yard overhauls in 1940/1941 and subsequent conversion to APD in 1942/43. Radar was unheard of.

On conversion to APD in 1942/43, new "state of the art" communications were installed, including new amphibious communications equipment, air and surface search radar, and new sonar.

THE THIRTY-TWO DD CONVERSIONS TO APDS

APD	NAME	CONVERSION YARD	DATE
1	*Manley*	New York Navy Yard	Feb. 1939
2	*Colhoun ~*	Norfolk Navy Yard	Dec. 1940
3	*Gregory ~*	Norfolk Navy Yard	Nov. 1940
4	*Little ~*	Norfolk Navy Yard	Nov. 1940
5	*McKean ~*	Norfolk Navy Yard	Nov. 1940
6	*Stringham*	Norfolk Navy Yard	Dec. 1940
7	*Talbot*	Mare Island Navy Yard	Mar. 1943
8	*Waters*	Puget Sound Navy Yard	Feb. 1943
9	*Dent*	Puget Sound Navy Yard	Mar. 1943
10	*Brooks ~*	Todd's Dry Dock, Seattle	Dec. 1942
11	*Gilmer*	Todd's Dry Dock, Seattle	Jan. 1943
12	*Humphreys*	Mare Island Navy Yard	Dec. 1942
13	*Sands*	IndMan San Francisco	Dec. 1942
14	*Schley*	Puget Sound Navy Yard	Feb. 1943
15	*Kilty*	Mare Island Navy Yard	Mar. 1943
16	*Ward ~*	Puget Sound Navy Yard	Feb. 1943
17	*Crosby*	Mare Island Navy Yard	Feb. 1943
18	**Kane*	Todd's Dry Dock, Seattle	Apr. 1943
19	***Tattnall*	Charleston Navy Yard	Sep. 1943
20	***Roper*	Charleston Navy Yard	Oct. 1943
21	*Dickerson ~*	Charleston Navy Yard	Aug. 1943
22	*Herbert*	Charleston Navy Yard	Nov. 1943
23	*Overton*	Norfolk Navy Yard	Aug. 1943
24	*Noa ~*	Norfolk Navy Yard	Sep. 1943
25	*Rathburne*	Puget Sound Navy Yard	May 1944
29	***Barry ~*	Charleston Navy Yard	Jan. 1944
31	*Clemson*	Charleston Navy Yard	May 1944
32	*Goldsborough*	Charleston Navy Yard	May 1944
33	*George E Badger*	Charleston Navy Yard	May 1944
34	*Belknap*	Charleston Navy Yard	Jun. 1944
35	***Osmond Ingram*	Charleston Navy Yard	Jun. 1944
36	***Greene ~*	Charleston Navy Yard	Feb. 1944

*   Only APD to participate in the Aleutians.
** Only APDs to participate in European Theater.
~   Lost in combat or by accident, 27 June 1940-2 September 1945.[17]

Troop Accommodations

On conversion to APDs the forward fireroom was removed and accommodations were provided for berthing 150-200 troops, plus head and shower berthing facilities and sick bay.

The APDs were used for many assignments. The following applies to most APD operations.

You called — We hauled:

1. Construction Battalion Seabees and supplies from place to place.
2. Army and Marine combat troops into various island operations.
3. Marine Raiders on "hit & run" operations.
4. American & Australian, Army, Navy & Marine Reconnaissance Teams.
5. Fiji Island Scouts.
6. Australian Coast Watchers.
7. "Various type passengers" to and from rear areas.
8. Casualties to rear area hospitals.
9. Underwater Demolition Teams (UDT) and/or munitions.
10. Coast Guard Weather Station Survey Teams.
11. Deck cargo of aviation gasoline in 100-gal. drums, ammunitions, and food.
12. Anything or anyone else that could be loaded/fitted aboard an "APD."

• **Troop reaction** varied from ship to ship and from troop to troop. A lot depended on the type of personnel transported. In most cases they liked the APDs. There were only a few scattered incidents where troops and ship's company didn't "mix." Our favorites were the Marines and the UDTs. When they left the ship they left it as clean as they found it. Some others did not, and our crew had to spend hours getting the "troop spaces" back in shape for the next operation.

• **On the APDs**, unlike many of the large transports, the 100-200 troops on boards were fed three hot meals a day, provided with a comfortable place to sleep, had access to a large, well-equipped sick bay and had their own head and shower facilities. Our C.O.—when troops were aboard for an operation—saw to it that they were provided with everything they needed. It might be a long time before they would have a clean bed and a hot meal again.

APD Amphibious Operations

Operations varied by the type of "troops" we were carrying:

• **Marine or Army Combat Landing Teams**, normally in company with several other APDs, LSTs, etc. Our function was to get the troops to the beach, unload their supplies and depart the area. Gunfire support was provided by destroyers and cruisers. The APDs guns were used primarily in antiaircraft defense with occasional "close in shore fire support." These operations were conducted throughout the Solomon Islands, New Guinea, the Philippines, Saipan, Guam and Okinawa.

• **Reconnaissance Teams** were usually dropped off at night, as quietly as possible. Get-in/get-out, come back later the next night and pick up. These operations were conducted throughout the Solomon Islands.

• **Underwater Demolition Teams**. Pre-invasion bombardment, clear the beaches, operations. This was done one to two days ahead of the landing forces. Get in as close to the beach as possible, make high speed runs parallel to the beach, and provide gunfire support when needed. These operations were conducted throughout the Philippines, Saipan, Guam and Okinawa.

• **Convoy Screen**. When not carrying troops, the APDs equipped with sonar were often assigned as part of a convoy screen. [At one point in the Solomon operations, they were assigned screen position when carrying troops, and this resulted in the sinking of the *McKean* (APD-5) with 12 officers and 140 crewmen and 185 Marines on board—a loss of 64 crew members and 52 Marines.] Following this, APDs carrying troops were placed inside the screen instead of being part of it.

• **Anti-Air Defense**. When finished with troop operations, and not returning for more troops, APDs were assigned AA stations. Our 3"/50 dual purpose, 40-mm, 20-mm and various .50-caliber machine guns could provide considerable support. During the operation at Okinawa, we were assigned AA stations for several days at a time.

CHAPTER 3

Biography of LCT Flotilla Five, from Crew Formation to Guadalcanal

D ue to the almost complete absence of individual Landing Craft, Tank (LCT) war diaries and action reports in the national archives, I jumped for joy when my distinguished historian/researcher, Samuel L. Morison,[1] uncovered two 1943 LCT Flotilla Five Action Reports.

Keep in mind that LCT skippers were not required to keep war diaries or logs, so written records of individual LCTs from World War II are few and far between. With such a small crew, there just wasn't time for paperwork. Presumably, LCT Flotilla and LCT Group Commanders kept a log and a war diary, but if they did so, they have not survived to reach the normal repositories of such documents.

About the time I was beginning to wonder if I could gather enough factual information to write this chapter, I came upon several new sources of information. First, I discovered there is an LCT veterans group of about 400 men who get together every year. Walter Minton, their former Reunion Chairman, not only provided me with a list of members, he spent hours ticking off the names of those he thought might have served in Flotilla Five LCTs in the Solomons in 1943.

Second, and this is a story in itself, I learned that about a dozen original skippers of Flot 5 still hold an annual reunion after all these years. I was elated to find this many seasoned skippers still above ground, and immediately set about interviewing each of them by telephone.

Third, while interviewing John McNeill, the original skipper of LCT-159, he offered me a copy of his self-published book, *The Voyage of the 159*, based on his personal diary. He also granted me permission to use any part of it in this chapter.

All told, I've talked to more than two dozen original crew members of LCT Flot 5. Excerpts from these interviews supplement the 159 story throughout the chapter.

We'll start the chapter by following John McNeill from April 1, 1942—the day he received orders to report to Midshipman's School—through amphibious training and LCT Flotilla 5 craft and crew formations. Then, we'll take a brief look at the design and construction of the LCTs, followed by the Flot 5 San Francisco shakedowns and sea trials.

Next, McNeill describes the ordeal of the 159 during an experimental tow to the South Pacific. Finally, John and his fellow Flot 5 LCTers relive their "on-the-job training" while under fire in the Southern Solomons as they prepared for the invasion of the New Georgia Group in the Central Solomons, code-named Operation TOENAILS.

Midshipman's School

On 1 April 1942, John A. McNeill received orders to report to the U.S. Naval Reserve Midshipman's School at Columbia University in New York. (The Navy V7 program recruited college graduates from the top half of their class.) John and his classmates would serve 30 days as Apprentice Seamen, after which those who were qualified would receive appointments as USNR Midshipmen. Midshipmen training would last three months and lead to the rank of Ensign, USNR—also known as a "90-day wonder."

McNeill reported for duty on 20 April along with about 800 other officer candidates. They were all given another physical, then issued Navy clothing, bedding and books, and assigned rooms in Furnald Hall or quartered aboard the *Prairie State,* the former battleship *Illinois* berthed at 136th Street on the Hudson.

Other future skippers of Flotilla Five LCTs in McNeill's class included Bob Capeless (LCT-62), Bob Carr (LCT-367), Tom McGann (LCT-377), Austin Volk (LCT-60), and George Wagenhorst (LCT-481). The class had its share of future celebrities, too, including: James Tobin (Nobel Prize in Economics), Cyrus Vance (Secretary of State), and Herman Wouk (author).

Austin Volk (LCT-60) took a circuitous route to Midshipman School. For starters, he joined the V7 program in 1940 while attending Brown University; then took a summer cruise in the battleship

New York as an apprentice seaman. He planned to enter midshipman training after he graduated from college in 1941, but couldn't pass the physical due to 19/20 vision in his left eye. So he wrote to the skipper of the *New York,* Daniel E. Barbey—later known as "Uncle Dan, the amphibious man" in MacArthur's Navy—to enlist his help. Barbey called the head of the Naval Reserve and, after Volk underwent another physical, he was accepted providing he successfully completed night school classes in solid geometry and theoretical trigonometry, which he did. And that's how he ended up in the first V7 class at Columbia University.

Carl Barrett (LCT-322) volunteered for Midshipman School while he was a corporal in the U.S. Army! "I was drafted into the Army in February 1941. Later on, I heard the Navy advertising that anybody with a college education could come to Northwestern and Notre Dame and be a 90-day wonder, so I volunteered. After the Army heard that, they said, 'Well, we'll send you to Fort Benning,' but, I didn't want any part of that. The Army had to release me but they weren't happy. I got my release order the day before we went on maneuvers in Louisiana. The General called me in and said, 'I'd rather you go to Fort Benning,' and I said, 'I don't choose to.' So, he says, 'Well, in that case, I'm not going to release you just yet.' So, he made me serve three more months in the Louisiana jungle."

Jack Johnson (LCT-182) went through Midshipman School at Notre Dame and Northwestern. Jack's memories are crystal clear: "We started with 900, and only 300 finished. They wiped you out if you blinked your eyes too much, or a shoulder drooped. I had a roommate who couldn't learn to swim. They had the best swimming instructors but he couldn't learn, so they wiped him out.

"Not long after Cmdr Jon Bulkeley, and what was left of MTB Squadron 3, carried Gen MacArthur and his party away from Corregidor to the Southern Philippines, the Navy interviewed us and I was one of them selected to go into the PT group under Bulkeley. There were forty of us that were picked out of that class of Midshipman's School that wanted PT-boats. Well, three days before we graduated, our orders were changed to the Amphibious Forces and nobody had even heard of that before. We had six days' leave after we graduated, then reported into Norfolk."

Indoctrination for the would-be officers began at once, and the pressure and discipline were intense. McNeill: "During this time, we were subjected to conditions and situations apparently designed to thin out those who did not have the aptitude for naval leadership. The staff was well qualified and hard as nails. Officers with frightening voices screamed words of ridicule at every move. None of us had ever experienced such treatment and some succumbed to the pressure. At the end of this indoctrination, a substantial number—perhaps 20 percent—were washed out of the school."[2]

The V7 program for college graduates was not exactly "a piece of cake" either, according to McNeill: "The curriculum... was largely in four categories—Leadership, Ordinance, Navigation and Seamanship. While we were not pushed physically, the academic load was awesome. Many of the textbooks of the Naval Academy were covered in a month and while I realize we were merely skimming over deep subjects, the total load was far greater than anything I had ever experienced in college. With the added pressure of the drill officers' verbal abuse, many of the Midshipmen fell victim to the frequent washouts."

By late July the pressure had lifted and the surviving Midshipmen were given liberty to buy their uniforms. John McNeill described the big day, 5 August 1942: "The graduation ceremony or commissioning was held aboard the *Prairie State* and Wendell Wilkie, Republican presidential candidate, presented the commissions. Each Midshipman walked across the stage, shook hands with Wilkie, and received his commission as an 'Ensign in the Naval Reserve.' At the conclusion of the ceremony we yelled and threw our hats in the air in the Annapolis tradition."

Amphibious Training

After a short leave, John McNeill and many of his Midshipman's School classmates received orders to report to Norfolk, Virginia, for amphibious training. Upon arrival at the base, they were detached to the amphibious transport *Samuel Chase* (APA-26) for training in ship-to-shore landing procedures.

Jack Johnson (LCT-182), a natural born storyteller, described the brief transport/small boat amphibious training out of Norfolk on the

Chase this way: "We went aboard that thing at 0900 one morning. It was raining to beat hell and there wasn't anybody topside and so we went down below... and were meeting people that had been to other midshipman schools. We also had about twenty Ensigns from the Naval Academy that were gonna be in this group. Well, shortly after they saw how screwed up everything was, the Academy boys decided they didn't want any part of the Amphibious Force... and asked for transfers, leaving it up to us Reserves.

"Anyway, that afternoon at 1600, I heard the whistle blowing, and looked out the porthole and thought I saw the pier moving. I ran topside and we were loaded with Army personnel and these LCVPs. That night at dinner we got these questionnaires about 'have you ever owned a motor boat or a sail boat?' and I put down yes because I'd had a 4-cylinder inboard-outboard on the Wabash River when I was 15 years old. So that evening a Yeoman knocked on the door and said, 'You're to report to the commander,' so I went topside to his quarters. He said, 'You're going to be commander of a group of LCVPs.' I said, 'Commander, until today, I've never even seen one of them.' He said, 'Well, don't let it out, but I haven't either.'

"Honest to God, you can't believe how screwed up it was and we had all of these Army guys aboard. Anyhow, the ship's crew would lower our boats on the davits... and then we would try to go alongside. It was so rough the first day we only managed a couple of these drills. The boats were heavy and they would swing out wide and... when they were up by the railing, it was 30 feet down. It was stupid, but nobody knew what they were doing.

"After 4 days or so we went back into Norfolk and they took all of us in the so-called Small Boat Commander's Group and made us skippers of LCTs."

After about two weeks of LCVP landing practice on the Chesapeake Bay, McNeill spotted a strange looking landing craft with only the number 001 for identification. McNeill: "Commander Wilson [training officer] was standing nearby and I asked him about the ship. He looked it up in a new landing craft manual and said that it was the *first* LCT (Landing Craft Tank, Mark V), and that it had an Ensign as Skipper and a crew of ten men. Its mission was to land tanks or vehicles on a beach. I immediately asked to be transferred to the

LCT training base which was at nearby Solomons, Maryland. The next day I was detached from the *Samuel Chase* and sent by LCVP to the Solomons Amphibious Training Base."

McNeill experienced a "sea of mud" between buildings enroute to his barracks, but this displeasure was soon forgotten when he discovered several of his midshipman classmates, including Bob Capeless, Bob Carr, and Austin Volk. Tom McGann and George Wagenhorst were also there. McNeill also met several new men, among them Jack Johnson and Bo Gillette. Little did they know at the time that they would all become life-long friends. In fact, more than a dozen of the original Flotilla 5 LCT skippers have been getting together once or twice a year ever since WWII. (The combination of shared training and hazardous duty creates a camaraderie that probably has to be experienced to be understood.)

Tom McGann (LCT-347) described the early amphibious training this way: "We were among the first groups that went through there. Both bases [Solomons and Little Creek] were just being established. In each case, they were big mud holes. It was our first exposure to LCTs. We had some Chiefs as instructors, and there may have been some officers, too, but nobody had any LCT experience. These things were brand new. We destroyed Chesapeake Bay. Fishermen have a lot of nets and poles and we just destroyed them because we didn't know what we were doing."

The new ensigns toured an LCT and began classes on the many duties of commanding a ship, however big or small it might be. About a week later, crews of enlisted men began arriving on the base to be assigned to each officer trainee. Bob Capeless (LCT-62) recalled the Solomons ATB training: "The training consisted of going out in the Chesapeake with a couple of old Chiefs and their regular crews... we would wander around for a few hours, with little opportunity to run the boat ourselves."

Crew Formations

The crew of an LCT (Mark 5) consisted of one commissioned officer and ten enlisted men. The LCTs were not commissioned ships of the Navy, so the one officer was designated as the Officer-in-Charge. It soon became evident that there would not be enough crews to go around. John McNeill, one of the officers to get short-changed, had a creative solution to this short-term problem: "One day as we were coming into the harbor I noticed a large group of men in an enclosure. Later I was told this was the brig and that these men were being held for minor offenses like absent over leave (AOL). I immediately went to the Training Officer and asked if I could recruit a crew from the brig. He finally agreed and I soon had ten men selected as my crew.

"I took them to a classroom and let each man tell me about his training, his ambitions and problems. I discovered that they all had several common situations. They had all volunteered within a week of Pearl Harbor—they all wanted to fight the Japs—and they were all bored with the inactivity and confusion in the Amphibious Force. They all had some skills that would be useful on a ship and they wanted to be called 'The Pearl Harbor Avengers.' They suited me perfectly and I had a crew.

"I began the training immediately. I let them know we were considerably behind the other crews and that I expected them to work twice as hard and soon become the best crew. Since there were only two LCT training vessels at the time, three crews would take turns operating each LCT out on the Bay. While ashore, the men attended classes on seamanship as well as their chosen specialty within the broader fields of the 'Deck Gang' or 'Black Gang.'"

Two weeks later, the new LCT crews boarded the *Princess Anne,* an ancient Bay Steamer, and chugged down the Chesapeake to the Amphibious Training Base (ATB) at Little Creek, near Norfolk. At Little Creek, the new arrivals immediately became part of a new flotilla being formed consisting of 36 crews divided into three groups of twelve.

Bob Gordier (LCT-67) had to be one of the youngest amphibians in Flotilla 5: "I lied about my age to get in as I had two brothers already in. I was 15 at the time and wasn't 16 until October 6, 1942."

At this early stage, the flotilla command structure was rather vague; however, Lieutenant Edgar M. Jaeger had been named the Commanding Officer. Jaeger was a controversial C.O. from the start. Here's how John McNeill remembers him: "He appeared to be in his late 40s and had served in a subchaser in World War I. While distinguished in looks and sincere in his patriotism, he looked more the part of a Girl Scout leader. Every afternoon he had the flotilla parade around with flags flying and band music blaring. With his wife at his side, he returned the salutes of the marching men.

"His idea of a war was far from reality. We were having little opportunity to handle the ships, with far more crews than the facility was designed for. I figured I only had about two or three hours of solo training at beaching and almost none at docking."

Another problem soon became obvious. There weren't near enough experienced cooks at Little Creek to fill the needs of the new flotilla so skippers Jack Johnson and John McNeill decided to create a cooking school. "It started with a bang," according to McNeill, "and collapsed the next day. We received orders to pack up, get aboard a train and head for an unknown destination." (That first day, Johnson was nicknamed "Cookie Jar," a name he carries to this day.)

Before boarding the troop train, let's examine some LCT details.

LCT Design and Construction

As noted in Chapter 1, the U.S. Navy had no amphibious landing craft in production at the start of World War II, although a few prototype designs like a 40-foot amphibious "sea sled" were reportedly tested in the late 1920s. The LCT can trace its lineage to the powered lighters used to land horses and vehicles during the ill-fated Gallipoli campaign of World War I. However, it was the curiosity and influence of England's Prime Minister Winston Churchill that renewed interest in a special vessel capable of carrying a tank directly to a beachhead.

Early U.K. Research and Development: Allow me to summarize the Brits' early R&D with excerpts from an article by historian Basil Hearde.

> Impressing his views on Admiral Maund, Chief of Naval Construction [for the Royal Navy], Churchill hammered his argument that if the Royal Navy had possessed ramped amphibious vessels of the type he advocated, the British Army might not have been forced to leave the cream of its armored equipment on the beaches of Dunkirk only months earlier. Few could counter the merit of the doughty Prime Minister's view, for indeed, much of the mechanized might of the Royal Army had been left behind to rust or be

captured, as the British Expeditionary Force beat a hasty retreat across the English Channel...

The evacuation from Dunkirk was a demoralizing blow to British morale and though 330,000 men were saved from capture, the Royal Army was left virtually devoid of any tanks, artillery or mobile equipment. Humiliated, Churchill vowed the English would never again be forced to suffer such a shattering exodus from a battlefield. It was a promise he was determined to keep...

The Prime Minister's idea called for an amphibious vessel capable of landing at least three 36-ton tanks directly onto a beach; a vessel able to sustain itself at sea for at least a week; a vessel with acceptable, if not commodious, crew accommodations, and a design simplicity whereby the craft could easily be built in separate unitized sections. These sections would make for easier shipment aboard large cargo vessels where they could then be launched at sea, assembled and loaded by the ships' cranes...

Taking the Prime Minister's mandate, Admiral Maund enlisted the skills of naval architect Robert Baker who, in a matter of three days, remarkably completed initial drawings for what would become a 152-foot landing craft with a 29-foot beam and a shallow draft. Ship builders Fairfield and John Brown agreed to work out details for the design under the guidance of the Admiralty Experiment Works at Halsar. Tank tests with models soon determined the hydrostatic characteristics of the craft's flat bottom hull, single rudder and blunt bow, indicating the craft could make ten knots on engines delivering about 700 shp to twin propellors.

LCT(1) UK Work now began in earnest and by November 1940, the first LCT Mark 1, yard number 14 was launched. The designers had transformed Churchill's visionary concept into an all-welded 372-ton steel-hulled vessel that remarkably drew only three feet of water at its bow. A 12-foot-wide hinged bow door ramp enabled tanks to exit onto beaches with a 1.35 slope gradient so they could wade ashore in water only three-feet deep. A second steel door behind the hinged ramp sealed the bow area from the tank well or tank deck. Flanking both sides of the landing craft were watertight, lengthwise, bulwark coamings that contained storage compartments which added to the buoyancy provided by the double bottom under the tank deck. Within the double bottom were ballast and fuel tanks that were plumbed to be able to change the fore and aft trim for beaching operations.

At the rear of the low-silhouetted vessel was a small boxlike bridge beneath which two 350-hp Hall Scott gasoline engines were crammed along with an auxiliary generator, batteries and pumps. The hull tanks contained fuel for a range of 900 miles. Aft of the engine room were equally cramped quarters for ten matelotes and a skimpy galley and meat locker. Behind the bridge was a tiny wardroom for two officers and mounts for a port and a starboard 2-pounder pom-pom machine gun.

Key to the LCT's concept was a large stern-mounted kedge anchor that was dropped while inbound to the beach. This anchor helped to keep the craft from slewing or broaching and with its powerful winch, enabled the craft to pull itself off the beach once the cargo was unloaded. The bow ramp was initially raised and lowered by hand cranks, but on later Marks, a powered winch assisted in ramp positioning.

Sea trials soon proved the Mk1 to be skittish and almost unmanageable in some sea conditions. During its difficult test course on the Tyne, the LCT's shallow draft made steering by the helm alone all but impossible and quick reversal of the engines mandatory. Below, the cork-lined crew compartment sweated profusely and the sound level was deafening. The engine spaces were no better, insufferably hot and so cramped the motor mechanics had to be of slight physical stature. Yet, despite its many shortcomings and ungainly barge-like appearance, the prototype LCT delivered its promise of handily putting tanks ashore on any beach.

Orders were immediately placed for thirty Mk1s while the designers set about correcting all that was wrong in the slightly larger (159') Mk2 version that was quick to follow.

LCT(2) UK In addition to a wider beam (31'), three 460-hp Paxman diesel engines replaced the Hall Scotts, and 15- and 20-lb armored shielding was added to the wheelhouse and gun tubs. Built in four sections, the increased length and beam also allowed storage for two rows of 25-ton tanks and enough diesel fuel to triple the Mk2's range to 2,700 nautical miles. In handling and reliability, the Mk2 would be a quantum leap ahead of its box-like forebearer.

Seventy-three Mk2 LCTs were under construction as the prototype Mk1s saw their first blistering action during the British evacuation from Greece and Crete early in 1941. As Churchill anticipated, the LCTs played a key role in saving much of the armored equipment that would soon serve them well in North Africa...

Winston Churchill was vindicated. The LCT had earned its first laurels in naval history even though seventeen of the Mk1s would be lost in the hard fighting of the Grecian operations.

With the development of the LCT, the Royal Navy now had the kind of beaching vessel amphibious warfare demanded. Fast unfolding events in North Africa and Sicily further proved their viability and other Marks soon were developed to fulfill a variety of needs.

LCT(3) UK Next to come was the Mk3. It would be even larger with an added 32-foot section giving a length of 192 feet and a displacement of 640 tons. Mk3 was accepted on 8 April 1941, and would be entirely prefabricated in five sections. The increase in length allowed it to carry five 40-ton tanks and all their related support equipment, or 300 tons of deck cargo...

LCT(4) UK Though the Royal Navy liked the higher load capability of the Mk3, it soon discovered several construction deficiencies. Quickly pressed into service without sufficient testing, combat operations demonstrated the need to add longitudinal stiffeners to the Mk3 (and later the Mk4s) in order to avoid torsional stresses to so lengthy a hull.

The soon to evolve Mk4 wuld be slightly shorter (187') but would have a much wider beam of almost 39 feet as opposed to 31 feet of the Mk3 and a displacement of 586 tons. The wider beam was intended for cross-channel operations where the ferrying aspect was critical for the fast unloading of raiding assaults as opposed to seagoing use for the transfer of tanks and vehicles to smaller landing craft. Better accommodation for the tank crews was also made possible by the increased beam. In each subsequent model, despite the size variances, the basic arrangement of bow ramp, long tank well and aft conning station would essentially be retained.

At a glance, the LCTs all looked to be much the same vessel— although they did contain a wide variety of interior equipment, communications, berthing and armament installations...

The LCT's versatility also led to the adaptation of many special purpose versions such as rocket craft (LCT-R), armored gunboats (LCT-G) and 76-patient hospital ships (LCT-H). Thanks to the simplicity of their construction, many were modified into other specific uses such as dredges, salvage, repair and mine craft. One even served as a floating bakery during the Normandy invasion...

As the war broadened in scope after Pearl Harbor, English LCT production increased. Three hundred fifty Mk3s were built (71 with

Sterling gasoline engines) followed by 865 Mk4s powered with two reliable 460hp Paxman diesels. These could carry nine M4 Sherman or six Churchill tanks. Carrying a load of 350 tons, the Mk4 would be built throughout the war, being the largest LCT production in English yards.

Testing in early assault operations, like the ill-fated Canadian commando raid on Dieppe in 1942, revealed shortcomings in the larger LCTs maneuvering ability. This led to the preference for shorter overall length in future variants, most of which were to be built in the U.S. England's hard-learned lesson in amphibious warfare would inure to the benefit of their Yank allies. Soon to be mass produced, American-made Mk5 and Mk6 LCTs, 160 of which were lend-leased to the Royal Navy, would be 117- and 120-footers, respectively, and both marks would be rated at about 285-ton displacement. These versions would result in the largest number of LCTs procured with 475 Mk5s and 965 Mk6s built by the war's end.[3]

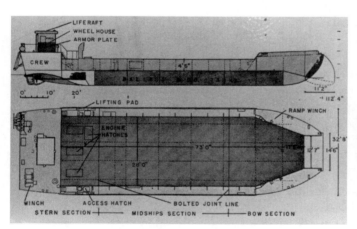

LCT (5) Landing Craft, Tank (Mark 5) drawings. American design, later superseded in production by LCT (6). Office of Naval Intelligence (ONI)226/1.

LCT (5) Collage. ONI 226/1.

With America's entry into the war, a whole new concept of amphibious warfare principles would be raised by the vast reaches of the Pacific Ocean. Due to the dire need for landing craft, the U.S. Navy's Bureau of Ships was quick to adapt any successful British designs already in existence.

The result by the spring of 1942 was LCT Mk5, a 114-ft. craft with a sizable beam of 32 ft. that could accommodate five 30-ton, four 40-ton tanks, or 150 tons of cargo.

Operational Use: A tank carrier designed for direct unloading on a beach slope of 1/30. Early LCTs were 114 ft. overall, had a 32-ft. beam, and a draft of a little over 3 ft. They were normally expected to carry four 40-ton tanks, or nine trucks, or 150 tons of cargo. Maximum speed was about 8 knots. The LCTs bridged the gap between the Landing Craft, Medium (LCM), and the Landing Ship, Tank (LST).[4]

	LCM (Mark 3)	LCT (Mark 5)	LST (Mark 2)
Length	50'	114'	328'
Beam	14'	32'	50'
Capacity	30 tons	150 tons	1900 tons

The LCMs were the largest landing craft carried by and identified with transports and cargo ships for ship-to-shore landings.

For the engineers among our readers, here are more U.S. Navy LCT specifications:

Crew: 1 officer, 10 enlisted men.

Capacity: (5) 30-ton, or (4) 40-ton, or (3) 50-ton tanks; or (9) trucks; or 150 tons of cargo. No troop accommodations.

Armament: (2) 20-mm AA.

Propulsion: (3) Gray 225-hp. diesels; triple screw.

Fuel: 11.12 tons fuel; 140 gallons lube oil.

The LCT(5) and later LCT(6) hulls were the same except the Mark 6 superstructure was offset to starboard so the craft could also be stern loaded. This modification also allowed the craft to be used in emergencies as an "unloading bridge" for an LST by mooring the two vessels in line. Other changes included the addition of accommodations for 8 troops.

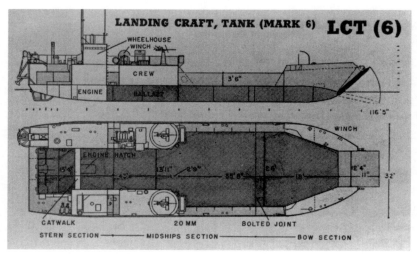

LCT (6) Drawings.   *Courtesy of ONI 226/1.*

LCT (6)-501.
ONI 226/1.

Although the LCT was not designed for long distances, it was a substantial diesel-powered, triple-screw vessel, capable of carrying three 50-ton tanks or nine trucks or 150 tons of cargo. It had a cruising radius of about 700 miles at 7 knots. (Later in the war, LCT flotillas made it all the way from Hawaii to the Philippines.)

Crew Accommodations   The living quarters on the stern of an LCT would feed and berth ten men and one officer. It generated its own electricity with a small diesel engine. Toilet facilities were hand-pumped heads that never worked properly.

LCTs were built by the following American Shipyards:[5]

Bison Shipbuilding Company
North Tonawanda, NY

Darby Products Company
Kansas City, Kansas

Decatur Iron & Steel Company
Decatur, Alabama

Jones and Laughlin Steel Corp.
New Orleans, Louisiana

Kansas City Structural Steel Co.
Kansas City, Kansas

Mare Island Navy Yard
Mare Island, California

Missouri Valley Bridge & Iron Co.
Leavenworth, Kansas

Mt. Vernon Bridge & Iron Co.
Ironton, Ohio

New York Shipbuilding Corp.
Camden, New Jersey

Omaha Steel Works
Omaha, Nebraska

Pidgeon-Thomas Iron & Steel Co.
Memphis, Tenn.

Quincy Barge Builders
Quincy, Illinois

Manitowoc Shipbuilding Corp.
Manitowoc, Wisconsin

Manitowoc Shipbuilding, which also built 28 submarines, was the lead yard in the design and procurement of all materials for the LCT program for all yards.

I had the pleasure of interviewing Art Zuehlke for this chapter. He headed up the hull division, which included the machinery and electrical, for Manitowoc during World War II. He was also in charge of developing the detailed drawings. I asked Art to explain: "We developed the plans for the LCTs based on a preliminary design that we got from the Navy. The Navy gave us the basic design and said, 'Here, this is what we want—go ahead and design them. It's a very hot program.' So we developed the design from their preliminary sketches. We had a higher priority for getting materials on that program than our submarine program. We had a demanding priority."

The LCTs were welded in sections in fabrication shops and, sometimes, hauled by truck or rail to the shipyards (many located on inland waterways) for further assembly.

Harry Denni, who was with one of the so-called cornfield shipyards, Kansas City Structural Steel, had this to say on the subject:[6] "At the time, the construction of these vessels was of the highest priority of any wartime construction for the reason that the main

Photos from top: LCT fabrication shop interior, shipyard exterior, tank loading demonstration, sideways launch. All circa 1942-1943. Courtesy Kansas City Structured Steel.

objective was the invasion of Normandy, which could not be accomplished without them.

"All of the vessels constructed by two of our competitors and ourselves on the Missouri River were taken over by the Coast Guard, and, on their own power, went down the Missouri and the Mississippi Rivers, either to New Orleans, or north on the Mississippi through the Great Lakes, Erie Canal, and down the Hudson."

LCTs were constructed in three watertight sections and capable of being transported disassembled on the decks of cargo vessels. (The U.S. Navy also experimented with towing an LCT behind a Liberty ship, as we will soon see, but abandoned that idea rather quickly.)

Later, as LSTs began heading overseas, fully-assembled LCTs were carried on their decks. When the LST reached her destination she was given sufficient list by manipulating ballast tanks so that the LCT launched itself over the side without any other assistance.

The first LCTs were completed during the summer of 1942 and crossed the Pacific and Atlantic in three ready-to-assemble sections on freighters. They arrived in the Pacific in December 1942, and in the Mediterranean in January 1943. They were the first of the new larger landing craft to be used offensively in the South Pacific.

Although LCTs were specifically designed to transport and land tanks on a shore-to-shore basis, it wasn't long before they were also being used to deliver vehicles of all types, as well as troops, ammunition, and supplies in all theaters of operation. With flat bottoms, shallow draft, and bow-ramps for close approaches to beaches, the LCT could also retract itself after offloading.

Down the Mississippi sail six LCTs built far from the sea on rivers and lakes. Ferry crews bring the Landing Craft, Tank downstream to New Orleans, where they are lifted aboard LSTs and sent overseas. U.S. Navy.

Powerful cranes load an LCT aboard an LST where it is secured to the deck resting on greased timbers or a system of rollers. U.S. Navy.

USS LST-318 launching an LCT in 1943. Courtesy Naval Historical Center.

A total of 470 Mark V LCTs were built by U.S. shipyards during WWII, of which 48 were lost in combat or by accident, and 160 were transferred to the United Kingdom under Lend-Lease.

Mark VI LCT production totaled 964, of which 27 were lost in combat or by accident, 17 were transferred to the Soviet Union, and 6 were converted to underwater locator minesweepers AMC(U).[7]

Troop Train West

And now let's return to the odyssey of Ensign John McNeill's land journey from Little Creek, Virginia.

The LCT Flotilla Five officers and enlisted men—some 400 strong—were bused to Norfolk where a train of Pullman cars was waiting. The "troop train" of new amphibians made its way south and then west to New Orleans amid rumors and theories of the ultimate destination. The next day, as the train pulled into New Orleans, the betting odds said their LCTs would be there awaiting them, but instead, there was a change of trains and a West Coast heading. Now everyone was pretty sure they would soon be fighting the Japs.

Flotilla Commander Jaeger appointed Ensign McNeill Officer-in-Charge of marching the men to hotels where they would be fed at stops twice a day enroute, since there were no dining cars on this train.

John McNeill: "The train stopped in Houston and immediately all of the other officers disappeared, leaving me with about 400 sailors to feed. I assembled the men near the train and a police car arrived to lead us to the hotel, which was about ten blocks away. The streets were filled with Army and Air Corps men who looked in amazement at this group of sailors this far inland. Naturally the air was filled with remarks about 'Swabbies being lost,' catcalls and jeers.

"We soon passed a bar district and the sailors began breaking ranks and heading for the bars. If I looked to right of the column, men on the left hid behind cars and jumped into bars. When we reached the hotel, I had lost about half of the men. This was fine as the capacity of the dining room was about 200. I called for ten policemen and began rounding up the stray sailors, several of whom were engaged in fights with soldiers. When I had fed the men and returned to the train, I had a conference with Lieutenant Jaeger about this episode. It was decided that each officer would be responsible for his crew being fed and this relieved me of that problem."

Just about every LCT skipper I've interviewed has a favorite C.O. story. Austin Volk (LCT-60) remembers Jaeger bringing his wife along on the supposedly secret troop train ride to the coast. Here's Austin: "She wrote all of these directives and so forth, 'You couldn't do this' and 'you couldn't do that' and would pass them out at mealtime.

"Of course, as soon as the other officers saw his wife, they wanted to bring their wives aboard...so they did...and then my men said, 'Well, we've got wives and girlfriends and we want them on the train.' I said go ahead and get them. Every time we pulled into a station, there would be larger crowds of people waiting for us. Jaeger was mystified by this and felt that Japanese spies had picked us up and were gonna blow the train up or something... We had some great times."

The train continued on to San Diego where no one was expecting the amphibians. Soon they were detached and sent by train to San Francisco and then by bus to Treasure Island ("TI" for short.)

Flotilla Five Organization

Landing craft flotillas were organized administratively into groups, then into divisions. Here's the original lineup for LCT Flotilla 5.

LCT GROUP 13
LCT Division 25—LCTs 58, 60, 156, 158, 159, and 180.
LCT Division 26—LCTs 62, 63, 64, 65, 66, and 67.

LCT GROUP 14
LCT Division 27—LCTs 321, 322, 323, 324, 325, and 326.
LCT Division 28—LCTs 367, 369, 370, 375, 376, and 377.

LCT GROUP 15
LCT Division 29—LCTs 181, 182, 327, 330, 351, and 352.
LCT Division 30—LCTs 68, 69, 70, 71, 481, and 482.

Significant Flotilla 5 Firsts
- The first mention of an LCT in RAdm Turner's Staff Log occurred on 19 December 1942, when the first 6 LCTs were reported at Noumea loading for Guadalcanal.[8]
- The first 12 LCTs to arrive in Guadalcanal were LCTs 60, 62, 65, 67, 70, 158, 159, 180, 182, 321, 325, and 369.
- The first 12 LCTs to get their bottoms crinkled in war operations in the South Pacific were LCTs 58, 60, 62, 63, 156, 158, 159, 181, 322, 323, 367, and 369.[9]

Treasure Island across the Lagoon from "Goat" Island. U.S. Navy.

San Francisco Shakedowns and Sea Trials

The Flotilla Five crews were mustered on TI and told that LCTs were being assembled nearby and would be arriving soon. A few days later McNeill was told to pick up his crew and take them to San Francisco's Pier 40 where LCT-156 was tied up and waiting for them.

The crew went to work at once attacking the mountain of crates containing the equipment necessary to operate and live aboard ship. McNeill had been told that the 156 was the first LCT(5) to be assembled on the West Coast and the first of the larger landing crafts, so he and his crew were both shocked and disappointed to learn the next morning that another crew would take over the 156. McNeill was assured that the change was a compliment to him and his crew but for security reasons, he would have to wait for the full story.

I opened the floodgates when I asked Bob Capeless (LCT-62) to describe his Bay Area sea trials and training. "The training in those awful tough waters in San Francisco on our own was something else. I ran into the Golden Gate Bridge once. It was always tough trying to dock along side a pier on the Embarcadero because of the tide. But, we picked that up gradually. I remember the first ship I unloaded at Guadalcanal. I got the damn thing loaded and started for the beach, and the water came pouring through under the ramp flooding the deck. I didn't think I was gonna make it to the beach. You learn by experience, but we were never taught a damn thing about it. We knew that they were designed for five medium tanks weighing 30 tons each. We were never told to think in terms of carefully loading the things."

Austin Volk (LCT-60): One of the "60s" more memorable training runs was to Redwood City in the South Bay to pick up a load of torpedoes. "We were all brand new. I told the officer who ordered us to make the trip, 'I don't even have a chart to go down there. I have no idea where it is,' and he said, 'Well, I'm gonna send the quartermaster over and he'll have a chart.' The quartermaster arrived and he was really potted, so I told him to hit my bunk, and not to worry, just give me the chart.

"We got down there about ten or eleven at night but, unfortunately, it was low tide. We ran aground and had to wait for the tide to change to back off. It was about 2200 the next night when we got back to San Francisco with our load of torpedoes. The freighter didn't want to load them because it was dark. So I finally told them that I would come alongside and might have to ram them but I was gonna get rid of them that night. We offloaded the torpedoes shortly after that! We operated there for two or three weeks and really picked up all our training around San Francisco Bay, what with the fog, strong tides and whatnot. It was interesting that we didn't have any accidents."

San Francisco waterfront. Courtesy Naval Historical Center.

Some of the skippers stayed in San Francisco hotels. Rank does have its privileges! Bob Carr (LCT-367) remembers his stay in the "City by the Bay": "I stayed on Treasure Island for two or three days and then ended up at the Fairmont Hotel. It was good duty. And then we got the boats. Somehow or other most of the crews were assigned to boats that were docked at the Embarcadero. We had the fun of trying to dock—we never had been on one of those things. The crew must of come from Ohio or Minnesota or something... never saw the ocean. So we had fun trying to dock these things in that San Francisco Bay current which was a pistol."

Jack Johnson (LCT-182) remembers being billeted at TI until it was time to pick up his boat at Mare Island. Here's Jack: "We were around the Bay Area for over a month. It would be foggy as hell but they would send us out...big ships coming and going. We would come within two or three feet of hitting something. That's how we got our training and it was great training. I would take friends for a ride around Alcatraz or up to Mare Island. When you'd get too close to Alcatraz, those big horns would boom, 'Lay off, lay off!' That was lots of fun.

"Then there's the time I was up at the Junior Officers' Club and I looked out and saw these tracers going over the San Francisco-Oakland Bridge...I looked out and knew that they had to be my crew. Well, I got in a cab and rushed back to Pier 40 and, hell, the guns were smoking hot, but everybody was in bed, so I knew we were in trouble. My crew had taken out all the regular shells and loaded the magazines with nothing but tracers. Navy personnel on Pier 40 were questioning everybody to see who was responsible. They took me to see our Commander Jones. He told me the Admiral was hunting for who did it last night and, I don't know how he knew my crew did it, but anyway he says, 'It's best we get you out of here.' That's how my crew and I got assigned to the first fully assembled LCT to be loaded aboard an LST headed for the South Pacific."

Now back to Ensign John McNeill and LCT-159. Two days after the false start with LCT-156, McNeill and his crew were bused to Pier 40 and assigned the LCT-159. Again they tackled the piles of crates and began the stowage of gear. Later that day, Skipper McNeill was told he would have to move to another pier the next morning.

McNeill: "The thought of getting the ship underway was frightening. With so little experience, I had almost no confidence and spent the night going over in my mind the procedures of moving the ship. I thought of the possibility of winds and currents, or my own inability, causing us to collide with the dock or another ship. There seemed to be so many variables that I could not gain enough confidence to calmly handle the ship. In any event, I realized I must not show this weakness to my crew. The great Hornblower stories came to me and I tried to wear some of the exterior of my fictional hero.

"The following morning a Lieutenant from the Port Director's office came down on the dock and told us to get underway and go up the Bay to the Esso Dock and take on fuel. I was paralyzed with fear. The LCT was tied up port side; the Port Director's gig was moored to a floating dock directly in front of me; a Barracks Barge was tied astern; and a large ship was alongside the left dock.

"I had been planning for this event and, although shaking inside, I went to the quarter deck and set the special sea detail; started the engines; cast off the spring lines; let go of the stern lines; ordered full left rudder, slow ahead on the starboard engine; and reversed the port engine. This should have started the stern to swing out into the fairway with no forward motion.

"Alas! The ship began to move ahead. Too late, we began pushing on the Port Director's gig and snapped the cleats from its deck setting it adrift under the pier. Quickly, I realized that my order to reverse the port engine had not been heard and we were going all ahead. I kept my cool and corrected the problem.

"The officers on the dock signaled me to back on out and ordered some men to retrieve the gig. The ship began to respond properly. The stern swung clear of the dock. I cast off all lines and backed beautifully into the fairway and straight down the slip into the Bay directly into the path of a harbor tug pulling a long string of barges. The tug was forced to back down with the following barges colliding with the tug. This commotion was mild compared to the lecture I received from the tug captain. With full use of a vocabulary gleaned from years of tugboating, I was told of his opinion of the Navy and of naval officers in particular. Later, I heard the Navy paid several thousand dollars in damages for my maiden voyage."

LCT-159 Towing Disaster

Two days later, Ensign McNeill was notified that he was wanted immediately in the Port Director's office in San Francisco. When he arrived, a meeting was in progress with an admiral and several captains and commanders sitting around a long table. McNeill summarized the meeting: "The Admiral began to explain that things were not going well in the South Pacific and that larger landing craft were desperately needed there. He mentioned that LCTs were available, but the planned use was delayed by the LSTs not being ready.

"He continued with alternate plans to get a group of LCTs into the needed area at once. One plan was to dismantle them... and load them as deck cargo on freighters. The problem was getting them unloaded in the South Pacific since it would require a large crane to lift each section.

"The second plan was to tow an intact LCT directly to the combat zone. If this could be successfully done, then an entire flotilla could be moved directly. A volunteer was needed and a Captain Powell, master of the SS *Ewing Young,* was present and just happened to be sailing for 'White Poppy' (Noumea) the next day. The Admiral said I had been recommended as the best choice and asked if I would volunteer for the mission.

"I think this was the most frightening moment of my life. I cannot remember what I said, except that I volunteered. The Admiral seemed pleased and told me to meet my crew at Pier 40 and that he would have a large staff available to get me prepared. He explained that specialists in all categories would look the ship over and suggest changes or alterations and that a large group of shipfitters, welders, riggers, and supply people would be on the ship all night.

"I walked down to the Pier and soon the 159 arrived. I called the crew together and told them about our assignment. I explained we had been selected to attempt a very important mission and that many risks were involved. I told them we would have no escorts and in the event of an attack, we would be cut adrift to fend for ourselves. Finally, I explained that I had volunteered for this duty and wanted them to feel they had another option personally, then asked for volunteers. They all stepped forward and I was indeed proud of them.

"Soon people were swarming all over the ship and bundles of

supplies were arriving. One group of shipfitters began welding huge gadgets to attach the towing bridle. We were to carry an LCM with an LCVP inside on our deck as cargo. Huge padeyes were welded on to attach turnbuckles and chains to the cargo. Life rafts and new lifelines were rigged for heavy seas.

"Several delays in rigging the towing bridle forced a decision to postpone the sailing one day. A large floating crane lifted the LCM on deck, then lifted a 36-foot LCVP and placed it inside the 50-foot LCM. These were secured with many chains and turnbuckles.

"Work progressed during the afternoon and several officers came and lectured me on shiphandling while being towed. It was decided to disengage the drive shafts from the engines and I had my men observe this so they would be able to get power if needed. Work continued and more problems arose. Later it was decided to postpone one more day...

"Next morning all was ready and a large crowd of LCT friends gathered for the farewell. At this point it was decided that a seagoing tug would escort us as far as the Farallon Islands—about 50 miles off San Francisco. The tug captain would ride with us through the ground swells off the Golden Gate and see that we were able to ride the towline. Since this was the first time an LCT ever went to sea, there were many questions that could not be answered this first day.

"Shortly after noon the tug took us in tow and came up astern the SS *Ewing Young*. I had decided to have half my crew transferred to the *Young* since there was nothing for them to do on the 159. Lieutenant A.Z. Kouri, my division commander, also rode aboard the *Young*. The towline was passed to the *Young* and secured and we were soon underway. We stood down the harbor, around Alcatraz Island, under the Golden Gate Bridge, and into the setting sun.

"Leaving or entering the United States via the Golden Gate Bridge, (or the Statue of Liberty in New York), is an emotional experience that is lost to air travelers. Inward or outward bound, I count it among my life's richest experiences.

"This first hour, although unknown to me until months later, was almost tragic. As the mainland slipped below the horizon, in gathering darkness on that late October 1942 evening, we met some inward bound ships. One excited lieutenant on a merchant vessel sighted the *Ewing Young* and detected a strange craft following in her wake. In the twilight he identified the 159 as a submarine and set off the alarm. A quick message to the Coast Guard informed them that no friendly submarines were in the area. The merchantman's gun crew now trained the 5" gun on the 159 and just before the 'open fire' command was given, the captain saw the towing hawser come out of the water on a large swell and then picked out our American flag.

"The 159 was taking the seas well and following fairly straight in the wake of the *Young*. The tug captain seemed pleased with our sea-worthiness and had the tug pick him up. We were on our own! Into the Pacific night we sailed."

One man stood watch in the wheelhouse at all times to steer the 159 to prevent her from wandering too far to the left or right. In the event the towline parted, or some other emergency, he was to sound the ship's horn. Another man stood watch to keep an eye on the cargo and the engine room.

Everyone is frightened by their first real storm at sea. McNeill: "The next day went well, the seas were moderate and the weather cloudy. That night the winds increased and the seas began to build up. The 159 began to roll and pitch and it became difficult to get up to the bow to check the towing gear. The next 24 hours the weather worsened and I estimated we were experiencing gale-force winds. The third night we had difficulty staying in our bunks, and several times someone was dumped on the deck.

"As dawn broke on the fourth day the seas were awesome. Visibility was very poor and we could barely see the *Young*. The radio malfunctioned and we lost voice contact with the *Young*. I had the crew wear their lifejackets at all times as seas began to come over the bow. I made my way to the bow and found an alarming amount of 'chafing' as the towing bridle rubbed against the bow of the 159. Returning to the cabin, I checked several turnbuckles holding the LCM and found them loose.

"The 159 would ride to the top of a wave and as the wave moved away, she would dive into the next wave, at times almost being suspended in the air between waves. The tension of the 12-inch manila towline appeared to be testing the limits of its strength. I realized that our situation was deteriorating rapidly, so I began to make plans to cope with a broken towline.

"As the morning progressed, the wind and seas increased and I thought we were in a hurricane. Wind-blown mist further reduced visibility and it appeared to me that the 159 was in danger of breaking up.

"Around 1100 the ship's horn sounded and I climbed the ladder to the wheelhouse and found that the towline had parted. I could not see the *Young*. I immediately sent the engineers below to connect the drive shafts and start the engines. The men were great. Soon we had power and I tried to bring the bow into the wind. The 159 wanted to lay in the trough of the waves and actually seemed to ride better there. I had been taught that this ship would be most seaworthy facing the wind. Nothing that I did, however, could bring the bow up into the wind. I would run full ahead down the trough, put the rudder full into the wind and reverse the windward engine with no response.

"Finally, I decided that since we were riding somewhat better abeam the wind and were heading east, I would go slow ahead and ride the storm out. I figured we were some 500 miles off Mexico or Central America and that we would head east until we reached land or were rescued. Later, however, the *Ewing Young* appeared upwind of us. She fired a messenger line over to us and we pulled a hawser over and secured the end. Next she sent a message, 'Abandon Ship,' and dropped a lifeboat on a line and four volunteers from the *Young's* crew brought the lifeboat alongside the 159.

"As I prepared to abandon ship, many thoughts went through my mind. I really would have preferred to ride the storm out on the 159 and either attempt to return to the USA or try the towing again. Since I had no choice, I made ready to leave the ship. I remembered stories I had heard about sailors who had lost their ship and all of their records, and who had to have their 'shots' all over again and wait months to be paid. I stuffed the crew's records inside my shirt and tied my lifejacket securely around myself. Then I remembered the tradition that the captain was the last person to leave the ship. Even in the fury of this awesome storm, I tried to remember any other things I was expected to do.

"After we had all managed to board the lifeboat, the *Young* began pulling it back with a winch, but the lifeboat became fouled with the hawser holding the LCT. The immense wave action put such a strain on the hawser that it about capsized the lifeboat, which was caught astride the hawser. Someone on the *Young* recognized the problem and cut the hawser with an ax. This set the lifeboat free, but also set the 159 adrift with no way to recover it.

"As the lifeboat was pulled near the stern of the *Young,* several enormous waves crested and broke over the *Young*. In this confusion, several men boarded her before the lifeboat came up on the weather side of the *Young* and another great wave smashed it against the side: I looked around and saw Anderson, the Boatswain's Mate, in the water. He had hit the side of the *Young* and was dazed. Together we began to climb up the *Young's* cargo nets and I tried to push him up with my shoulder. About halfway up, he collapsed and fell on me and we both fell back into the drink. We began to climb the nets again, but this time we reached the gunwale and climbed over on the deck. Immediately we were helped into a cabin.

"Captain Powell was there and asked the gun crew to sink the 159. He turned to me and shook my hand and, as if nothing had happened, said, 'I am happy to have you aboard.' Not to be outdone with his coolness, I replied, 'Thank you, Sir. Will you see that my men are fed?' I am sure that food was the last thing that any of us were thinking about. We laughed about this many times later on.

"Before the gun crew could get into action, the 159 disappeared into the mist and gathering darkness. A message was sent to the Navy simply saying 'LCT Lost.'

"The storm continued for a few more hours. Two of the lifeboats were washed overboard and several of the Kingfisher aircraft deck cargo lost their wings or were damaged. I was assigned a cabin and given some dry clothes. I got into a hot shower and will forever remember how great it felt.

"The Navy canceled its plans to tow LCTs across the Pacific. I was very disappointed and felt I had failed in a very important mission. (Of course, I did not know about this for two months.)"

The SS *Ewing Young* passed south of Tongatabu and Samoa and then westward to New Caledonia and around Amity Shoal into Noumea Harbor, code-named "White Poppy." As the *Ewing Young* pulled into the harbor, there appeared to be a hundred or more merchant ships and dozens of warships laying at anchor.

Noumea, New Caledonia

The LCT-159 crew was taken ashore and trucked to a large "Survivor's Camp" (later nicknamed "Halsey's Rest Camp"), a tent city mostly made up of crews of sunken ships from the Solomons' battles. John McNeill was temporarily detached from LCT Flotilla Five and assigned to the Small Boat Pool at Isle Niue as a courier. Consequently, he visited many of the ships that were making history during the early part of the war.

Before we go any further, let's catch up on the status of the Flot 5 crews we left in San Francisco. Most if not all of them had taken delivery of their boats at Mare Island or at a pier in San Francisco, but departure dates for the South Pacific were very uncertain due to the severe shortage of shipping. Consequently, the Navy had three options for delivery of these 114-foot landing craft to the war zone: sail them, tow them, or haul them. Because of its size, each LCT was specifically designed to be shipped in three sections as deckload on a freighter.

LCTs were designed for the shore-to-shore movements of troops and supplies, but not for distances like San Francisco to Guadalcanal. Towing was also ruled out based on the ill-fated LCT-159 test. Hauling, the third option, had its challenges, too. In addition to the availability of freighter deck space, there was the need for jumbo cranes to load the three sections—the aft section containing the

Solomon Islands, Santa Cruz Islands and New Caledonia.

Shipyard workers prepare to join two sections of an LCT.
Courtesy of Kansas City Structural Steel.

engines weighed an estimated 75 tons. And, of course, you had to have a similar crane at the other end to unload the sections. Big cranes were available in San Francisco and the Seabees would soon have a huge crane mounted on pontoons to offload the LCTs in Noumea, New Caledonia. (Later, as LSTs came on line beginning in early 1943, each LST would carry a fully assembled LCT on its deck as it headed overseas.)

As for the LCT crews, most lived in their boat's quarters on the deck of the freighters while enroute. A few freighters had passenger compartments. Others had a spare cabin for the LCT skipper only.

It wasn't long before the Flotilla Five LCTs began arriving at Noumea in sections as deck cargo on Liberty Ships. (Each ship carried five sections or 1-2/3 LCTs) As they were urgently needed at Guadalcanal, LCT unloading received first priority with the new floating crane. The crane was brought alongside the Liberty Ship, the sections were unloaded into the water, then placed in a floating dry dock and bolted together.

Lt Ameel Z. Kouri was given command of the first six LCTs to arrive and quickly prepared them to depart 20 December 1942 on their maiden voyage to Guadalcanal.

A few days after Kouri's division left for the 'Canal, McNeill spotted a ship entering the harbor with the LCT-159 on board. He soon learned it had no crew and was his to command. Lt Ashton L. Jones arrived on another ship and the 159 was quickly offloaded, placed in the floating dry dock, and McNeill was reassigned as Officer-in-Charge. (McNeill also learned that the 159 was found by a picket destroyer adrift and in good condition off the West Coast of Mexico. A tug was called from San Diego and it was towed back to the U.S. and then steamed back to San Francisco.)

LCT-159 Restoration Skipper McNeill rounded up his crew and went to work. According to all hands, "The 159 was a wreck." After being towed back to San Francisco, it was left unattended at a dock where 72 other LCTs were being outfitted. No one thought it would ever be used again, so everything on it that could be lifted without a crane was removed. The perishable food, such as the meat in the refrigerator, had to be cleaned out first. McNeill was furious. As he put it: "We hosed down the entire inside of the living quarters and then repainted everything. Even then, the smell of the rotten food lingered for a few days.

"Mr. Jones and the other LCTs gave us any spares that they had, but we were far from livable or being ready for sea. I made up an exaggerated list and went to RAdm George Fort's flagship to report the 159's condition. At first the Admiral was very cold, but finally called a supply officer and had him look over my list. The Admiral instructed the supply officer to completely equip my ship at once. Not realizing how small an LCT was, he overdid it. The 159 was overnight the best found ship in the flotilla."

Two days after leaving the dry dock, McNeill was ordered alongside the USS *McCawley,* affectionately called "Wacky Mac" by the sailors and used as the Flagship by the Commander, Amphibious Forces Pacific, RAdm Richmond Kelly Turner.

McNeill: "Soon I was boarded by Admiral Turner, Admiral Fort, and the world famous Admiral 'Bull' Halsey, along with a dozen or more Captains and Commanders. I was told that I was temporarily relieved of command and that the Admirals and their staff wanted to test the LCT for its capabilities. A Captain got the ship underway and stood down the harbor at full speed. As he approached an anchored cruiser he gave the order 'full left rudder,' not knowing an LCT had a completely flat bottom. As the ship began to slide sideways into the cruiser, I whispered to the Captain that I would suggest he back the port engine quickly. He grasped the situation and ordered full astern on the port engine just in time to make the collision a minor one.

"The Admiral then asked me to take command again and demonstrate some of the capabilities of the ship, including some landings or beachings. I was thrilled to stand among these famous men and demonstrate the abilities and peculiarities of the LCT. It was especially an honor to have Admiral Halsey aboard. As they left the ship when we returned to the *McCawley,* Admiral Halsey said to me, 'Get ready to sail, Skipper, we really need her at Guadalcanal.'"

Twelve LCTs had arrived in Noumea by this time, counting the first six that had left for Guadalcanal on 20 Dec. 1942. A.L. Jones made preparations for the second six to depart as soon as possible.

Significant LCT Firsts These first 12 LCTs, which made up Group 13 of Flotilla Five, proudly claimed several significant firsts in amphibious warfare. They were the *first* of the larger U.S.-built landing craft to operate in World War II. They were the *first* U.S. group to land on enemy-held beaches; the *first* to engage in combat; and the *first* to engage in a forward island-jumping operation. They were the only large landing craft in Task Force 61, the "Spit Kit Expeditionary Force," which made the *first* island-to-island landing in the war in "Operation CLEANSLATE."

After filling water and fuel tanks, taking on food and other stores, each LCT took on about 900 drums of aviation gasoline and other cargo. Meanwhile the skippers met with Convoy Commander J.D. Sweeney, Captain of high-speed transport *Stringham* (APD-6) and picked up their sailing orders and charts. The LCTs were to follow the *Stringham* in two Vs of three.

The LCTs carried no navigational equipment other than a small compass plus a set of local charts. They simply followed their escort. In the event a storm or enemy attack separated the formation, it was every ship for itself.

Solomons Here We Come The convoy departed Noumea early on 26 December 1942. Bob Capeless (LCT-62) remembers day one of the eight-day voyage from Noumea to Guadalcanal like it was yesterday: "It was a fascinating trip...eight days. Four days to Espiritu Santo and four days to Guadalcanal. The first night out there were six of us...the second six LCTs to leave for the 'Canal. We were following an old World War I converted destroyer and when dawn came, I was the only one with the destroyer. The rest had just disappeared.

"Commander John Sweeney, skipper of the *Stringham,* the destroyer transport that would escort us on later missions, hightailed it back to us at flank speed and shouted: 'Steer a course of 350'—I think that was it—'and I'll go round up the others.' It wasn't until later in life, I began to think what the hell would have happened if he had never came back. I didn't have the vaguest notion where we were and had no navigation equipment worth a damn. That was just the first day. But that's how we learned the business. You're going all night and you're desperately trying to keep the guide ship in your sights."

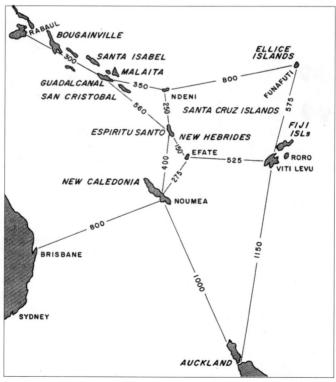

Approximate South Pacific distances.

The convoy arrived at Espiritu Santo in the New Hebrides on the 29th. So far so good. The experience improved everyone's seamanship. The next day the convoy headed northwest towards the Solomon Islands.

Emotions continued to build now. McNeill: "It is difficult to explain my feelings as we steamed into the Coral Sea and watched the semi-security of Espiritu Santo sink into the horizon. In two days we would be a part of the great struggle at Guadalcanal. They say fear usually is greatest before an action and gradually recedes with involvement, unless some traumatic experience occurs. I was filled with fear, but also anxious to 'do my thing in the war.' I realized how critical the battle at Guadalcanal was and that we must win there. Already the Battle of Midway and the Battle of the Coral Sea had stopped the forward motion of the Japanese, and now we must start pushing them back."

Late New Year's day 1943, San Cristobal Island in the Southern Solomons was sighted. Later that night a storm created heavy seas for the convoy for about two hours but at dawn all ships were accounted for. The convoy returned to steaming formation and before long entered the Indispensable Strait and proceeded through Lunga Channel into Iron Bottom Sound. The convoy had reached Guadalcanal, that little speck on the globe upon which the eyes of the entire world were focused—the field of battle in the Pacific.

The LCTs were to discharge their cargo of AV-gas directly on Lunga beach, the main unloading point for Henderson Field. However, a Condition Red from Cactus Control warning of an enemy air raid called for a quick change of plans, so the convoy headed for Tulagi Harbor, code-named "Ringbolt," about 19 miles north of the 'Canal.

The convoy arrived in Tulagi Harbor that afternoon and was soon united with the other six LCTs under Lt Kouri's command. Of course, in addition to receiving their first assignments, the new arrivals heard many wild stories about life in the Solomons.

Southern Solomons Service and Training

On 3 January 1943, the LCTs returned to Lunga Point to unload the AV-gas. Upon arrival off Lunga, the Beachmaster assigned the LCTs to various positions on the beach. The scene was one of organized confusion. Large pontoon barges powered by outboard motors were being unloaded onto the beach, then the supplies were loaded into trucks and hauled off to various dumpsites.

A long line of trucks backed up to the LCT ramps and working parties of Marines, Seabees, and Army personnel were soon unloading the ships. The gasoline drums were rolled down the ramps and hauled directly to Henderson Field and/or the nearby fighter strips.

The new Flotilla Five LCTs were soon performing the many valuable functions for which they were designed. One service they were well-suited for was hauling cargo from the long-haul cargo ships to the beaches. Here was the drill: Early each morning, the freighters, mostly merchantmen, would anchor about a mile from shore. The LCTs would pull alongside and take on about 150 tons of cargo for delivery to the beach. At night the supply ships left the immediate area since the anchorage was not protected against submarines.

The Mule Pack Outfit   LCT-159 had a challenging first assignment made necessary because the Japanese had managed to get a large gun up in the hills where its shells could reach one end of the beach. John McNeill described his first local hauling job: "Among the ships to be unloaded was a Liberty Ship lifting the 47th Field Artillery, a mule pack outfit. Mules could move howitzers and other artillery over terrain that machines could not cross. The mules were brought up from Noumea and our job was to land them on Kukum Beach. I came alongside the ship and about 40 mules were lowered to my deck in slings, each one with a soldier to manage it. Then several cylinders of oxygen and acetylene were lowered for some reason. As we headed for the beach, the heat from the sun set off the safety valves on the gas cylinders and the resulting noise panicked the mules.

"I had been taught to drive the LCT hard into the beach at full speed to get the bow high enough to lay the ramp on dry land. This I did, and the result was to knock the mules off their feet. The ramp was dropped and these frightened animals looked up and saw the first dry land they had seen in six months. Then I learned about a stampede. The mules were uncontrollable as they started down the ramp, dragging their attendants with them. The bottleneck at the bow of the ship presented a minor problem, but slowed them down very little. As soon as they reached the hot sands of the beach they behaved just like mules, they began wallowing. It was impossible to

Guadalcanal Cargo Handling, 1943. Courtesy Claude Gulbranson.

control them until they had finished. They were then led away to their corrals. This procedure continued throughout the day with the help of other LCTs until several hundred mules with their equipment were unloaded. A few days later the gun in the hills was silenced and I knew the mules had done their job."

The work along the beaches continued. Each morning the LCTs would meet several freighters after dawn and make numerous trips back and forth to the beaches. The weather was generally good and a bulldozer was available to push them off the beach when the tide left them aground while unloading.

Solomons Organized Crime   One day John McNeill decided a game of bribery was in order since, as he put it, "the merchant ships were so eager to get unloaded." He talked to the other LCT skippers and together they decided to "organize crime in the Solomons."

Here, in McNeill's own words, is how this "caper" was launched: "Each morning as we approached the freighters we would stop about 100 yards abeam and holler over to the Captain with a sad story about being out of food. Unless a quick offer was made we moved on to the next ship. The results were startling! Each morning the freighters had men holding up hams, fresh fruit, steaks, sacks of flour, beer, whiskey, boxes of cigars, cigarettes, electric fans, or anything else they thought we might want.

"We soon developed this to a fine art. Since everything was expendable on a battlefront, it seemed no one was held accountable for such items. When we came alongside a ship to unload her, I would visit the Captain, usually being entertained with a big meal. Then my list of needs was discussed. It was unbelievable. They were so eager to get unloaded they would agree to anything if we would only hurry. While I was visiting the Captain, our cook would visit the galley and present a list of his needs. The Gunner's Mate, the Electrician, the Boatswain's Mate, the Machinist, the Quartermaster, all had their lists and usually received their needs. We were soon 'rolling in riches' and the freighters seemed to be happy since we worked much harder."

Condition Black   One afternoon Cactus Radio announced a "Condition Black" warning. This meant an invasion or attack by sea was near. All sea-going ships left the area and the landing craft went to the Tulagi area. The LCTs were instructed to enter Hutchinson's Creek, a small bay behind Gavutu and Tonambogo Islands that penetrated a short distance into Florida Island, and tie up alongside trees so as to be shielded from aircraft and hidden from the sea approach.

Tulagi Island in foreground is 18 miles north of Guadalcanal. It was the capital of British Solomon Islands. The island in the center is Makambo – headquarters of LCT Flotilla 5 and area PT boats. National Archives.

Lt Jones had informed his skippers that a large Japanese Task Force was gathering at nearby bases and that their aircraft were in position to deliver a major strike. It was thought the enemy was preparing to bring in a large force and attempt to recapture Guadalcanal. That night a few aircraft flew over Tulagi and dropped bombs, but they did little damage. The next day Mr. Jones told his division the Japs had been turned back by a large Allied air attack, so the LCTers could return to work.

Makomba Base   The Flotilla Five LCTs frequently tied up at the Burns-Phillips dock on Makomba Island near Tulagi, usually in nests of three, to share electricity. PT boats also shared the island facilities. One of the boats, the PT-109, was skippered by Lt Jack Kennedy, who was destined to become president of the United States.

Cape Esperance End Run

In late January 1943, the 159 and five other LCT pioneers were selected to move an Army regiment around Guadalcanal's Cape Esperance and make a landing on Marovovo Beach. The skippers were instructed to go to the 'Canal for a briefing on the operation.

Here is a condensed version of John McNeill's record of this historic action with additional input from RAdm Morison: [10]

"When we arrived at Lunga Beach, we were picked up by a jeep and taken to headquarters on Guadalcanal. A tent had been set up with charts, maps and photographs of the landing area. The operation was explained in great detail and we met and talked to the officers of the Army unit and the destroyers that were to escort us. While we were there we also learned about the Battle of Rennell Island which was fought the night before on the west side of Guadalcanal. We had lost another heavy cruiser, the *Chicago,* to a night attack by torpedo planes.

"In the early hours of 1 February, the 159 moved onto the beach at Kukum and began embarking units of the 2nd Battalion, 132nd Infantry. Six large trucks came aboard first, each with a machine gun mounted on the open cab. Then several hundred rounds of artillery ammunition and many boxes of supplies and food were loaded. I remember the troops so vividly. They sat among the palm trees along the shore and talked and smoked.

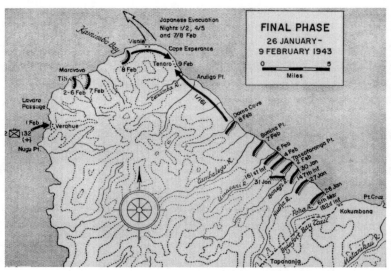

Guadalcanal Final Phase, 26 January to 9 February 1943.

"Once again APD *Stringham* was to lead us, although we were to proceed independently, about five miles apart. This was to confuse the Japanese about our intentions and to separate any forces that attempted to intercept. We were also escorted by four fine and famous destroyers, the *Fletcher, Nicholas, Radford,* and *DeHaven,* and by Henderson Field fighter planes. I was to depart fourth in order, followed by Bo Gillette in the 367 boat.

Embarkation of Troops   "At 0400 1 February, the troops came aboard and we got underway. Our instructions were to head directly for Savo Island and turn to the west just before reaching Savo. We reached Savo around 1000 and I made my turn westward, clearing Cape Esperance far enough away to stay out of range of the Japanese artillery.

Zeros Attack   "When we reached a point about three miles from Savo, the lookouts reported four Zeros approaching from the north... I quickly turned towards the aircraft in order to clear all my guns, to reduce our exposure, and to give the Army guns an opportunity to fire. When I gave the order to open fire I was astonished at the firepower of the Army. In addition to the machine guns on the trucks, the soldiers were all firing all of their weapons including rifles and BARs. The effect was so massive I first thought that we had been hit, but I saw the Zeros had turned away in face of this defense.

Cape Esperance on Guadalcanal at left, and Savo Island in the distance. At center, a destroyer steams what became known as "Ironbottom Sound." Courtesy of National Archives.

"Soon we could see the first three LCTs and the *Stringham* at Marovovo Beach. When I reached a point about a mile from the beach, one of the destroyers came alongside and reported that the troops ashore were advancing rapidly and that I was to change my destination to Komimbo Bay, which was 2 or 3 miles closer to the Japanese lines...

Bettys Suddenly Appear   "I looked up and saw several twin-engine 'Bettys' at close range coming from over the island. It was so sudden that we did not get off a single shot, but one of the destroyers picked one off with a salvo of a 5-inch shell with the new radio proximity fuse. These aircraft were returning from a strike at Henderson Field and were as surprised to see us as we were to see them. I changed course and proceeded easterly back towards Cape Esperance. The destroyer remained alongside and was indeed welcome. When we sighted Kamimbo I picked out an open beach and started in.

Troops/Cargo Offloaded   "As we approached the beach, a lookout shouted and pointed towards a submarine on our port side. I quickly identified it as the wreck of the Japanese submarine I-1, which I recalled was beached after being shelled and rammed by the New Zealand corvettes *Kiwi* and *Moa* two nights before. I continued onto the beach and dropped my ramp. The troops quickly ran ashore and the trucks drove off. In addition to the troops, I also had aboard about a dozen 'Malaita Boys,' natives of the island of Malaita, who were to help unload the ammunition.

"About this time I heard a commotion on the bow followed by an explosion. Looking out, I saw the bow was covered with blood and human remains. We had been told to pick up any prisoners or Japanese wounded. The soldiers had wounded a Jap in the skirmish, I had heard earlier, put him on a stretcher and started to put him on my ship. They had failed to search him and when he realized that he was taken prisoner, he had pulled the pin on a hand grenade and lay on top of it, which had spread him across the bow of the 159.

Unfriendly Ships In Area   "Soon Bo Gillette arrived with the 369 and began unloading. I still had considerable ammunition aboard to unload when I was called to the bridge. It was Cactus Radio calling, asking our location. They gave me the startling news that 21 unidentified ships were in my area and that I was to make best possible speed for Tulagi. I figured this was Admiral Tanaka with the 'Tokyo Express' and that I had best see how fast an LCT could run.

"I hollered over to Bo Gillette and he made the same decision. We both retracted from the beach and headed for Tulagi. Radio Cactus called again and reported the 21 ships to be unfriendly, adding their best wishes for a speedy return.

"As we headed east the destroyer *DeHaven* (DD-469) came alongside. This is one of the most vivid memories I have of the war. The *DeHaven* was freshly painted and I remember how neat and powerful she looked. The Captain walked across the quarter-deck and said something to the signalman. The signalman turned to me and slowly sent me the following semaphore message, 'Good Luck.' Then I remember how handsome the Captain looked and how his 'scrambled eggs' looked on his cap as he saluted and waved to me. He then turned to the OD and said something and the *DeHaven* sped away to oblivion. This was about 1700 with another hour or so of daylight left. I sent word to the engine room to give me all that we had.

"The sea was calm as we headed around Cape Esperance staying just outside what I considered to be the range of the Jap guns. At this time three converted destroyer minelayers were laying a minefield across the anticipated path of the 'Express.'

USS DeHaven passing north of Savo Island, 30 January 1943. She was sunk on 1 February 1943 in these waters by a Japanese air attack. Photo by USS Fletcher (DD-445). Courtesy National Archives.

LCT-181 coming alongside Fletcher (DD-445) with survivors of DeHaven (DD-469) aboard. DeHaven had been sunk by Japanese air attack on 1 Feb. 1943, the day this photo was taken off Guadalcanal. Courtesy National Archives.

USS DeHaven Sunk   "The bow lookout suddenly screamed, 'Look, Skipper!' and pointed at the *DeHaven* which was about four miles ahead of us. I swung my binoculars around in time to see 14 Val bombers already in their dive on *DeHaven*. I could hear Cactus Radio announcing 'Condition Red' but too late for poor *DeHaven*. Three bombs made direct hits and a near miss mined the hull. Commander Charles E. Tolman was killed and within two minutes the *DeHaven* had joined the graveyard of Ironbottom Bay.

"This triggered one of my rare emotional explosions. Cursing and crying, I screamed at the Japs, daring them to come within our range. I was so mad that I felt like standing on the bow of the 159 with a claymore and taking on the entire 'Tokyo Express.' We soon passed over the spot where DeHaven went down and found nothing remaining."

Ranking high among the exploits of LCTs was the remarkable rescue of the 146 survivors of the destroyer *DeHaven,* sunk off Savo Island in February 1943. Two LCTs, the 63 and the 181, under constant threat of attack by Japanese planes, lowered their bow ramps and actually scooped the men from the sea to safety. During this brief action, the machine guns of LCT-63 and LCT-181 also shot down a Japanese plane. Unfortunately, the *DeHaven* took 167 of her crew with her to the Ironbottom graveyard.[11] Now back to John McNeill:

The Race For Tulagi   "As darkness fell over Ironbottom Bay, our two LCTs rang up every turn our engines could make. I had hoped to reach the edge of Savo before the 'Tokyo Express' entered the Bay. Glancing at the chart, I could find no easy out. Our only chance was to try to hug the shoreline of Savo and either beach there or continue down to the south side and make a run for Tulagi.

"I continued in the darkness towards Savo Island. Bo followed closely. Every eye was searching the northeastern area for the approaching Japs. I considered several situations that might develop—all were bad. The crew behaved beautifully. While I know they were as scared as I was, everyone did his job perfectly. The two 20-mm guns and the two .30-caliber machine guns were constantly manned and ready to fire. All others held a Springfield rifle. However insignificant this was, we intended to give it all we had.

"Approaching Savo, I considered beaching and 'heading for the hills,' but decided to do this only if discovered and attacked. I turned east and ran close to Savo's shore where I knew the water was deep and free of reefs. We were now into Ironbottom Sound and quietly passing Savo. I realized then I did not know how to find Tulagi from this direction. I did not dare use a light to consult a chart. Then I remembered the 'Malaita Boys' on deck. I sent the chief down to ask if any knew how to find Tulagi. One came on deck and stared into the darkness for several minutes. Then he pointed to a position near the port bow. With my binoculars I picked out a mountain that I could guide on. It would be about 8 or 9 miles to Tulagi and I knew the next hour would tell the story.

"Suddenly the lookout screamed, 'Ships ahead!' Before I could react, two PT boats zipped past us, barely avoiding a collision. We both continued on our courses and in a few minutes an airplane dropped a brilliant flare over us. This was a typical Japanese prelude to attack. Without radar, they had an observation plane illuminate the target. Nothing happened. I suppose that since we were leaving the area, they did not consider us a threat.

"We began to see gunfire in the Cape Esperance area which we thought was the Japanese firing at the PT boats. Several flares were dropped behind us by the Japanese, who had detected *Fletcher, Radford,* and *Nicholas* trying to get into position for an attack. Then we saw a violent explosion, which was Jap destroyer *Makigumo* exploding in the minefield.

LCT-159 Returns To Base   "I began to feel that we might have escaped the Japs, but we still had a few miles to go. I knew that by now we were being observed by gunners on Tulagi. Then I remembered the recognition signals had just changed and I had forgotten the new answer to a challenge. I ran to the signalman and told him to watch in the direction of Tulagi and if a challenge signal was made, to answer 'LCT 159 returning to base.' Shortly I saw the challenge light and held my breath, knowing that many big guns were trained on us. We answered and Tulagi replied 'Proceed.' As we rounded the buoys and entered Tulagi, I was indeed a thankful man.

"We continued to see flashes in the sky during the night and wondered about the PTs. Around dawn the survivors of the eleven boats began to return to base. Three of the boats were sunk and PT-48 went aground on Savo but was later rescued."

Author's note: The CinCPAC report[12] covering the strike at Cape Esperance on 1 February 1943 confirms the LCT skipper's story.

Evacuation of Guadalcanal

The increased runs of the 'Tokyo Express' in early February, in combination with intensified air activity, gave the impression that the enemy was again undertaking an offensive move in force. Increased operations of Japanese landing barges in the Southern Solomons gave the impression that they were ferrying troops by night between the Russell Islands and Guadalcanal. Actually, the craft were evacuating troops and probably played a major part in the withdrawal from Guadalcanal.

Admiral Nimitz and his staff summed up the evacuation of the 'Canal with these words:

On the morning of 8 February another large number of empty landing barges were found floating off Esperance and later a few abandoned ones were found in the Russells. These were the last indications of Japanese troop movements off Guadalcanal. It appears that on the night of 7-8 February, exactly 6 months from the day of our landing in August 1942, the Japanese withdrew from Guadalcanal. Simultaneously, the strong fleet north of the Solomons retired to bases in the Carolines, carrier air groups operating ashore in the Solomons returned to their ships, and most of the land-based aircraft brought to the Solomons for this operation flew to New Guinea.

On 8 February our troops encountered only occasional patrols southwest of Esperance and no resistance to the west. Medical stores, rations, and unused weapons were captured in quantities. On 9 February our main body joined forces near Esperance with the enveloping detachment from Verahue, ending the campaign on Guadalcanal. [13]

John McNeill's reaction to the news of the evacuation was shared by thousands of U.S. servicemen in the Solomons: "It was very difficult for all of us to accept. After the long and bloody battles ashore, at sea, and in the air, and believing all the recent activity was an attempt to recapture the island, we could not believe the Japs had fled. Even 'Tokyo Rose' reported that after 'slaughtering the American troops on Guadalcanal, the Imperial Japanese Army had moved on to new battlefields.'"

Boredom, Humor and Heroics

"Scrappy" Kessing   More than one amphibian had a favorite Captain Oliver O. Kessing story for me. He was one of the best known characters in the Navy and, reportedly, a Naval Academy classmate and close friend of Admiral Halsey. As commander of Naval Base Tulagi, he gave orders and dispensed hospitality at Government House, Tulagi.

It was Kessing who ordered Halsey's famous slogan painted above the fleet landing at Tulagi, in letters two feet tall:

" KILL JAPS, KILL JAPS, KILL MORE JAPS! "

One of the LCT Flot 5 skippers (he prefers to remain anonymous) told me this Kessing story: "Seems there were these two doctors stationed on Tulagi in 1943. One of them was a real clown. He somehow got hold of a parrot and put him up in a cage. He kept that bird company every chance he got for a month or so. Then one day the two docs got Captain Kessing to pay them a visit to see their new friend. When the three of them walked outside to see the bird, the good doctor said to the Captain, 'You know what you're supposed to say to a parrot, right?' And, of course, the Captain, right on cue, said, 'Polly want a cracker?' With that the parrot answered, 'Fuck you, Captain!' Those were the only words he knew! He just kept repeating them. This doctor had spent a month teaching that bird just those three words!" (Kessing went on to command advance bases in Bougainville and Ulithi later in the war. He eventually was promoted to Commodore by Halsey.)

Hand Grenade Close Call   Austin Volk (LCT-60) and his crew had a close call hauling Jap POWs while in the Southern Solomons: "About the middle of February [1943], we went up the line to pick up these prisoners near Cape Esperance in the northern part of Guadalcanal. The Army had picked them up and they were mostly debilitated—malaria, malnutrition, pretty far gone. As the Army brought them up the ramp, one POW had his arm bound up. Two Corpsmen came to pick him up and put him on a stretcher and as he passed me, I heard what sounded like a cap pistol go off. (The Japanese armed their grenades by tapping them on a surface, instead of pulling a pin, then throwing them.) As soon as I heard that, I went over the side.

"The Corpsmen saw or heard him do this and flipped him over as they dropped him. He landed on his face and stomach and blew himself up fortunately. Those hospital corpsmen were really on the ball. If they hadn't flipped him, they would have gotten the blast."

Artie Shaw Entertains   Here's a quickie worth telling even if the LCT storyteller prefers to remain anonymous: "Artie Shaw was doing his bit to entertain the troops. After he finished his gig, he climbed this hill—maybe 75 to 100 feet high—with a bunch of sailors following him. They followed him right into the head and he asked one of them why they were there. They all answered, 'We want to see the prick that screwed Ava Gardner!'"

Lessons Learned Four of the first skippers to reach the Solomons, Austin Volk (LCT-60), Richard Easton (LCT-71), Ed Burtt (LCT-68), and Carl Barrett (LCT-322), received orders in mid-April 1943 to return to New Caledonia to join the staff of Landing Ship Flotillas, South Pacific. Here's how skipper Volk described the new duty: "We returned to Noumea on LST-446. [LST-446 was on its way to Australia to temporarily join Admiral Barbey's VII Amphibious Force.] The staff down there at Landing Ship Flotillas had no experience running these ships... so they put us in charge of training the new arrivals coming in from the States. They were also concerned with how the new landing craft were operating and what could be done to improve them.

"We gave the new skippers tips on training their crews, showed them how to offload their boat from the deck of an LST, how to beach at the Isle of Pines and offload cargo, and so on. We got it done pretty quickly actually.

"As far as improvements were concerned, the Landing Craft Flotillas staff was surprised to learn we had to scrounge around for refrigerators and cut part of the hull away to get some air into the crew's quarters because there wasn't any ventilation. So they asked us to come up with suggestions for a new or improved LCT which we did. Most of our ideas and suggestions were incorporated into the LCT(6) when it came out about six months later, including better crew quarters, improved ventilation, a larger stove, and stern loading."

Johnson Head Most LCTers I've interviewed sooner or later bring up the story of the "Johnson head," a.k.a. "Johnson Crapper." So I asked Ensign "Cookie " Johnson to elaborate: "I was the inventor but my patent never went through. Well, we carried a lot of Marines around, you know, and we only had one head on the 182... and I couldn't stand to have my crew clean it anymore. So I went to the Seabees at Tulagi and told them what I wanted. I had become pretty good friends with the top Seabee over there. He says, sure. So they took and bent a piece of pipe around, then attached this flat metal thing used to hold a life preserver on it... Then we took our toilet seat off the toilet and put it on there, bolted it down. Then they cut a piece of canvas and hung it around the back of our new crapper and then we put toilet paper there in a box.

"It was great except when you had following winds or seas, you'd get a bidet [a.k.a. crotch wash]. It was a lifesaver. Of course, you weren't supposed to do that. You were never supposed to alter anything on a ship unless you got permission from the Bureau of Ships.

"That was the most successful contribution I made during my entire service in the Navy. And pretty soon other guys began to copy it. I think every LCT in our Flotilla had one put in. Later on, we got recognized for it."

Russell Islands Shuttle

Skipper McNeill describes both the challenges and the boredom on the shuttle runs to supply the Russells: "The trips to supply CLEANSLATE became the mission of Flotilla Five. We eventually moved about 16,000 men and a mountain of equipment to Banika Island. The Japanese did not discover our move for two weeks which gave us the opportunity to become firmly secured.

"The LCTs did the job well. We would load during the day at Guadalcanal and leave the beach around dark. Usually three to six LCTs made the trip escorted by an APD. We would arrive in the Russells around 0200 and begin unloading. The first Jap air attack occurred on 6 March, but we were never the primary target.

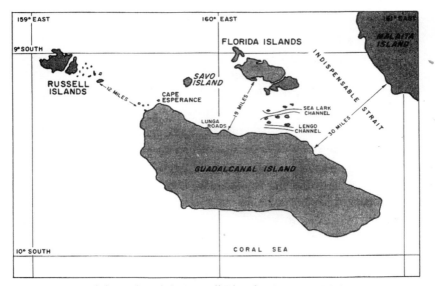

Guadalcanal and the Russell Islands. Courtesy U.S. Navy.

LCT-326 unloading at Banika Island (Russells) at Lever Coconut Plantation, Mar. 1943. Courtesy John McNeill.

"Our departure depended on the type of cargo. With some construction material, it sometimes required a full day to unload, but generally we were back at Tulagi early the second night. Since there was only one officer on an LCT, it was generally the procedure to remain on deck from the time of departure from Tulagi until the return, usually 36 to 48 hours.

"Then with one night's rest, the cycle was repeated. This awesome physical challenge expedited the training of the Boatswain's Mate to relieve the Skipper for short periods of rest. While I felt my Bos'n, a Chief Petty Officer, was very competent, I felt full responsibility for the ship and usually stayed on the bridge.

"The activity of unloading and the intense heat during the day prevented any sleep. However, sometimes I would doze for a few minutes in the shade of the wheel house. On a few occasions a Japanese plane would detect us at night by observing the phosphorescence of our wake and strafe us. The 159 escaped any damage from these attacks.

"I did not keep a record of how many times I went to the Russells— I would guess at around twenty-five. Some of the ships developed engine trouble and all quickly wore out the strut bearings on the main propulsion shaft. We had no dry dock and no spare bearings, but we did have Lt Ameel Z. Kouri, the incredible Wheaties salesman, who later was offered the presidency of General Mills.

LCT(5) Landing Craft, Tank (Mark 5). ONI/226.

Changing LCT propellers and strut bearings at low tide with no dry dock available. LCTs were pulled on and pushed off beaches at high tide by large bulldozers. Courtesy John McNeill.

"Lt Kouri, 'A.Z.' to all the skippers, learned to drag us backwards up on Gavutu Island with a bulldozer and replace the worn out bearings with his new invention, while the tide was out. The time of low tide allowed very little work time, so it required a couple of days to change all the bearings.

Where to Next? "With April came an enormous buildup of men, ships and supplies. The new and larger landing craft, LCIs and LSTs, appeared in considerable numbers. Guadalcanal, now called 'Mainyard,' became a larger base with miles of men and equipment. Flot Five reached its quota of 36 ships and Mr. Jones was promoted to Flotilla Commander. Flotilla Six LCTs also began to arrive and it was obvious that preparations were being made for a major move towards Japan."

Shortly thereafter, McNeill and the other Flotilla Five skippers learned that top secret plans had been completed for the next Solomon Islands campaign—code named "Operation TOENAILS." The relative inactivity of the last few months had come to an end.

We'll rejoin LCT Flot 5 in our next book, which will provide complete land, sea, and air coverage of the 1942-1943 Solomons campaigns from Guadalcanal to Bougainville. Stay tuned. But before I wind up this Chapter, let's fast forward to 1944 and a group photo taken of several original Flot 5 LCT skippers on leave following the successful Solomons campaigns.

LCT Flotilla Five reunion in Washington, DC, 1944 while on a much deserved leave following the Solomons campaigns. Courtesy of John McNeill.

CHAPTER 4

Biography of LST Flotilla Five, from Amphibious Training to Guadalcanal

The LST was and is still a marvel, and the officers and men who manned them hold a high place in my affections.

—Admiral Richmond Kelly Turner

W hen you compare the almost complete absence of archival information available on LCTs and LCIs, my sources for this chapter border on "information overload." Consider this: In addition to the War Diary of Captain G. B. Carter, Commander LST Flotilla Five, my primary sources include several command histories of individual Flot 5 LSTs including the 446, the first LST to arrive in the South Pacific. I also had the good fortune to locate and interview the late Rogers Aston, LST-446 Gunnery Officer and First Lieutenant, and to receive permission to use excerpts from his WWII memoirs.

Another LST featured in this chapter is LST-398. I've also interviewed more than two dozen plankowners of Flot 5 LSTs, thanks to the assistance of the United States L.S.T. Association, and Mel Barger, author of *Long Slow Target*.

First, I'll summarize early amphibious training, such as it was, then I'll describe how crew and flotillas were formed. This will be followed by LST design and construction; shakedown cruises and sea trials, maiden voyages, and Southern Solomons "on-the-job-training" in preparation for the invasion of New Georgia in the Central Solomons—code-named "Operation TOENAILS"—and the first use of these revolutionary new shore-to-shore landing ships.

Amphibious Training

By mid-October 1942, Camp Little Creek was barely in "usable condition" according to LST Flotilla Five amphibian trainees. In fact, there were only a few barracks and practically no camp facilities. Food had to be cooked in tin containers on field kitchens borrowed from the Marine Corps. There was no hot running water for the kitchens or laundry. Furthermore, there was no Ship's Store, Post Office, or Recreation Hall. The net result: serious griping and a low morale factor among both ship's company and trainees.

Martin "Flags" Melkild, LST-398, believes Camp Little Creek deserved its nickname, "Alligator Camp," because when he arrived on 15 October 1942, "rainwater still covered the grounds and if you stepped off the boardwalks you were ankle deep in mud."

To paraphrase Flags, the barracks were tarpaper shacks framed with two-by-fours and heated by two antiquated coal and wood-burning stoves that needed constant tending. The double-decker bunks, also made of two-by-fours, had chicken wire bottoms to support sagging sailors. There were no lockers, so everyone lived out of their sea bags.

The bathhouse, connected to the barracks by a boardwalk, had corroded pipes resulting in water unfit for drinking or washing clothes. Sea water retrieved from the pier in a bucket and salt water soap were used to do one's laundry.[1]

Solomons ATB Here's how the LST-446 command historian described the arrival and training of the original crew. "The officers came straight from indoctrination schools and the men came from boot camps and specialists' schools. On 11 September 1942, they were placed upon a cattle boat at Norfolk, Virginia and sent on their way to the Solomons, Maryland ATB."[2]

Following a 14-hour trip without food, the future officers and crew of LST-446 arrived at the Solomons base and received their initiation into the amphibious force. They were greeted by pouring rain, unpainted and half-finished buildings, mud up to their ankles, and the loud ["sucker"] cries of a vast number of enlisted personnel.

At that date, Solomons ATB was a counterpart to the battlefield in the Pacific bearing the same name, and the subsequent experience upon that latter island base proved almost preferable to the rain-soaked, insect-infested base in Maryland, where fresh drinking and bathing water was rationed severely and often unobtainable.

Officers and men wandered aimlessly about within the confines of a high steel fence thrown around the base, with nothing to occupy their minds or hands except constant speculation about the meaning of the word "amphibious."

Denied the privilege of shore leave, and offered no constructive education in the task ahead—not even a glimpse of a picture of the ships they were later to command—reserve officers listened with hope to the few Mustangs[3] billeted with them in the enlisted men's barracks when they promised, "The regular Navy is nothing like this," but had misgivings when the statement was followed with, "But I don't know about this amphibious force. What is it anyway?"

LST-460 was featured in a BuPers magazine article entitled "The Temporary War of LST-460."[4] In the article, one of the 460 officers recalled the amphibious training during the winter of 1942-43 this way: "Training was sometimes so fast that if you bent over, you missed most of it. We had one week of training at Norfolk, then we went out to the West Coast to take over our ship."

At Norfolk as many as seven crews were training aboard one LST at the same time, all trying to squeeze into quarters meant for one, and trying to learn about the ship without stumbling over each other.

Crew/Flotilla Formations

In the previous chapter, 36 crews were selected for LCT Flotilla Five while most of their landing craft were still under construction. The crews were then shipped to San Francisco to await the arrival and assembly of their LCTs.

For LST Flotilla Five, form ups worked somewhat differently. For example, the crews of LST-446 and her Kaiser-built sister ships were assembled at Solomons ATB and shipped to Portland, Oregon, to await the commissioning of their ships; whereas the crews for the first 12 Flot 5 LSTs built on the East Coast were formed up together.

Before going any further, please remember the early Flotilla Five LSTs were all manned by U.S. Navy personnel. However, the U.S. Coast Guard, although relatively small in number,[5] manned 30 LSTs and served in all theaters of operation.

Flotilla Five LSTs

The 18 LSTs that *initially* made up Flotilla Five were built in four different shipyards and commissioned between 27 November 1942 and 13 March 1943. They were the first LSTs assigned to the South Pacific. Here they are by shipyard and date of commissioning:

Kaiser, Inc., Vancouver, Washington

USS LST-446	30 November 1942
USS LST-447	13 December 1942
USS LST-448	23 December 1942
USS LST-449	31 December 1942
USS LST-460	15 February 1943
USS LST-472	13 March 1943

Newport News (Virginia) Shipbuilding and Drydock Co.

USS LST-395	19 December 1942
USS LST-396	23 December 1942
USS LST-397	28 December 1942
USS LST-398	02 January 1943
USS LST-399	04 January 1943

Norfolk (Virginia) Navy Yard

USS LST-339	23 December 1942
USS LST-340	26 December 1942
USS LST-341	28 December 1942
USS LST-342	28 December 1942
USS LST-343	09 January 1943

Charleston (South Carolina) Navy Yard

USS LST 353	27 November 1942
USS LST-354	27 November 1942

USS LST-339 and USS LST-340 at time of launch. Note the competitive rivalry between shipyards. Courtesy Naval Historical Center.

LST-446 would be the first LST to arrive in the South Pacific, as well as the first to see service in the Solomons. She arrived at Guadalcanal on 8 March 1943, followed closely by three of her Kaiser LST sisters: 447, 448, and 449. (These early birds would soon be loaned to "MacArthur's Navy" for the unopposed occupation of the Trobriand Islands off New Guinea on 1 July 1943.)

The 12 East Coast-built LSTs would arrive at Noumea, New Caledonia, the afternoon of 14 May 1943 after completing a voyage that spanned 67 days and some 9,000 nautical miles—Captain Grayson B. "Chick" Carter, USN, Flotilla Five Commander in LST-340 with his LST "chicks" 339, 341, 342, 343, 353, 354, 395, 396, 397, 398, and 399.

Seven (39 percent) of the first Flot 5 LSTs would be lost before the war ended: LSTs 342 and 396 from submarine torpedo attacks,[6] the 448 from a bombing raid; the 447, 460, and 472 from Kamikaze suicide attacks; and the 353 from an accidental ammunition explosion.

LST-340 became the first LST battle casualty of WWII when she took a direct bomb hit off the 'Canal on 16 June 1943. She was salvaged, repaired and put back in action for the Marianas campaign only to sustain serious storm damage on 29 July 1944. Her final duty: redesignated as barracks ship, *Spark,* 20 October 1944, in Tanapag Harbor, Saipan.

Twenty-four Flot 5 LSTs earned the Navy Unit Commendation for WWII service. Collectively, they also earned a total of 79 battle stars! But we are getting ahead of ourselves.

LST Design and Construction

Much has been written about the design and construction of landing ships and craft. Who would get credit for the designs? Were they American or British? However, there are two key points no one argues about: The urgent need for LSTs in 1942, and which home front warriors came through when the chips were down.

The following special study—condensed by the author—was originally issued in July 1944. It helped me appreciate the critical decisions that had to be made by the President, Joint Chiefs, War Production Board, and Allied planners each time landing craft production snafus[7] created delays in launching major campaigns such as North Africa (TORCH) and Normandy (OVERLORD).

Even though I was a 16-year-old welder working on LSTs and Liberty ships during the summer of 1942—waiting to turn 17 so he could join the Navy—I obviously didn't have a clue as to what went on in Washington. Oh, I knew there was an urgent need for ships, everyone knew that. But I didn't realize how close we came to losing the war due to many factors far beyond the control of any shipyard worker.

Amphibious warfare in the Pacific required ships with ocean-going capabilities that could also be "beached" in the course of landing operations. This requirement was met with the design and production of the Landing Ship, Tank (LST) that was used in combat for the first time in the Central Solomons.

The forerunner to the LST was a U.K. Bachaquero class vessel—a converted British shallow-draft merchant oiler designed for work on Lake Maracaibo and consequently, they became known to the Brits as "Maracaibos." The three merchant conversions had the now-familiar bow doors and were capable of transporting 18 heavy Churchill tanks or 22 medium tanks directly on steep beaches. (Americans first witnessed the Maracaibos in action at the North Africa landings at Oran in November 1942.)

At Churchill's instigation, the British Chiefs of Staff forwarded to their American counterparts the concept for a large ship that could land tanks directly on a beach. They requested that Americans take responsibility for its development and mass production.

Scarcely one month before Pearl Harbor, John C. Niedermair, Technical Director of Preliminary Ship Design for the Bureau of Ships, prepared a rough sketch of what eventually became the Landing Ship Tank. The British had specified a design to go on a beach with a slope of 1 foot in 100 feet (1/100). In Niedermair's words:

> The design had to have two conditions: one, it had to be able to cross the ocean with enough draft to get there; and then, when you got to the landing area, you could pump the tanks dry and go on the beach. Instead of taking the 1/100 slope, I decided that to make this design successful you would have to design it for a 1/50 slope, and that's the way we designed it.

The sketch was finished the same afternoon that Captain

Cochrane came in with the dispatch. That same night I took it home and made a larger drawing, one-sixteenth inch to the foot, and brought that in. They made copies of that and flew it over to England. Then Admiral Carling and a [British] team came over and worked with the Bureau in the development of the detailed plans.[8]

In less than a year from the time of Niedermair's sketch, the first LST was commissioned. More than 1,000 were produced during the war, mostly by inland shipyards never before involved in classical naval ship construction.

The first standard U.S. Navy LST floated out of a building dock at Newport News, Virginia, in October 1942. The overall length was 328 feet—longer than a football field—with a beam of 50 feet. These vessels were capable of transporting a load of 2,100 tons of cargo and about 150 troops. Speed and endurance: 10.8 knots maximum; 6,000 miles radius at 9 knots.

The LSTs employed the principle of submarine diving tanks; e.g., when they blew their ballast tanks, the draft was reduced for unloading tanks and other vehicles through the bow doors—although the perfect beach gradient to accomplish this was seldom realized.

War Production Board Study [9]

Prior to the beginning of World War II, our familiarity with the construction of landing craft was scant indeed. It was not until 1937 that a close approximation to the new smaller-type landing craft was developed. This was the 35- to 50-foot tank lighter, which was capable of carrying one light tank.

During 1940 and 1941, as the prospects of war grew daily, the Navy let contracts for the tank lighter and for other light types of landing craft including the Landing Craft, Personnel (Large); Landing Craft, Personnel (Ramp); and Landing Vehicle, Tracked.

In November 1941, the British asked the United States Navy to develop a large landing craft of real ship dimensions. This craft, according to the British, had to be capable of undertaking long ocean voyages and of carrying and depositing on enemy held beaches many heavy tanks and other heavy equipment. Thereafter, with the aid of a group of British consultants, the Bureau of Ships developed the preliminary design of the LST, a large ocean-going craft of 1,490 tons.

The preliminary design of this ship was practically complete by the end of December 1941.

The first large landing craft construction program started in April 1942, only four months prior to the Guadalcanal landings, and ended in the spring of 1943. The second program, anticipating the invasion of western Europe and the Pacific operations, originated in August and September of 1943, and reached its peak in deliveries during May of 1944.

Landing Craft Program On 7 December 1941, this country had ready for use only a limited number of miscellaneous types of small landing craft and an additional 1,700 on order. During the first quarter of 1942, the Navy Department's Bureau of Ships slowly began letting contracts for more varied types of landing craft. For the first time, Landing Ship-Docks (LSD) and Landing Ship-Tanks (LST) appeared on Navy purchase orders.

But the Navy still did not consider the landing craft program a very urgent one. By virtue of being placed in the eighth group in the Navy's Shipbuilding Precedence List published on 18 January 1942, landing craft had a very low priority. One of the reasons for this low-priority designation for landing craft during the first quarter of 1942 was the menace of the German submarines, which required concentration on building vessels for anti-submarine work, principally destroyer escorts. Work was scarcely started on this program, however, when the landing craft program was interposed in the Navy's total program. Construction of LSTs was subsequently undertaken at six of the eleven yards constructing destroyer escorts in the spring of 1942.

Foreshadowing the North African campaign, a conference was called at the White House on 4 April 1942, which stressed, among other things, the urgent need for landing craft to be used in future operations. As a result, the Bureau of Ships was ordered to provide 600 fifty-foot tank lighters (LCMs) by 1 Sept. 1942. Subsequently, the anticipated campaigns in the Pacific added to the requirements until the first landing craft program bulked as one of the most important in the Navy's shipbuilding list.

Production Goals By July 1, the landing craft program for 1942 called for the construction of more than 12,000 vessels.

Production Challenges   The landing craft program faced almost incalculable difficulties. The program was in competition for materials and components with scores of other urgent military programs. Although landing craft were placed alone in the first preference group of the Navy's Shipbuilding Precedence List on July 1, timely deliveries of materials and components were far from assured. Moreover, the landing craft program was the first multiple, mass-production ship program undertaken by the Navy.

Because of the magnitude of the landing craft program, contracts had to be let to many small boat yards, structural steel plants, and other metal-working firms located thousands of miles away from deep water. By June 30, contracts had been let to 5 Navy yards, 22 major private yards, 11 minor private yards, 12 small boat yards and 29 manufacturing companies. Of this total, 21 were located in the Mississippi River-Great Lakes water sheds. They, together with many firms on the coasts, had to acquire the know-how of constructing landing craft. In that attempt, thousands of mistakes were made and thousands of man-hours lost.

The landing craft program ordered by the White House conference of 4 April 1942 got off to a slow start. To make certain of obtaining the 600 fifty-foot tank lighters by 1 Sept. 1942, the Bureau of Ships let contracts for 1,100 such craft on April 16 and 22.

LST-23 launching 13 March 1943 on the Ohio River at Dravo Shipyards, Neville Island near Corapolis, P.A. Courtesy of Thomas Robson.

By May 1942, the first fifty-foot Bureau of Ships-designed lighter was available for testing against a comparable craft designed and built by the Higgins Corporation. As a result, 1,000 tank lighters in this program were changed to the Higgins design on May 29.

Meanwhile, the Bureau of Ships had been busy adding to the few orders let in the first quarter of the year for other types of landing craft. During April, May, and June 1942, additional contracts were let for 160 LSTs, 340 LVTs (Landing Vehicles, Tracked) and for the first 251 LCTs (Landing Craft, Tanks) weighing over 100 lightweight displacement tons. In June, contracts were also let for the first 350 LCIs (Landing Craft, Infantry), of 175 lightweight displacement tons.

According to its May and July schedules, the Bureau of Ships expected many types of landing craft to attain peak production in August, September, and October of 1942, presumably in time for the units to be used in the North African Invasion.

The extreme urgency of the program was evidenced by the change in the status of landing craft on the Navy's Shipbuilding Precedence List from the 10th group on March 1 to a position alone in the first group on 1 July 1942. In fact, completions did rise rapidly—in tonnage from 1,457 to 15,806. That in itself was a considerable accomplishment, considering the difficulties involved and the woefully short period of time that intervened between the letting of the contracts and the scheduled delivery dates: LCTs of over a hundred lightweight tons that had been ordered in April were being delivered in August. But by August 1, it was apparent that the program was falling short of the May and July goals of the Bureau of Ships.

Deliveries   None of the 1,000 Higgins fifty-foot tank lighters ordered in May by directive of the April 4 White House Conference were delivered in July. Only 118 of them were delivered in August and another 111 in September. The entire 600 required by September 1 were not delivered under this program until late November.[10]

WPB Participation   Reflecting official concern over the lagging landing craft program, the President gave instructions to WPB head Donald M. Nelson in August 1942 that landing craft were of such urgency, the program should interfere, when necessary, with any other program where such interference could not be avoided. Excerpts from the proposed scheduling procedure:

To implement the program, the Navy engaged the Bethlehem Steel Company to organize an office in New York to act as Material Coordinating Agency for the program, and the WPB appointed L. R. Boulware...to supervise the priorities and expediting aspects of the program. To carry out his responsibilities, Boulware was given special delegation of priority authority by J. A. Krug, Deputy Director General for Priorities Control. To work under Boulware's direction, a Landing Craft Specialist was appointed for every War Production Board Regional Office.

It was agreed between Krug and Admiral Robinson on August 24 that the Navy Bureau of Ships was to be held responsible for coordinating delivery dates in all purchase orders for all materials and components needed for the program; that the Materials Coordinating Agency would be responsible for preparing a detailed construction schedule, which would serve as a master production program; and that Boulware and his Landing Craft Specialists would be responsible for resolving bottlenecks in the flow of materials and components by the usual WPB field procedures and by the use of directives where necessary.[11]

LST Profile and Specifications

To bottom-line this profile, here's how the U.S. Navy described the LST in 1944-5:[12]

Operation Use: Ocean-going ship designed to land waterproofed tanks or vehicles over a low ramp on a 1/50 beach slope.

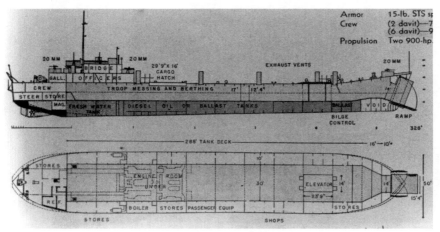

Landing Ship, Tank drawings. USN Office of Naval Intelligence (ONI 226).

Description: An American design, later the United Nations standard. Elevator and hatch service main deck where miscellaneous vehicles and cargo are stowed. Starting with LST-513 and excepting LST-531, main deck ramp was substituted for elevator. For inaccessible landings, sectional pontoons or earth causeways were used, LCT(5) or (6) may be carried in sections or as a unit on main deck. UK Designation-LST(2).

Armament: One 3"/50-cal. D.P. (omitted when 40s available); one 40-mm (seven authorized); six 20-mm (twelve authorized). The bow and stern guns were upgraded to twin 40-mm power-driven, director-controlled mounts as they became available.

Propulsion: Two 900-hp diesels; twin screws.

Fuel: 1,060 tons diesel oil.

Officer's Country was the area below the wheelhouse, chartroom, and radio shack. The crew's sleeping quarters were below deck aft. Troop quarters ran along both sides of the ship on the tank deck.

With a maximum speed of 10 to 12 knots, they lived up to their nickname, "Large, Slow, Targets." LSTs in the South Pacific were also dubbed "Green Dragons" because of their camouflage colors. With meager antiaircraft armament and damage control facilities, concealment was frequently their best defense, but the hundreds of LSTs which helped win the war certainly did not do so by hiding.

Landing Ship, Tank collage showing 2-davit design with early armament, later reinforced as shown by the diagrams. These illustrate the ultimate armament for both the 6- and 2-davit designs. ONI/226.

LST Ships Tour

Charles J. Adams, Jr., (LST-281), a frequent contributor to *Scuttlebutt,* gave readers a nostalgic tour of an LST recently. Here is his article in a condensed/edited format.[13]

Over the years, we've heard many catch words attributed to the LST. 'Landing Ship Tank' didn't seem to suit a lot of the Navy's punsters, so it became Large Slow Target, Large Stationary Target, Large Snapping Turtle, and my favorite, Lousy Stinkin' Tub. No matter what they called them, they were one of the most practical ships in the Navy— especially designed to discharge men and equipment directly on hostile beaches.

The first time we saw the ship, we thought, 'This has got to be the ugliest ship in the Navy.' Only 325 feet long and 50 feet wide, it weighed a mere 3,800 tons. Not a big ship in the fleet, by any means. The exterior was not a bit impressive, but inside she was a wonder of practicality.

The bottom of the ship, or fourth deck, carried ballast (water and fuel) and housed the engine rooms. The main engines could be run together or separately. The ship's electric power was supplied by three smaller auxiliary engines.

The tank deck included the third deck which was rimmed by scores of storage rooms, and the second deck, which was surrounded by eating, sleeping and recreation quarters for the crew and passengers. The tank decks were quite functional even when not loaded with equipment. Some days, lines were strung across with the crew's laundry. When in port and empty, various sports were played on the tank deck and/or movies were shown.

Though built to transport tanks, trucks and a multitude of other war materiel, it soon became apparent that the tank deck would have many other uses. A most effective employment of the tank deck was as an emergency medical facility utilizing portable cots. It could carry hundreds of wounded men to hospital ships and land-based surgical stations.

Forward, the huge enclosed tank deck ended with a cleated perpendicular ramp. On beaching, the bow doors were opened outward and the great ramp was lowered by chains, so tanks, trucks, and other equipment could rumble onto the beach. High on the forward portside was a ramp-control room. The bow doors and ramp could be operated from there. Vehicle traffic also could be directed from this station. In case of power failure, there was a standby method to operate the bow doors and ramp. Should they fail to engage power drive, a series of manually operated cables was put to use.

When vehicles were warming up they produced carbon monoxide, and there was a warning device that sounded a clanging noise when excessive fumes filled the air.

Astern of the main deck was the deck house or 'officer's country,' which included the officer's quarters, mess and galley. (It was off-limits to enlisted men.)

Above all this was the ship's wheelhouse and chartroom containing the 'Steering Wheel,' and all the navigating paraphernalia needed to keep the ship on course. The wheelhouse was surrounded by four AA-guns and a 3"/50 stern gun. (This armament would be upgraded later on.)

The aft end of the ship contained added crew quarters, the mess hall, and galley. The poop deck contained a stern winch to operate the stern anchor to pull the ship from the beach after loading or unloading operations.

Top-side cargo fluctuated according to the needs of the operation ranging from fully-assembled LCTs and vehicles of all types, to supplies, ammunition, and drums of gasoline. Pontoons to assemble 'rhino ferries' were also conveyed on our port and starboard sides.

Up another ladder we find the 'flying bridge,' an enclosure that enabled the ship to be commanded at sea by phone and/or voice tube. Atop all this were the masts with the all-important radar and the ship's red, white and blue commission pennant.

LST Flotilla Five Maiden Voyages

In this section, we'll chronicle the maiden voyage of Kaiser-built LST-446 and her pioneering crew as they make their way to the South Pacific from the West Coast. In the process, it makes the history books as the *first* LST to arrive at Guadalcanal. Then we'll follow the first 12 East Coast-built LSTs to join Flotilla Five as they transit the Panama Canal enroute to the Solomon Islands.

USS LST-446 Early History[14]

As I mentioned earlier, one of the most valuable resources for this history has been plankowner Rogers Aston, the first LST-446 Gunnery Officer and First Lieutenant—the officer responsible, in general, for a ship's upkeep and cleanliness (except machinery and ordnance gear), boats, ground tackle, and deck seamanship.

Between our interviews and his memoirs,[15] he added immeasurably to the factual data in the ship's "Command History."

By the way of background, Rogers volunteered for the U.S. Navy in April 1942; was sworn in with the rank of Ensign—Deck Volunteer Probationary (DVP)—in July 1942; graduated from Northwestern as a Deck Volunteer Special (DVS) in October 1942; and was detached to the Solomons ATB on 26 October 1942. While there, he was assigned to Crew No. 4019—to crew the LST-446 then under construction at the Kaiser Shipyard at Vancouver, Washington.

Author's note: I report sadly that Rogers Aston passed away in July 1999. During World War II he achieved the rank of Lt Commander, and was awarded the Legion Merit with combat V for valor, the Navy Marine Medal for heroism, and the Commendation Medal with five stars.

The initial LST-446 crew was composed of 7 officers and 68 enlisted men—although it would increase to about 110 men later on.

On 5 November 1942, the officers and men assigned to man LST-446 were placed aboard Solomons ATB buses at 1800 and handed orders to report 9 November 1942 to the Navy Receiving Barracks, Portland, Oregon. The enlisted men were provided with rail transportation from Washington, D.C. to Portland. The officers were denied transportation requests and, consequently, forced to use their own initiative to obtain transportation to the coast. Despite these difficulties, all officers and men reported to the Receiving Barracks, Portland, on 9 November, with the exception of two officers who were unable to borrow money for the trip for several days.

The Receiving Barracks were not yet completed, nor was the Officer-in-Charge expecting them. However, after expressing his regrets, he proceeded to make them as comfortable as possible.

On 30 November 1942, almost a month after their four day rush to the West Coast, the officers and men saw their first LST when they boarded the LST-446 at 0900 to supply and provision her prior to departure from the Kaiser yards across the Columbia River in Vancouver, Washington.

John "Monty" La Montagne (LST-448) gave me several choice tidbits during our interview. For starters, Charles Roeschke "loaned" him to the 446 in November 1942 "to help those people out."

Here's Monty:

Roeschke was the 448 Exec. Zitinfield was our skipper, initially. I was supposed to help the 446 get commissioned while we waited for our ship. I wasn't even there for the commissioning ceremonies. I was over there just trying to give them a hand because they were short-handed.

When I went aboard the 446, I went to the Captain's cabin to introduce myself. When I walked into his cabin and looked at him I said, 'Coach Schwartz, what are you doing here?' He was my high school coach. He looked up and says, 'John, what are you doing here?' I said, 'Same as you,' and he says, 'Come on in and close the door.' He was my coach at South Pasadena High School. So I went in and closed the door and he said, 'Sit down.' He had a big stack of papers in front of him. Then he said, 'I don't have a clue as to what I'm doing.' 'Well, I'm gonna tell you,' I said, 'I don't either.' He said, 'I need all the help I can get,' and that's the way we kinda left it.

Author's note: LST-446, one of the first West Coast-built LSTs, was laid down on 15 June 1942 at Kaiser's Vancouver shipyard—my employer at the time.

Outfitted with British signal flags, ensign, and jack, the ship was hardly prepared for commissioning as a U.S. naval vessel. However, a United States ensign, jack, and commission pennant were soon borrowed for the occasion; so on 30 November 1942 at 1300 hours, LST-446 was duly commissioned. Of all the officers and men aboard, only two had ever been to sea before: a second-class motor machinist mate and a warrant carpenter.

The ship was docked on the Columbia River at Portland until 10 December, when she departed for Astoria, Oregon, at the mouth of the Columbia, where she remained for four days taking on additional supplies.

On 15 December, the 446 departed for the open sea commanded by Lt H. A. Schwartz, USNR. Since no one aboard had been trained in navigation, it was arranged for the LST to follow a coast-wise tanker until the latter turned off course to enter San Francisco harbor. The 446 proceeded alone to San Diego, arriving without mishap the evening of 20 December 1942.

After a short period of trial and training runs and experimental beachings, Lt Schwartz was replaced at his own request by Lt W. A. Small, USN. Lt Small enforced a rigid discipline upon the ship and began the training of officers and men for the job ahead.

On 1 January 1943, the ship proceeded north to the Mare Island Naval Shipyard, in Vallejo, California where much work was done in fitting-out and remodeling. At this time, though inexperienced, the officers and crew of the 446 devoted their every hour to the challenge of preparing their ship for combat, even though faced with a lack of interest on the part of officers ashore. (The ship was the first of a new amphibious vessel type and therefore, still without an organization ashore to service her needs.) In spite of this handicap, the fitting-out and reconstruction was completed on time in order to proceed down the bay to San Francisco to await departure of a convoy.

Maiden Voyage of the LST-446

On 22 January 1943, the 446 joined a convoy headed for Pearl Harbor in the midst of a heavy storm which was sweeping the California coast. It was only through the insistence of the C.O. and Cmdr Roger Cutler, LST Group Commander, that the ship was permitted to proceed. However, the ship could only maintain a speed of about five knots in the heavy sea; within a few hours, all sight of the convoy had been lost. Nevertheless LST-446 proceeded alone while her shallow draft and flat bottom construction made her roll, pitch, pound and vibrate, violently throwing materiel and personnel about her deck. Soon two thirds of the officers and crew were seasick and totally incapacitated. The entire operation of the ship was now maintained by one-third of the personnel, even though most were barely able to maintain their feet while standing watches of 12 hours or longer without food.

The third day out, the sea subsided somewhat; galley fires were lighted and prepared food was served for the first time since leaving port. During this entire period, three inexperienced young radiomen maintained a Fox schedule watch, copying everything with pencil, since the ship was not yet equipped with typewriters.

On 1 February, the 446 arrived at Pearl Harbor in the wake of the convoy which had lost her outside San Francisco. She remained there for further fitting-out and for inspection by senior officers of all branches of the U.S. armed services.

Keep in mind, there had never been a ship like the LST—a 328-foot ship with a fifty-foot beam, designed to be purposely run aground under combat conditions. The bow of the ship had great doors and a waterproof ramp lowered as a bridge to the shore. This was their first look at an LST. Here's how Rogers Aston depicted the inspection:

All of the ranking officers in Hawaii came down to visit this unique craft. An added interest was the LCT—a Landing Craft weighing 134 tons—lashed to our main deck and to be launched at Guadalcanal.

I was officer of the deck as a spanking new ensign. As I stood at the gangway on the quarter-deck, a large limousine drove up to the dock. Marine orderlies snapped to attention as a distinguished-looking admiral made his way up the gangplank. He saluted the quarter-deck and asked for permission to come aboard. I returned his salute and granted him permission to come aboard.

There is a great protocol when an admiral comes aboard but,

being a '90-day wonder,' I knew nothing of what was expected of me. We were so short-handed I did not even have a messenger to send for the captain.

The admiral approached me and stopped about two feet away. My heart sank. The admiral smiled, held out his hand, and said 'My name is Nimitz. What's yours?' 'Ensign Aston,' I gulped. The Commander in Chief Pacific Fleet (CinCPAC), had won a lifetime admirer.

Rogers Aston, LST-446 Gunnery Officer, is ready for action.
Courtesy Rogers Aston.

On 7 February 1943, LST-446 departed for the New Hebrides alone and without escort, arriving at Espiritu Santo on 22 February, where she delivered her San Francisco cargo of 29 6x6 U.S. Army trucks and the LCT-182 [Jack "Cookie" Johnson, Officer-in-Charge].

Hugh Comer served in LST-446 from the time it left San Francisco until August 1943. He was one of two Supply Officers on the staff of Group 13 Commander, Roger Cutler. During our interview, I asked Hugh if he remembered when Admiral Nimitz came aboard the 446 in Pearl Harbor to inspect it. Hugh's response: "No. I hid when he came aboard, but I have a little story about 'Uncle Roger' [Cutler] for you. It was during our next stop in the New Hebrides. We hung around Espiritu Santo longer than he thought we should, and so late one afternoon when they opened the torpedo net for a submarine, we just went on out. We went all the way to Guadalcanal without any orders. He was always lucky—the whole ship was lucky. We had a very happy ship."

Since he was on Cmdr Cutler's staff, I asked Hugh if he had a battle station during General Quarters. His reply surprised me: I didn't really have one. I had a suitcase with a strap long enough to go around my neck. I would put the pay records in it, and if I had enough room, I'd put the money in there too. If not, it would just go down. But we didn't carry much money; we never went anywhere it was needed."

On 5 March 1943, the 446 departed Espiritu Santo for Guadalcanal. She arrived on 8 March safe and sound—a major accomplishment when you consider that these officers and had little or no previous training in the tasks assigned to them. Rogers Aston summarized the maiden voyage of LST-446 with these words: "The 446 had cruised from San Francisco to Guadalcanal alone and unescorted at an average speed of nine knots. Only one member of ship's company had ever been to sea before. I think its a prime example of the effectiveness of the American ability to develop know-how. They were pretty ingenious. They started with a blank slate and got those ships up and running beautifully in a matter of just a few months. This notable accomplishment by a pioneer group of sea-going 'civilians' was chronicled by the Associated Press. AP also nicknamed the 446 the 'Lone Wolf.'"

LST-446, the "Lone Wolf," was the first LST to arrive in the South Pacific. Courtesy Naval Historical Center.

Southern Solomons Service and Training

On the day of arrival, the 446 crew made several demonstration landings on Guadalcanal beaches for the benefit of various amphibious commanders. Objective: to determine which 'Canal beaches would be available for future use by the remarkable new landing ships. The 446 was run hard aground several times while executing orders from "higher authority," but was always extricated by the hard and tedious labor of the ship's crew.

The CO of the 446 created quite a stir when he sent off a report a short time later to OPNAV, CinCPac, BuSHIPS, and half-a-dozen afloat commands, enumerating on the trials and tribulations of a new type of ship operating in the Southern Solomons. He objected strenuously to his ship "being loaded while the ship was beached." The CO continued, "An LST is the only ship in the world of 4,000 tons or more that is continuously rammed onto and off of coral, sand and mud."[16]

Despite this dim view of what became a very routine function, the arrival of LST-446 was a very real advance in the readiness of RAdm Turner to conduct Operation TOENAILS, the upcoming invasion of the New Georgia Island Group.

During her first few weeks of duty in the Guadalcanal/Tulagi area,

LST-446 often anchored in Purvis Bay, a banana-shaped deep-water bay off Florida Island, a few miles west of Tulagi.

The 446 made the first LST cargo run to the Russell Islands, about 30 miles northwest of Guadalcanal, on 11 March 1943. All operations to the Russells at this time were carried out under cover of darkness without the aid of lights of any kind. Over the next five weeks the 446 would make nine additional trips to the Russells, transporting hundreds of troops and thousands of tons of cargo.

With the exception of one load of 1,500 drums of aviation gasoline and diesel oil, all cargo was 100% "mobile loaded" upon 6x6 trucks. Cargo loads ranging from 500 to 700 tons were completely off-loaded in 45 minutes to 2 1/2 hours. Such speedy operations were only made possible by the fighting spirit of the ship's crew with full cooperation of Marine Corps personnel. (These 446 operations in the Russells, and later at Woodlark Island, were reportedly unequaled for speed of performance, with the exception of LST-447 which later discharged a mobile load at the Russells in 18 minutes.)

In his memoirs[17] Rogers Aston describes a peaceful midwatch— the duty between 0000 (midnight) and 0400—with evocative details most sailors will reminisce about, in spite of the griping that took place when one pulled the midwatch:

Strangely enough, I enjoyed the midwatch. I missed sleep but it was the quietest time of the day. While underway, as officer of the deck, I was stationed on the bridge or in the Conn at the top deck. The engine rooms were, of course, manned as was the radio shack. A helmsman and leehelmsman held the ship to course and a signalman was close at hand.

The ship was completely blacked out and there was little talk. The ship seemed to sleep. I could hear the wind through the rigging and the soft whisper of the sea washing by. The sky was filled with the eternal glory of the stars, the sailors' friend. The Southern Cross was a familiar sight and the breeze had a cool freshness far removed from the depressing heat in the steel compartments below.

The OOD monitored the combat frequency on the radio and a strange mystic, almost musical, sound whispered softly from God's eternal universe. My mind and heart crossed the miles to home and loved ones.

A ship likes to gossip as the superstructure murmurs to the deck and the lifeboats tug softly at their lashings. War was hidden in the soft comfort of night and I was at peace with myself.

Aston's midwatch could easily have taken place on one of the 446's shuttle runs to the Russells. Of course, when in a war zone, there are many nights when conditions are anything but peaceful.

Big April 7 1943 Air Strike

Here is a condensed version of the action that afternoon as witnessed by Rogers Aston, LST-446 Gunnery Officer:

We noted much activity among the large naval ships in Purvis Bay-Tulagi on 7 April 1943. The cruisers and destroyers got underway mid-morning, and departed southwest at a high speed. We all wondered at this hasty scramble to depart Purvis Bay.

Our ship was notified mid-day that we were to get underway at once, and to depart Purvis Bay. A destroyer, that I am unable to name, [most probably the *Taylor*] preceded us out through the torpedo net at the mouth of the bay. Her flag hoist advised us of a pending Japanese air strike.

Radio Cactus (Guadalcanal) notified us that a large group of bogeys (unidentified aircraft) were coming down the Slot toward Ironbottom Sound. Cactus then reported that they were signing off and that a large group of bandits were over the 'Canal.

The 7 April raid (and subsequent 16 June strike) were part of Fleet Admiral Yamamoto's "Operation I" campaign, promised to the Emperor as compensation for losing Guadalcanal. The operation was meant to be a crushing air offensive to rub out the shipping and one or more of the Southern Solomon bases recently won by the Allies.

The number of attacking enemy planes totaled an unheard of 110 Zeros covering 67 Val dive bombers. Their targets: Allied shipping in Ironbottom Sound, including RAdm Ainsworth's task force of three U.S. cruisers and six destroyers, plus three dozen other vessels of corvette size or larger in Lunga Roads and Tulagi Harbor.

To intercept this massive onslaught—greater than any Japanese air raid since Pearl Harbor—76 Air Solomons' ("Airsols") fighters were scrambled at Henderson Field. At 1400 the Russell Island radar screen became milky with traces of bogeys. An hour later, Zeros whipped down on our fighters over Savo Island and the air battle was on. Airsols had the edge from the start; but while the fighters engaged high overhead, Vals slipped into the Sound unmolested.

Now back to Rogers Aston:

At 1510 hours, a bomb dropped a short distance behind LST-446. Two 500-pound bombs struck the USS *Kanawah;* she stopped dead in the water and lay burning as a fire and rescue party from LST-446 came alongside with hoses. Two injured men were found in the *Kanawah's* engine room and transferred to the 446 for medical care and several bodies were located.

I guess we had been aboard the *Kanawah* about 20 or 30 minutes when the *Menominee* came alongside and said they would take charge. Those of us from the 446 returned to our ship.

Aston singled out three LST-446 men who performed "above and beyond" that day: Gunner's Mate Milton Crook, who rescued the two men in *Kanawah's* engine room; Pharmacist Mate McWilliams, a member of the fire and rescue party; and Doctor Hank Benson who treated the wounded. Aston summarized the rescue efforts of the 446 crew with these words: "We were pleased to find that the two survivors from the engine room were not seriously injured. The smell of that burning ship was so strong and sharp, that it is a thing I will always remember. I felt we had done a good job. We probably saved two lives and did our best for the fallen crew."

Aston also described the rude reception of their sister ship LST-447 in these words: "The LST-447 arrived at Guadalcanal just in time for the April 7th attack. A Japanese pilot parachuted out of his burning plane and landed in the water near the 447. The pilot waited until he was opposite the bridge of the ship and then pulled a pistol and fired at men on the bridge. The rails of the ship were lined with infantry destined for Guadalcanal. A hundred rifles sighted in on the Japanese pilot and riddled his body. It was proof that the Japanese troops were more than ready to die for their Emperor."

Air intelligence credited our fighter pilots and anti-aircraft gunners with 27 Zeros and 12 Vals on 7 April, not counting the cripples who fluttered into Munda that night.

Allied air losses were 7 Marine fighter planes—all but one pilot was saved. Two U.S. ships, destroyer *Aaron Ward* (DD-483) and tanker *Kanawah* (AO-1) were sunk along with New Zealand corvette *Moa,* while *Adhara* (AK-71) and *Tappahannock* (AO-43) suffered damage.

There were some lighter Flot Five moments, too. Rogers Aston related two humorous stories to me in one of our interviews—both having to do with the "amphibious brass." Aston:

A ship always likes to keep its commander happy. Our flotilla skipper, Captain 'Chick' Carter, enjoyed an occasional libation, and ice was a definite luxury. One evening at the cocktail hour, Carter ordered the 446 to beach at Lyon's Point in Carter City to deliver ice. The beach was flat and shallow, so we decided we had better land at a pretty good speed so our ramp would reach dry ground. When we 'hit the beach,' we slid farther ashore than we expected.

Carter City was comprised of a cluster of small prefab plywood huts. As we slid up on the beach, to our horror, we crashed into Captain Carter's quarters, reducing it to a pile of kindling. The mailman may ring twice, but the 446 never made another ice delivery at Carter City—once was more than enough!

Another time, we were ordered to come in and unload some cargo at Lunga at Guadalcanal. The current in the channel was strong, and a brisk side wind made the LST drift. The LST had a terrible problem with drifting. The wind would blow against the side and it was just hard to steer, so we were having trouble staying on course. We varied our engine speed and course, trying to go aground at a marker we could see on the shore—a tall pole topped with a red flag.

There was a man on the beach near the marker and he waved his arms and dashed about wildly. We did our best to bring the 446 into the marker. The nearer we got, the more excited the man on the beach became. When the ship finally slid up on the beach, we missed the red flag by some twenty-five feet. As it turned out, the flag marked a beached Japanese torpedo and we were just damn lucky we didn't land on it, because it might have gone off.

Admiral Fort, Commander, Landing Craft Flotillas, South Pacific, was there to meet us. They had put down some marston mat—the kind they make airstrips out of—and we had missed it by the width of our ramp. So the Admiral, pointing to the matt, shouted, 'What do you think we laid this mat down here for? I wanted you to land on it.'

Our Executive Officer, a fellow by the name of R. J. Mayer, hollered back, 'Take it easy Shorty, this isn't a cab. We can't just land it exactly.' Somebody then said, 'That's Admiral Fort' and Mayer went into hiding, but the Admiral didn't come aboard.

Later, when we retracted from the beach, everybody said, 'Where's Mayer?' So we began looking for him. One of the cabins was empty but there was Mayer in the upper bunk, laying there in the dark waiting for us to get off the beach because he didn't want to run into the Admiral.

Harold Breimyer (LST-448) remembers their ship's first "engagement" in the Solomons this way: "We unloaded supplies at the Russell Islands...sneaking in under cover of darkness and completing the unloading in 18 minutes, or so they told us. I find the figure scarcely credible, but it was on wheels—roll-on roll-off equipment and trucks. That was the only time we were really scared. After a while, you just live with it and the fear kind of disappears."

On 18 April, following several more shuttle runs to the Russells, LST-446 departed for Noumea, New Caledonia, with three sister LSTs. Cmdr Roger W. Cutler, Flot 5 Group Commander, had received orders to proceed to Townsville, Australia, in the 446 in company with Flot 5 LSTs 447, 448, and 449. As it turned out, they would be on loan to RAdm Daniel E. Barbey's VII Amphibious Force, part of "MacArthur's Navy," for about three months. Mission: The "occupation" of the two small Trobriand Islands, Kiriwina and Woodlark, in the Coral Sea just north of Milne Bay, New Guinea. (The four Flot 5 LSTs would be joined in Noumea by LSTs 334 and 390 for the Trobriands campaign.)

Now, let's join the crews of the first 12 East Coast-built Flot 5 LSTs at Solomons ATB as they form up and prepare for their shakedown cruise before departing for the South Pacific.

Maiden Voyage of the East Coast Flot 5 LSTS

By the time land-based training was completed, each new amphibian was assigned to a ship's crew. Each crew was then scheduled to board a LST training ship for a brief training cruise on Chesapeake Bay which consisted of various ship drills like General Quarters, fire, and abandon ship exercises. For most, it was their very first time to even see an LST.

About a week later each crew received orders to board and load-in supplies for their new ship as soon as it was ready for commissioning. That meant an almost unbearable wait for some crews since commissionings were spread out over six weeks: LSTs 353 and 354 on 27 November; LSTs 339, 340, 341, 342, 396 and 397 in December; and LSTs 343, 398 and 399 in early January—located in three different shipyards in Virginia and South Carolina.

When the ships were commissioned and all supplies and provisions had been safely stored, they proceeded to an anchorage off Little Creek, Virginia, to await further orders.

According to Martin "Flags" Melkild, his first "sea story" took place while LST-398 lay at anchor off Little Creek one cold morning in February.

The 398's LCVP liberty boat was returning with stragglers from the previous night's liberty when the inexperienced Coxswain (Cox'n) hit the portside of the ship with sufficient force to trip the bow ramp. The net result: the stragglers began floundering in the Bay in their peacoats. Flags, on signal bridge duty, illuminated the hapless sailors and Quartermaster Ed Draper sounded General Quarters, rousing all hands. The bottom line: the hapless and soggy shipmates were all hoisted aboard, then the sleepy-eyed crew secured from GQ. [18]

Liberty in Norfolk during WWII was not all that great, according to most bluejackets. It can best be characterized by the neighborhood signs that said, "Dogs and sailors, keep off the grass!" However, some lucky crew members always managed to get 72-hour passes to visit Washington, D.C. and that's quite another story.

New York Shakedown Cruise

On 16 February 1943, the Flot 5 LSTs weighed anchor, formed up in columns, and proceeded to take up position in a convoy in Hampton Roads, Virginia. Orders had been received to proceed to New York City. The voyage would also serve as a shakedown cruise—a period of adjustment, clean-up, and training after commissioning or major overhaul. In Flag's words:

Our group of inexperienced officers and sailors were going to brave the Atlantic Ocean for the first time! As I recall, only three aboard our ship had been to sea before. Soon after leaving our safe anchorage in Hampton Roads, our ship, with its high-riding bow, pointed her way into the Atlantic. We were totally unprepared for the worst storm to hit the Atlantic Seaboard that winter.

The ship rolled and pitched and with each breaking wave, sprayed salt water over the entire ship. It soon became necessary to tie a lifeline to anyone moving about topside. Seasickness seemed to be the order of the day and sea legs were hard to come by. [19]

As the convoy proceeded up the coast, weather conditions improved but it remained bitterly cold. But not too cold for antiaircraft practice against a towed target sleeve, or for the signalmen to run up tactical signals by flaghoist in order to practice evasive maneuvers from a lurking U-boat.

New York City   All eyes were on New York as the harbor pilots conned the LSTs past the Statue of Liberty, lower Manhattan, and the skyscraper view of the city, then proceeded up the Hudson River to drop anchor near George Washington Bridge.

The skippers went ashore to a Port Director's meeting to make arrangements to load cargo at various docks in lower Manhattan and/or Bayonne, New Jersey. Over the next two-plus weeks the Flot 5 LSTs filled their tank decks with various cargo, ranging from pre-fab bundles of corrugated steel for Quonset huts to U.S. Army trucks. While tied up to the loading docks, civilian paint crews boarded each vessel and changed their colors from navy gray into tones of green, yellow, and brindle-brown in undulating waves of camouflage. Scuttlebutt began to circulate as to the Flotilla's destination.

A large floating barge with a jumbo crane pulled alongside each

A 112-ton Mark V LCT is hoisted aboard an LST to ride piggy-back to battle. Courtesy National Archives.

USS LST-334, Flot 5 with LCT-481 on deck. Courtesy Naval Historical Center.

LST during their New York stay. The barge crew would begin by placing large squared timbers across the main deck. After they were in place, the timbers were covered with a layer of grease, then planks were added to form a skid plate. The next operation: hoist aboard a 112-foot by 32-foot Landing Craft Tank (LCT) and ease her down on the skid plates. The LCT was then secured to padeyes welded to the main deck. (The LCT was now ready for a long piggy-back ride!)

When the LCTs were fully secured, all regular and extra ballast tanks were filled with diesel fuel. While all of this activity was going on, most crew members lucky enough to have families living in the Northeast received short leaves. Others had more liberty than money.

Two or three days before departure, the LCT crews consisting of an Officer-in-Charge, usually an ensign, and 9 or 10 bluejackets, re-ported aboard each LST to accompany their landing craft. Then each ship paid a brief visit to Brooklyn for degaussing—whereby the ship's magnetic field is neutralized for protection from magnetic mines—followed by the necessary compass checks in the outer harbor. They then returned to anchor off Brooklyn, ready for departure on their maiden voyage. During one of these ship movements, LST-341 ran aground and was forced to delay her departure for hull repairs. (She would catch up with her flotilla sisters in Panama.)

Here Come the Amphibians

On 9 March 1943, eleven Flot 5 LSTs stood out from New York under the command of Captain Grayson B. Carter, USN, in LST-340 and joined a mixed convoy consisting of 16 merchant ships, the 11

Flot 5 LSTs, plus escort vessels *Fury* (PG-69), PCs 553, 554 and 555. Lt W. F. Jones, USNR, in gunboat *Fury* was the escort commander.

Capt Carter and his staff, of 7 officers and 10 enlisted men, were still working to complete the organizational structure of Flotilla Five and numerous other tasks. The flotilla would be divided into three groups commanded by Commanders Slawson, Crenshaw and Cutler (the latter already in the South Pacific in LST-446).

Altogether, an estimated 1,100 new amphibians went to sea that day, serving in the 11 LSTs, the 11 LCTs and on the Flot 5 staff. The seven-day trip to Cuba was filled with problems, "opportunities in work clothes" and training drills. The problems were largely steering and engine room-related difficulties. They were to occur so frequently during the voyage, they were soon considered standard operating procedure—well, almost. It certainly reinforced the need and value of the service schools for motor machinist mates (motor macs). Then there was the night LST-399 was rammed in the stern by the 353, requiring temporary repairs until she could reach port.

On-the-job training for all hands started on day one and would be never ending—the Flotilla Commander would see to that. There was a drill for everything, or so it seemed, ranging from gunnery practice, to abandon ship, to flag hoist and signal light drills. General Quarters (GQ) sounded early the first morning: all hands to battle stations with life jackets an hour before sunrise—a procedure that would be followed the rest of the trip while at sea.

Since it was a well known fact that German U-boats still considered these sea lanes excellent hunting grounds, Capt Carter issued the following special instructions: "In the event of a submarine attack, counter attack. Do not scatter unless to go towards submarine, if sighted. If torpedo wake passes you, turn at once toward the source of attack and parallel track. Do not hesitate to ram if possible. Use 3-inch gun freely. Use 20-mm if within range."

Four submarine sightings were reported by radio dispatch before the convoy reached Cuba, but no subs were seen by the Flot 5 ships. On more than one occasion, the Convoy Commander had to remind the new LST skippers to darken their ships at night and/or preserve radio silence.

Temperatures ranged from bitter cold the first day, to tropical heat in the Caribbean. The seas were for the most part moderate, although the heavy swells along the coast made the LSTs roll. However, on the fifth day the convoy ran into a violent storm off the tip of Florida. Here's how Flags Melkild described it:[20] "All ships in the convoy were tossed about like corks. As one looked forward to the bow of the ship from the bridge, it would seem that with each rise and fall of the ship between waves, our ship would surely break in two! It became increasingly hard to keep one's footing, and next to impossible to serve food in the ship's galley, as pots and pans kept flying off the galley stove. But for the time being, food certainly wasn't number one on one's mind, as most had succumbed to seasickness."

On 15 March, the mountains of Cuba could be seen to starboard and Haiti to port as the convoy slowly wound its way through Windward Passage. The next day LST Flotilla Five arrived in Guantanamo Bay and dropped anchor at 1253.

GTMO, or "Gitmo," as it was called, was still under development as a major naval operating base equipped with ship repair facilities, fuel depot, supply depot and other related activities. The site acquired by lease from the Cuban government in 1903 completely encircled the bay, and the greater part of the water was navigable, forming an excellent land-locked harbor.

Soon after arrival, Capt Carter and some of his staff met with the 11 LST skippers and the Masters of any merchant ships scheduled to join a new convoy the next day bound for the Canal Zone. In the meantime, some 89 bluejackets boarded LST-340 to await further assignment. It seems the Flotilla Commander had sent a dispatch to the Gitmo Base Commander several days earlier requesting some experienced hands to be apportioned among the Flot 5 ships.

Cuba—Panama Canal

On 17 March, St. Patrick's Day, LST Flot 5 became part of another convoy consisting of the 11 LSTs and 15 merchant vessels escorted by the destroyer *Tattnal* (DD-125), PCs 461 and 462; SCs 1031 and 1039; and the *Bodega,* a Coast Guard vessel. The Escort Commander was LCdr May in the *Tattnal.*

LST-395 caused more than a little stir when she dropped out of sight the night of 17-18 March. Allow me to condense/paraphrase Flags Melkild's account of the incident:[21]

18 MARCH 1943

0645 The LST 395, in position 34 in convoy, was reported missing to Captain Carter on discovery of her absence.

0716 To the Escort Commander, Captain Carter flashed: "395 Not In Sight x Have You Any Information Of Her Whereabouts?"

0730 LCmdr May's reply: "Sorry But No x Will Investigate."

0747 Captain Carter asked the LST 399 (her convoy position was 24, to the port of 395): "Have You Any Information About The 395 x Did You Observe Her Drop Out Of Formation x If So What Time?

0802 To the LST 342 he signaled: "LST 395 Not In Sight x Have You Any Information?"

0815 The LST 342 answered: "395 Not Seen Since Midnight."

0900 The LST 399 responded: At About 2030 Last Night One LST Was Observed Leaving The Formation x At About 2130 She Was Out of Sight Astern x She Appeared To Be Making Way Slowly."

0907 The *Tattnall's* Commander flashed: "Plane Will Search 100 Miles Astern For Missing LST."

1214 Captain Carter to the *Tattnall:* "Suggest Planes Renew Search x Best Info We Have Vessel Left Convoy About 2100 Last Night x If Located Please Ascertain Visually The Trouble Fear Main Engine May Be Broken Down And Green Personnel Aboard Probably Unable To Make Repairs." Then Capt Carter added: "When And By Whom Will Proper Base Authorities Be Notified Of Our Straggler?"

1307 The *Tattnall* signaled: "When Plane Returns Will Send Following x Search 60 Miles To Eastward Of Convoy Then 140 Miles To North x Report Missing LST By Radio When 60 Miles From Convoy x Request Additional Aircraft To Join Search x Contact LST 395 By Radio And Send Us Any Information They Might Get x If Ship Located, Find her Trouble."

1900 To all ships in this group, Captain Carter issued this order: "Each Ship Check Up Each 15 Minutes Throughout Night On Presence Of Ship Astern Of It And Record Time Should Any Absentees Be Noted." This order was in force for the remainder of the voyage westward.

19 MARCH 1943

0725 At the expiration of morning twilight came the reassuring message for the *Tattnall:* To GTMO LST 395 Proceeding With Difficulties To Engine x Navy Blimp Watching In Daytime x At 1420 Queen From Guantanamo sent PC And Tug x 395 Doubtless In Port At Present."

0730 "Thank You Very Much x Greatly Appreciate Your Help In This Matter" Captain Carter flashed back.

0815 Here came the ultimate reassurance from the *Tattnal:* "Our Lost Sheep Arrived Safely In GTMO At 9:30 Last Night." All hands were relieved to hear this news which Captain Carter signaled to the LSTs of his Group: "395 Safe In GTMO."

0915 To the Escort Commander, Capt Carter remarked (by blinker): "It is Reassuring To Know Our Straggler Only Stubbed His Toe."

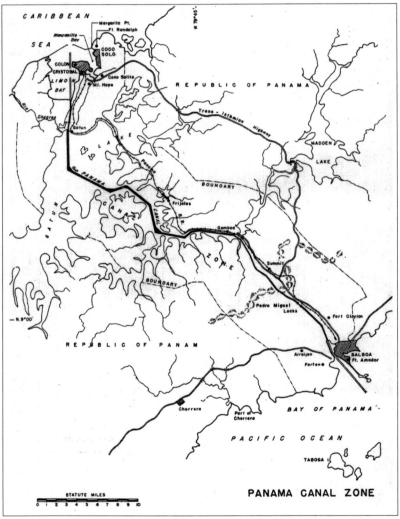

Panama Canal Zone. Courtesy of BuDocks.

Engine and steering problems continued to plague the flotilla. The 398 underwent both engine and telemotor trouble on the 19th and was forced to drop back to a rear position in the convoy in order to safely shift to hand-steering. Her skipper also notified Capt Carter: "Complete repairs beyond capacity of ship's force because of lacking spares."

As the convoy drew nearer its destination, the crews were preoccupied with cleaning their uniforms in anticipation of liberty. The air was hot now. Sunburns could be seen on the crew of every ship.

On 21 March 1943, thirteen days out of New York, ten Flot 5 LSTs cleared the breakwater and submarine nets at 0942 and proceeded to moor alongside piers 1 and 4 at the Submarine Base at Coco Solo, Canal Zone. (The 395 was undergoing repairs at GTMO and the 341 was in a following convoy expecting to catch up soon.)

The naval shore establishment on the Atlantic side of the Canal Zone was primarily limited to an air station for seaplanes and the submarine base at Coco Solo, bounded by Margarita Bay on the west and Manzanillo Bay on the south. Colon and Cristobal, across Manzanillo Bay, were the liberty town options.

Coco Solo Sub Base   Flotilla Commander Carter and all LST skippers immediately met with the sub-base authorities, determined what facilities were available, then agreed upon a lengthy list of needed repairs. As an aside, the skippers were also given some tips and advice for liberty hounds.

Flags Melkild described liberty in the "Zone": "As the sailors explored things ashore and reported back their findings to fellow shipmates, one could find the true meaning in the calypso tune we had sung on the way southward: 'Drinking Rum and Coca Cola' and broads ashore— 'Working for the Yankee Dolla'!"

While at the sub base, the LST crews were realigned by transfers between ships and supplemented by the new men who joined the flotilla at GTMO. However, all ships would still be undermanned.

On 23 March, Radio Guantanamo informed Capt Carter that LSTs 341 and 395 would depart GTMO on the 26th in convoy.

On 28 March, LSTs 339, 340, 353, and 398 took on pilots and proceeded to transit the locks of the Panama Canal.

Flags Melkild: "Our ship proceeded through Gatun's three sets of locks, elevating her 85 feet to man-made Gatun Lake, in 110 minutes. As we rose to each new elevation, a donkey engine running along a cog railway would pull us into the next lock, until we reached the Gatun Lake elevation. After we crossed the 32-mile Gatun Lake, we passed through the 9-mile Gaillard Cut. Then we dropped down via the Pedro Miguel and Miraflores Locks to arrive at the level of the Pacific Ocean. Finally, we traversed another 8 miles of canal before arriving at the town of Balboa." [22]

The six LSTs that had remained behind at the Sub Base transited the Canal during the following two days. The last of the original East Coast-built Flot 5 LSTs, the 341 and the 395, finally caught up with the flotilla in Balboa harbor the night of 31 March.

The next morning, Capt Carter met with all 12 of his skippers to hand out sailing orders and offer some last-minute advice. Carter would be running his own show on the next and longest leg of the maiden voyage as the Convoy Commodore with two escorts: SC-742 and APc 4. [23]

That night the Flotilla Commander sent two secret dispatches to the Bureau of Ships in Washington, D.C.: One described the many LST equipment problems, with suggested solutions. The other was a laundry list of spare parts and supplies urgently needed upon arrival at the next destination.

Capt Carter also received a secret dispatch that night from the Operations Officer, 15th Naval District, Balboa. It read: "Depart With Craft [Enumerated Above] From Balboa At 1300 Zebra 2 April And At Speed Advance Nine Knots Proceed Bora Bora Via Route Furnished x Arrive 25 April x No Enemy Activity Reported Along Route But Same Possible x Arrival Bora Bora Report COMSOPAC For Onward Routing To Destination All For SOPAC Except APc 4 and SC 742 For SOWESPACFOR."

Flags' memories of the last 398 liberty in the Canal Zone: "A bus took our liberty party into Panama City, the capital of Panama. Here again were the bars and the hustlers—much like we'd encountered in Colon... with cheap liquor served to the blaring tune 'Rum and Coca Cola.' Some setting for our final liberty before the long voyage across the Pacific." [24]

Operation Order (2-43) called for alignment of the LSTs into three columns of four ships each. Annex A to the Op Order detailed the communication plans while Annex B contained Capt Carter's special instructions. A condensed summary follows:

Distance between LSTs in column...300 yards. Interval between divisions in column...1200 yards. If necessary, ships will be taken in tow...LST 354 and 395 stand-by as towing vessels in order named.

Leading ships will make quarter-hour checks on ships astern of them, noting their presence and general condition. Darken ships completely at sunset without further orders...All hands will be at General quarters one hour before sunrise...Each even day, weather and other conditions permitting, ships will test automatic weapons. [25]

The instructions also included detailed procedures in the event of breakdown and/or separation from the convoy, as well as attacks by submarine, aircraft or surface vessels. A separate enclosure described the approaches to various South Pacific islands and ports.

Panama—Bora Bora

On 2 April 1943, LST Flot 5 steamed out of Balboa harbor at 0700 into the Gulf of Panama and set course of 155 degrees. By 1000 surface and antiaircraft gunnery practice had commenced. Firing was at a tug-towed target and a plane-towed sleeve, respectively.

Crew of 3"/50 during gunnery practice. Courtesy Naval Historical Center.

At the conclusion of the exercise, Capt Carter signaled his ships: "Surface Firing Just Witnessed Was Of A Very Low Order x If We Even Hope To Stand A Chance Against The Enemy Definite Improvement Must Be Made x Commanding Officers Will Take Steps To Have Pertinent And Applicable Parts Of Chapter 43, Bluejackets Manual, 1940, Explained To Gun Crews, Also Elementary Principles Of Exterior Ballistics x Sight Setting Pointing And Communication Drills Will be Regularly Held." [26]

As we said earlier, on-the-job training would be never ending. But the intensity had just increased, and for good reason. The next day the flotilla held an hour flag-hoist drill, only this time the Commodore signaled "Well Done."

The convoy continued on its course without major incident. There were numerous reported operational difficulties and breakdowns, including one from the APc 4, but so far none was critical.

On 8 April, the Commodore served notice on all hands that the convoy would be entering the realm of "His Majesty King Neptunus Rex" on the ninth, and that an appropriate signal would be displayed when crossing the equator.

Trouble is like bananas, it comes in bunches. One ship after another reported trouble it seems. To quote Flags again:

The 398 was forced to use hand steering. The 395 reported, 'One Engine Disabled.' The 339 had a leaky fuel pump in the port engine. An engine was disabled on the 342, and the 340 had engine and fuel-line trouble. [The next day, 9 April, was not much better.]

At *0517*, the 395 signaled the Commodore: 'Port Engine Not Holding At Any Speed x Proceeding On Starboard Engine Only.'

0520 Commodore Carter slowed convoy from 9 knots to 5 knots.

0520 The 395 signaled: 'As Port Clutch Will Not Hold At All believe It Must Be Ruptured x Will Require 8 to 12 Hours To Install Spare x May Be Necessary To Secure Starboard Engine Also To Prevent Drag Revolving Port Shaft.

LST-354, designated as the No. 1 towing vessel, was directed to make preparations to tow the 395. About two hours later, the Commodore signaled the convoy: "The 340, 354, and SC-742 Are Going To Stand By 395 x Proceed With Remainder Of Group On This Course At This Speed x We Will Probably Overtake You At Sundown."

LST Bridge Scene. Commanding Officer shoots the sun as a signalman sends a message with semaphore flags. Courtesy of U.S. Army.

Pollywogs to Shellbacks   King Neptune presided over the ceremonies on the Flot 5 LSTs the afternoon of 9 April in spite of problems on the 395. For starters, a Jolly Roger flag was run up the mainmast of each ship to signify the presence of the King. Here are a few excerpts from Flag's account of the ceremonies on the 398 after his Majesty had appointed his court made up of sailors who had previously crossed the equator:[27]

The tank deck of the LCT provided an excellent, secluded spot to conduct the ceremony being well screened from the prying eyes of expectant Pollywogs.

Several petty officers, including quartermaster Draper and signalman Melkild, felt they should be part of the court's team, and made plans to disrupt His Honor's Court. Once the ceremonies started, the disrupters crept up over the bow ramp of the LCT and brought to bare a full blast of salt water directly on King Neptune and his court!

His Royal Highness, as befitting his office, ordered the troublemakers brought before him for speedy trial. After being convicted and sentenced the villains were allowed to make bail in order to take their place in the line dispensing just punishment to the other Pollywogs. [Who said justice is always fair?]

Meanwhile, some of the 398's Pollywog officers who had dressed as pirate impostors, were sentenced to stand lookout duty from the crows-nest—a bo'sun chair run up and secured to the yard-arm. They were given a pair of binoculars, consisting of two beer bottles taped together, and required to report sightings on the horizon.

By the end of the afternoon, all Flot 5 amphibians had become Shellbacks in spite of the rude interruptions by unruly Polliwogs.

By the next morning the 395 and her tow ship, the 354, had dropped out of sight. The Commodore slowed the 340 and SC-742 to 5 knots and the two lost sheep soon reappeared.

LSTs 340, 354, 395, and SC-742 increased their speed to 10 knots shortly before noon and sighted the main Flot 5 formation at 1254. The 12 Flot 5 LSTs, together again by 1503, increased their speed to 10 knots steaming on new course 255.

The seas were calm and the skies clear as the flotilla sailed forever southward. While on watch, the crews were entertained by flying fish and the occasional school of porpoises.

There would be one breakdown after another over the next two weeks—mostly engine and steering difficulties. The Motor Macs were challenged at every turn of the screw, or so it seemed. The Commodore and the two escort skippers had their hands full keeping tabs on each LST, especially at night. But, as the saying goes, "Experience is the best teacher." That's important, because the Flot 5 crews were to have precious little training time prior to combat once they reached the Solomon Islands.

On 13 April, Capt Carter sent each Group Commander and all skippers a confidential letter via the guard mail directing them to review *Notes on Amphibious Warfare No. 1 of March 1, 1943,* a critique by commanders who had witnessed the North African and Guadalcanal amphibious operations in 1942. Carter's letter also said:

During the present passage of LST Flotilla Five we are blessed with one of the most wonderful opportunities we will ever have for training. Not only have we the *Time*...we have the *Facilities* with which to work. And we have had, are having, and it is hoped will continue to have, absolutely ideal weather.

These conditions must be taken advantage of in such manner that the conduct of any future operations in which we participate will give us no cause for regret.[28]

The convoy continued on course 253 at 8.5 knots expecting to sight landfall on Good Friday the 23rd. On 16 April Capt Carter issued the following notice to each ship:[29] "A Standard Watertight Closure Bill For An LST Is In Process Of Being Drawn Up x It Is Expected It Will Be Ready By Arrival Next Port When All Damage Control Books Will Be Brought Into Conformity With It."

The escorts received six secret dispatches on the 16th advising of more Jap sub sightings in South Pacific waters, mostly near the International Dateline. Recent training sessions have included navigation school; recognition signals and communication relay exercises; 3"/50 bore sighting and sightsetting drills, 3"/50 surface target practice, and 20-mm firing practice. The navigation school was being conducted by Cmdr Crenshaw. He emphasized the need to improve navigational preparations for entering and leaving ports. The ships were also given a reminder—one of many on this voyage—not to send unimportant messages by visual light during twilight hours.

Capt Carter would usually spend a couple of hours after supper on the signal bridge of the 340. Melkild recalls: It was cool with delightful breezes. It also offered a balcony seat to a spectacular sunset, and a moonrise extravaganza. Tonight the moon, full and powerfully bright, rose above a screen of alto-cumulus clouds banked low on the eastern horizon, with such luminous brilliance you could tell time by your watch's second hand two hours after sunset."[30]

Land was sighted by the 340 lookout at 1330 on 22 April and relayed to the other ships by flag hoist signal. The island was one of many in the Tuamotu Archipelago northeast of the Society Islands. It was also the first land seen in 20 days. The 22nd was also payday—sure to boost morale a bit further.

Captain Carter sent the following message to each skipper that afternoon:

"Expect To Enter Port Tomorrow Shortly After Noon x Take Steps To Have Ships Clean And Neat Appearance. Enlisted Personnel Topside Are To Be In Whites."

The following morning several of the smaller Society Islands were sighted at 0631 and then someone spotted the majestic twin peaks of Bora Bora on the southwest horizon. The convoy was greeted by a seaplane followed by rain squalls. Shortly after noon, a small craft came out of the harbor and signaled, "Picket boat with pilots will meet you west of the entrance approximate five miles on your present course."

When the convoy was within a few miles of the harbor, the signal tower on Bora Bora challenged, then asked for the call signs of each ship. The replies were flashed immediately.

Seven pilots were spread out between the 14 ships aligned in single file astern of LST-340. Lt S. A. Upson, Operations Officer of the base, acted as the 340's pilot and guided the Flagship into Teavanui Harbor.

Fifty fathoms of chain thundered out of the LST hause pipes into 13 fathoms of water at 1432. Flot 5 had come some 4,600 miles since Balboa and about 6,600 nautical miles since leaving New York. Not bad for a bunch of greenhorns, fast-becoming old salts.

Bora Bora, in the Leeward group of the French-owned Society Islands, is 140 miles northwest of Tahiti, the center of government.

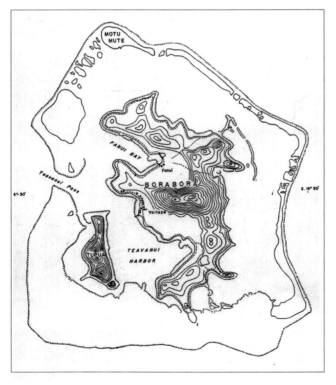

*Bora Bora
(Society Islands).*

The island is small—about 4-1/2 miles long and 4 miles wide. A steep barrier reef, a mile or two offshore, almost completely encircles it; the natural passageway through the reef is curved, adding protection to the harbor. Vaitape, on Teavanui Bay, was the principal town. When the U.S. advance base expedition of Seabees arrived in 1942, the population was about 1,400 with less than half a dozen permanent white residents.

The Bureau of Yards and Docks' great WWII program of advance-base development in the Pacific got its start here. It's an interesting story.

On Christmas Day, 1941, Admiral King, already in Washington but not yet formally installed as COMinCh, requested the War Plans Division of CNO to "proceed at once to study the matter of a fueling base in the central South Pacific area—the Marquesas, Society, or Cook Islands." Five days later CNO recommended that the base be established in Teavanui Harbor on Bora Bora, in the Society group, which was under control of the Free French government. The CNO division also recommended a seaplane base, suitable harbor facilities, and the installations necessary for a defense detachment of 3,500 men. Admiral King approved the recommendations the day they were made.

The code name for the base was BOBCAT. The importance of establishing and holding such a base to facilitate the use of Allied shipping routes from the U.S. and Panama to Australia, New Zealand, and the Southwest Pacific was obvious.

The First Construction Detachment—later assigned to the First Naval Construction Battalion (Seabees)—landed on Bora Bora on 17 February 1942. Their efforts would be rewarded later when the island's tank farms supplied the ships and planes that fought the historic Battle of the Coral Sea.

The detachment would also keep an organized crew available for the repair of convoys of recently commissioned LSTs, LCIs, YMSs, and subchasers which passed through Bora Bora on their way to the Southwest Pacific. The "Bobcats," as they were nicknamed, repaired refrigerating plants, diesel engines, electrical wirings, and occasionally performed a major overhaul job. [31]

For the next seven days, the Flot 5 LST crews were kept busy making needed repairs and catching up on routine maintenance. All hands scanned the beaches, but topless natives in grass skirts failed to materialize. And liberty, what there was of it, was very restrictive. This was understandable in retrospect, since the LST personnel almost outnumbered the natives.

Soon after the ships dropped anchor, natives in outrigger canoes were everywhere, offering to barter fresh fruit, necklaces, and hula skirts for coins—just like in the movies.

On 25 April, Easter Sunday, church services were held ashore for all flotilla personnel wishing to attend. The Catholic shore party attended mass in a native church—pole construction, thatched roof, and mat floor. The U.S. Army detachment had brought in a portable organ so Gregorian chants could be sung. The Protestant service was conducted by a Navy Chaplain in a serene park-like setting under the palms. War, and all of its horror, seemed light years away at the moment. The amphibians, all decked out in their best tropical whites, were disappointed when they were promptly returned to their ships after the services. However, they were soon consoled by a sumptuous holiday dinner consisting of roast turkey and all the trimmings.

On 27 April, Capt Carter sent a dispatch to BuShips with a laundry list of spare parts urgently needed, with instructions to ship them to Noumea in time for the convoy's arrival. Carter also asked each LST skipper by guard mail to advise him as to day and time of sea readiness.

Flags Melkild offers this amusing "last night in Bora Bora" anecdote which I've condensed:

It was during the midwatch... All was peaceful and quiet except for some muffled voices coming from the fantail. On closer observation, it appeared to be 'Bull' Bison, our first-class cook, along with pharmacist mate, first-class 'Doc' Wiggins. They were stealthily climbing aboard from an outrigger. 'Bull' had grown up in New Bedford, Massachusetts, where he had learned to speak a polyglot of French and Portuguese. Through the French-speaking natives, he had contrived a trip ashore.

[It seems that once on the beach] 'Bull' and 'Doc' were invited to a party...a luau featuring roast pig and native hula dancing. [32]

Well, you get the picture. I'm sure that sea story improves with age, much like fine wine.

Bora Bora-New Caledonia

On 30 April 1943 at 1100, LST Flot 5 steamed out of Teavanui Harbor following escort vessels SC-742 and APc 4. The shore signal tower flashed, "Bon voyage and good hunting, Commander Carter, Base Commandant."

Speed 9 knots, standard convoy speed. At 1400, all ships tested their 20-mm and 40-mm antiaircraft weapons by firing at target sleeves towed by two Bora Bora-based planes.

Before a new day dawned, four LSTs experienced troubles—the 398 with its port main engine out being the most serious. Lieutenant Tweedle and Chief Motor Mac Stansell, the Flot 5 trouble shooters, were transferred from the 340 to the 398 at 1146—now in tow by the 354. Diagnosis: Port main engine right-bearing cam shaft. Fifteen hours to repair. At 1802 the 398 relayed a signal to the flagship that they were underway, estimated 8 knots in tow.

On 2 May, the Commodore notified all ships to prepare for gunnery practice. The target: a submarine model built on the flagship. It would be towed by escort APc 4.

By 1400, the LSTs were aligned astern of the flagship which followed SC-742. The subchaser would fire first when the target was abeam. Ammo allowance: 20s, 20 rounds; 40-mm, 4 rounds; and 3"/50, 4 rounds. Estimated distance: 1,200-1,500 yards. Speed: 8 knots.

Convoy of LSTs enroute to South Pacific, 1943. Courtesy Naval Historical Center.

The target practice lasted more than an hour as each ship tried to sink the tiny target. The Commodore's reaction: "The shoot today was a tremendous improvement. Intend to fire for record Tuesday." Meanwhile, the 398 remained in tow, speed 8 to 9 knots.

As the days passed, there were little reminders that the convoy was nearing the war zone. One example: No dumping of garbage during daylight hours. It could disclose the convoy's position to an enemy sub. Speaking of submarines, the 340 decoded a dispatch on 3 May advising of a sub contact almost directly on the scheduled course of Flot 5. The dispatch triggered a Commodore guard mail letter (delivered to each LST skipper by an escort vessel).

Some key excerpts: "The Unit Commander in possession of information which indicates considerable enemy submarine activity along our present route and in contiguous waters. All hands to be informed of this menace and cautioned to be ever more vigilant in standing their watches...Lookouts must be alert and Modified Condition Two [constant manning of 40-mm and 3"/50 guns] must be maintained... Pay particular attention to watertight integrity. The use of lights must be held to a minimum and used only when provoked by absolute emergency."[33]

No one expected this trip to be a pleasure cruise, far from it. What with standing watch and participating in the various drills and training programs Capt Carter scheduled, there was precious little time to just lay back. What little downtime there was, was spent reading, playing cards, fishing off the fantail or in plain old bull sessions over a cup of coffee.

On 4 May, the Commodore scheduled another surface shoot. Only this time, the gun crews of each ship would compete with each other for a prize. Carter announced the competition with these words: "In view of the fact that the record practice is to be scored on the basis of the fall of shot only, point of aim should be at waterline immediately and directly below the "bull." A prize of $65 will be awarded on 'winner take all' basis."

At 1140, the APc 4 (nicknamed "Little Charley" or "Apple Cart") closed the flagship to receive orders for the afternoon competition. At 1415, Capt Carter issued the skipper of APc 4 the following instructions: "Take Station As You Did For Last Sunday's Shoot x Two-

Block Baker When Ready x Stream Target With Bulls Eye In It x Take Rakes Carefully And Keep Record Of Them x Deliver Them To Us As Quickly As You Can After The Shoot x After Shoot Pass Target To The Last LST In Column x Steam At 6 Knots."

The shoot in midafternoon was confined exclusively to firing by 3" gun crews... four rounds by each of the 13 ships. Later, after the shoot and determination of the results, Capt Carter turned to the communication officer on watch aboard the 340 and said, "Send this message: Shooting Was Excellent x I Couldn't Possibly Say Who Won x As Soon As Rakes Are In Will Announce Winner."

The results of the shoot were delivered to the Commodore that night by "Apple Cart" skipper, Lt (jg) Edwards. The 395 was judged winner with a score of 46.25 on her four rounds and later collected the $65 prize. Second place went to the 398 with a score of 48.75. LST-395 also won side bets with the 340 and 341. The Commodore was more than pleased with the results of the competition. His guard mail letter said it all: "This kind of shooting spells no good for the enemy which is exactly what we want. So, get behind your guns...use them skillfully and intelligently. They stand between you and Davey Jones' Locker."

Dispatches continued to indicate Japanese sub activity—this time near the Fijis. The subchaser refueled and took on provisions from LST-339, then resumed her station ahead of the convoy with orders to "Keep a sharp lookout for subs." As if anyone needed another reminder, the 6 May morning radio news contained sketchy information from Admiral Halsey's Noumea headquarters on the sinking of Allied vessels in the Pacific.

The night of 7-8 May, the barometer tumbled as gale force winds whipped up and visibility turned poor. But there were no collisions and all ships were accounted for, although the 341 and 353 were far out of position. That same morning the convoy turned the corner below Point Easy and "headed for the barnyard." It also lost a day when crossing the Date Line later that night.

On 12 May, the 397, which had indicated fuel-line troubles earlier, pulled ahead of the 343, her division leader, at 1655 with obvious steering difficulties. Her flag hoist signals read: "Disregard My Movements, Maneuvering With Difficulty, And Vessel Not Under

Command." A collision followed. LST-343 sent the following report to Capt Carter: "397's Side Plating Open From Main Deck To TwoFeet From Water Line x Damage This Vessel Negligible x 97 Directed To Pump Ballast From Forward Tanks."

The gash in the 397's side could be seen from considerable distance. Capt Carter directed the 343 to stand by the 397 and take her in tow if necessary. Both ships then fell astern, joining the company of the APc 4 and the 354. (The Little Charley had broken down earlier and the 354 had been ordered to stand by in case Charley needed a tow.)

The convoy resumed standard speed after the 397 reported her engines undamaged and her maneuvering abilities unimpaired. Cmdr Crenshaw was instructed to investigate the collision and make a formal report upon arrival in port. However, he chose not to wait. He sent Ensign Van Horne aboard both ships to investigate the damage the following day. Crenshaw's report to Carter read: "397 Has No Underwater Damage x Degaussing Cable Cut x Maximum 260 Port Engine x 343 Bow Doors Sprung And Jammed. Will Require Removal."

In spite of the many mechanical failures the flotilla has had to correct, Capt Carter expressed his sincere belief in the LST. In fact, at the noon meal on the 13th, he predicted the new landing ships and craft would "win the war" for the Allies.

On 14 May, New Caledonia was sighted at 1115. On the approach into the harbor bustling with activity, many airplanes were spotted overhead and scores of ships at anchor—from carriers to tin cans, and patrol craft to merchantmen.

LST Flotilla Five had finally arrived at anchor in Port Noumea at 1518 local time. The convoy had traveled some 9,500 nautical miles in 67 days, with plenty of on-the-job training to boot.

During the next two weeks, LST crews were kept busy unloading cargo—including the LCTs which had been riding on the main decks piggy-back style the entire trip—and making repairs. Training also continued. Six men from each LST were detailed to attend antiaircraft school for four days.

Noumea, at the southern end of the island of New Caledonia, was fast becoming the main fleet base in the South Pacific, assuming the extensive functions planned originally for Auckland, New Zealand.

Noumea served as a staging area for the development of other advance bases, such as Guadalcanal; and on November 8, 1942, became headquarters for the Allied Commander of the South Pacific. (This move put Admiral Halsey 1,000 miles closer to the action, but still out of range of land-based Jap bombers.)

New Caledonia is almost entirely surrounded by a barrier reef, with a spacious channel varying in depth from 20 to 50 fathoms, between the shore and the reef.

It was a Free-French colony during WWII and had under its administration several outlying islands—the Isle of Pines, the Loyalty Islands, the Wallis archipelago, Futuna and Alofi, and Huon Islands. New Caledonia inhabitants include Melanesians, Europeans, Walliseans, and Tahitians.

Noumea was already a major advance base and would soon play a significant role in many Pacific campaigns. Most any sailor who made it to the South Pacific went through Noumea at one time or another. You could call it "Pearl Harbor South."

Liberty in a French colony was close at hand! But first, the cargo had to be unloaded and LCTs launched.

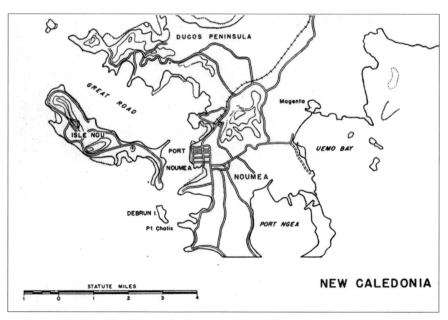

New Caledonia. Courtesy of BuDocks.

Navy oil tankers went alongside each LST and removed surplus diesel fuel, then the LSTs proceeded to designated beaches to offload cargo. Next came the LCT launch. Here's a paraphrased version of how Flags Melkild remembers the 398's successful launch of LCT-145—with an audience of brass, yet.

It was evident that our ship had been selected to carry out the first such launching, as evidenced by the arrival of many high-ranking officers. Chief Bos'n mate Bennett and his deck hands began by releasing turn buckles and chains that had secured the LCT in place. LST-398 was then ballasted to take on an 11-degree list to starboard, and all that remained was a signal to Chief Bennett to sever the last remaining cable.

When the signal was given, all eyes watched as the big 114-foot LCT began slowly moving along the greased skid plates picking up enough momentum to clear the ship's starboard side. She hit the water on a slight angle, which created a shock wave nudging the 398 gently aside. Amongst cheers, LCT-145 had arrived safely!

Launching operations had gone off without a hitch and compliments were freely offered by the visiting officers.[34]

Ensign Willard E. Goyette, USNR, and his 10-man crew also disembarked the 398. After several island-hopping days, LCT-145 would join her "early-bird" sisters at Guadalcanal—some having been there since December 1942.

While riding the hook in Noumea harbor, the LSTs spotted at anchor the *McCawley* (APA-4) flagship for VAdm. R. Kelly Turner, Commander Amphibious Force, South Pacific. The signalmen of Flot 5 were kept busy exchanging communications with the big boss and his staff.

Liberty was finally granted, once the ships were unloaded. A liberty party from each LST hit the beach in their whites with the usual query: "Where are the broads?" There were several pubs in Noumea town plus USO and Officer's Clubs. Thousands of soldiers, sailors, and airmen filled the bars and clubs and spilled out into the streets. And in addition, Shore Patrol and Military Police were everywhere, monitoring their every move. The SPs and MPs also policed the long lines at the government-run pink brothel, while in a nearby park a U.S. Marine Corps band played the familiar pop tune, "Rum and Coca Cola," made popular by The Andrews Sisters.

Flot 5 Planning and Preparation

The June 1943 War Diary of Commander LST Flotilla Five bottom-lined the U.S. Navy's Task Organization in the South Pacific.

TASK ORGANIZATION[35]

Commander in Chief, US Navy	Adm Ernest J. King, USN
Commander in Chief, Pacific Fleet	Adm Chester W. Nimitz, USN
Commander South Pacific Force	Adm William F. Halsey, Jr, USN
Commander Amphibious Force, South Pacific	RAdm R.K. Turner, USN
Commander Landing Craft Flotillas, South Pacific	RAdm G.K. Fort, USN
Commander LST Flotilla Five	Capt G.B. Carter, USN

All operation orders were generated by Admirals Turner or Halsey. Captain Carter spelled out the status of the LST Flot 5 organization as of June 1943 in the War Diary as follows:

FLOTILLA ORGANIZATION

Commander LST Flotilla FIVE   Captain G.B. Carter, USN

LST GROUP THIRTEEN

*Commander LST Group THIRTEEN   Commander R.W. Cutler, USNR

LST DIVISION 25	LST DIVISION 26
*LST 446 - Lt J.C. Adams, USNR	LST 339 - Lt J.H. Fulweiler, USNR
*LST 447 (FF) - Lt F.H. Storms, USNR	LST 340 - Lt W. Villella, USN
*LST 448 - Lt C.E. Roeschke, USN	LST 395 - Lt A.C. Forbes, USNR
*LST 449 - Lt L. Lisle, USNR	LST 396 - Lt L.W. White, USN
^LST 460	LST 397 - Lt N.L. Lewis, USNR
^LST 472	LST 398 - Lt B.E. Blanchard, USNR

LST GROUP FOURTEEN

Commander LST Group FOURTEEN   Commander P.S. Slawson, USN

LST DIVISION 27	LST DIVISION 28
*LST 334 - Lt C.J. Hawkins, USNR	LST 353 - Lt L.E. Reynolds, USNR
*LST 390 (FF) - Lt J.J.P. O'Brien, USNR	LST 354 - Lt B.E. Robb, USNR
LST 341 - Lt F.S. Barnett, USN	~LST 208
LST 342 - Lt E.S. McCluskey, USNR	
~LST 166	
~LST 167	

LST GROUP FIFTEEN

Commander LST Group FIFTEEN   Captain J. S. Crenshaw

LST DIVISION 29   **LST DIVISION 30**

LST 343 - Lt H.H. Hightmeyer, USN

LST 399 - Lt J.W. Baker, USN

~LST 485

~LST 486

~LST 487

~LST 488

* Operating with ComSoWestPac.

∧ Enroute from continental United States

~ Whereabouts unknown

(The six Flot 5 LSTs "operating with ComSoWestPac" arrived in the South Pacific earlier, as detailed under "LST-446 Maiden Voyage.")

Captain Carter continued to fly his flag in LST-340 (FF). Cmdr Cutler (Group 13) was in LST 446 (GF) at Townsville, Australia; Cmdr Slawson (Group 14) was in LST 342 (GF); and Capt Crenshaw (Group 15) was in LST-343 (GF). As of 1 June, six LSTs were operating in the Guadalcanal area, six were still in Noumea, and six were in Australia.

The Flot 5 LSTs still in Noumea got in some valuable night and early morning beaching practice simultaneously and separately following "Commander Landing Craft Flotillas, South Pacific Confidential Doctrine of 1943" guidelines. Following the drills, all LSTs stayed busy making last minute repairs and taking on supplies, water, and cargo. Most of the cargo was mobile, belonging to the U.S. Army and Marine Corps.

LST-340

Ensign Tony Tesori, LST-340 gunnery officer is not your usual "90-day wonder." His route to amphibious duty was quite different. He enlisted in the Navy in January 1942. As an outstanding college athlete and high school director of athletics, he qualified for Commander Gene Tunney's education program for the Navy.

From Norfolk, Virginia, where he served as Chief Petty Officer,

Tesori went to the navy pier in Chicago, Illinois, and became an Ensign. Shortly after returning to Norfolk, he was assigned to duty with the Atlantic fleet and took part in the invasion of North Africa. Tesori:

> I served as a wave boat commander on the USS *Calvert* (AP-65) and spent time rehearsing with U.S. Army Rangers in the Chesapeake Bay during the months of July and August 1942. Later I sailed with the *Calvert* to join a huge armada of transports, destroyers, battleships, and a carrier on their way to North Africa. We put our troops ashore at Safi.

> Upon returning to Norfolk, Virginia, in December 1942, I was assigned to LST-340 berthed in Norfolk. Capt William Villella assigned me to the Gunnery Officer slot because as he put it, "you are the only one who has had combat experience." As little as that was, I became the Gunnery Officer.

Here's how Tesori remembers the last two days in Noumea:

> LST-340 loaded up with 250 Army troops. Our tank and top deck were both loaded with trucks, jeeps, and other equipment intended for our trip to Guadalcanal. I even went ashore and 'requisitioned' a jeep for the Skipper, so he could get around on shore when we got there. My fellow officers and I spent some time ashore at the Officer's Club before departing, and saw Artie Shaw, the noted band leader, and some other celebrities who were there to entertain the servicemen. [36]

Noumea—Guadalcanal

On 10 June 1943, Task Unit 32.7.2 got underway for Guadalcanal. It was composed of LSTs 340, 341, 343, 395, 396, and 398 with *Trevor* (DMS-16) and *Ward* (APD-16) serving as escorts.[37] Capt G. B. Carter, USN, Commander of the Task Unit, and Capt J. S. Crenshaw, USN, Vice Commander, were aboard the 340 and 343 respectively.

Friendly aircraft staged a mock dive-bombing attack on the LSTs the first morning—an enlightening experience for the new amphibians. Later, gunnery practice was conducted against trailed sleeves.

At 1600 the *Trevor* was seen flying Emerg. Unit 136, warning of sound device detection of submarines. The flagship immediately relayed the hoist to the convoy and the convoy began to maneuver in order to avoid possible torpedoes. *Trevor* dropped two depth charges. In a few minutes *Ward* dropped a depth charge. According to the War Diary, "This was only a test emergency exercise to get the convoy alert."

There was more gunnery practice on 11 June and because the weather was so ideal, the Task Unit Commander... "suggested LSTs be painted." Sound familiar to you old salts? There were also more LST engine troubles: 341 (fuel injector) and 396 (one engine disabled).

Bob Hilliard (LST-396) shared one of his memories with me. The story begins in Noumea. The 396 was loading "thousands of cases of beer for Guadalcanal." Here's Bob:

At the time, we had two auxiliary engines and I was in charge of the emergency generating power. Anyhow, they had to come in the bow doors with the beer and up the passageway past the emergency generating room...so every once in a while we'd slip a case down into the bilges.

I don't remember how many cases we had in there, but one night between Noumea and the 'Canal we had a party in the battery room just off our machine shop. That's where we kept and charged all our batteries.

The next morning the Captain—or maybe it was the Engineering Officer, I'm not sure now—tried to find out what was going on. To avoid detection, we had to dump our GI cans full of beer overboard. We still had some in the engine room plus more cases in the bilges so the electrician told them, 'You can't go in there because we're degaussing the batteries and it's full of acid in there. Nobody goes in there now.'

That night we got rid of the rest of the beer—it was probably headed for the Army anyway.

On 12 June, the sea became moderately choppy after a change of course. Flot 5 War Diary: "The LSTs, a.k.a. "tubs," rolled with the greatest of ease. The Army personnel, including Army officers, failed to attend chow lines and the rail of the ship was lined with sick soldiers. The sailors and officer personnel of the ship did not notice it as they had seen many days of this slow rolling motion."

The following day started out with a 0640 breakdown report from the 395 concerning a ruptured air line; General Quarters at 1230 reported an unidentified plane sighted low on the horizon; and four

EMERG VICTOR signals. The first three resulted in calls to GQ. The fourth was a laugher. The Flot 5 War Diary explains: "1511 "EMERG VICTOR 125." General Quarters. LST 398 signaled that a white plane almost overhead was still in sight. The Commodore immediately told them to take a shot at it. LST 398 fired three rounds 3"/50 at it. *Trevor* reported radar screen clear. By this time the staff officers had noticed the white object which the 398 took for a white plane. It turned out to be Venus, the planet which was very bright at that time of day although the sun was near it. This was a phenomenon which few had ever witnessed.

Here's how Martin "Flags" Melkild (LST-398) described this "shooting:"
> The bow lookout reported to the Conn sighting an object high in the zenith, a few degrees to starboard. The officer, who was at this time conning the ship, after viewing the sighting through his binoculars, summons for gunnery officer Ensign O'Leary. Not being too sure of what it was, he in turn summons the executive officer. Finally, Captain Blanchard was summoned and, after a brief parley was held...he directed the 3"/50 gun crew on the fantail to fire four rounds at this object.
> The end result of these gun bursts: a terse comment by signal light from Captain Carter: 'Cease fire, you are shooting at Venus.'[38]

Ensign Fred V. Johnson, USNR, LST-398 OOD, during the shoot, downplayed the Venus "embarrassment" with this entry in the 398's Log: "1200-1600 Steaming on course 027'T. GQ 1230-1245. Airplane spotted by escort, 0225, type unknown. 1440-1545 plane overhead, 5 rounds from 3" gun fired - no hits. 1540 changed course to 355'T. All secure."

The big question: Who really spotted Venus? According to Flags, the "398 Venus shoot" became one of those sea stories repeated time and again among amphibians throughout the Pacific.

At 0727 on 14 June the Task Unit met up with LST-397 and its minesweeper escort *Hopkins* in a planned rendezvous. (The 397 had left Noumea on 2 June for Espiritu Santo to discharge cargo.)

Two friendly escort patrol planes provided additional coverage for the rest of the voyage, but the lead escort suggested that each ship monitor their radios for aircraft warnings from Guadalcanal.

The following instructions were received by all ships at 1115 hours:

"In event of night air attack, unless otherwise directed, do not fire at planes; only fire at planes that you have a fair chance of hitting. Concealment is one of the best defenses under present conditions. Be at General Quarters as directed and from sunset to one hour and a half thereafter."[39]

LST 341 was trailing along behind the convoy after experiencing a breakdown. Her skipper was given course and mileage data in case he couldn't catch up.

The new LST crews got their first distant glimpse of Guadalcanal Island at 0610 on 15 June 1943. The Diary entry says it all: "Our minds immediately went back to the description which each one had in his own mind of the place where the Marines landed and fought so gallantly against those yellow-bellied enemies of ours. Now we're getting a glimpse of the place. We're all eagerly awaiting the close-up view."

Southern Solomons Operations

The Flotilla Five Commander and his staff went about the business of getting the ships ready to unload their cargo upon arrival. The following diary messages explain the planning involved:

1. 'Each ship submit to me immediately upon arrival copy of cargo manifest.'
2. 'Ships earmarked to discharge cargo Guadalcanal should take steps now to have it ready for discharge immediately upon arrival.'
3. 'Submit memorandum report times unloading tank deck and main deck cargo with pertinent comments.'
4. 'Now is a good time to dump garbage and trash.'
5. 'Intend to make every effort to have ships having cargo for Guadalcanal beach and unload upon arrival. Be governed accordingly.'

As the Task Unit neared Koli Point two LSTs were spotted on the beach. The 0930 Diary entry was both amusing and serious: "We learned that one of them was the 399 which had been sent up several days prior to our Noumea departure. Of course we were all eager to know what it had been doing. The reply was 'Ferry service to the Russell Islands and a front seat at all the dog fights.'"

The Convoy anchored off Koli Point at 1355 on 15 June 1943. "It was pouring rain; it never fails to rain as we near our destination. It rained at Bora Bora, at Noumea, and now here at Guadalcanal."

Capt Carter left immediately for Camp Crocodile to meet with Adm Fort and Cmdr Slawson. In the meantime, LSTs 340, 341, 395, and 398 were directed to await beaching instructions. LSTs 343, 397 and 396 were to anchor and await movement orders for a trip to the Russell Islands later in the night. The escorts were to join the screen off Koli Point.

Instructions were received at 1525 to beach LSTs 340, 341, 395 and 398 at Beach Able at Koli Point. Unfortunately it was not possible to get the 340 far enough upon the beach to allow the trucks to be driven off. The 340's officers and crew and Flot 5 staff officers were still at work at 2130 building a ramp to unload the cargo of trucks when a Condition Red sounded.

The Flot 5 War Diary summarized that first night with the following entries:

2130: All personnel were told to leave the 340 except the gun crews and special sea detail, so down the open ramp door all the sailors, soldiers and some officers went wading through three feet of water off the bow ramp to shelter in foxholes on Koli Point. The raid was over Tulagi, the sky over that American base was lighted with streams of 20-mm and 40-mm gunfire, and bursting 90-mm shells. This lasted for approximately half an hour when "All Clear" sounded. Then as the personnel entered the boat another Red Alert was sounded and they returned to the foxholes like foxes. These seemed to be the most secure places against our slant-eyed enemy.

Most of the night was spent in trying to get the 340 on the beach in order to get unloaded but due to changing tides, condition of the beach and cross currents, the idea was abandoned and in the wee hours of the morning the officers hit their sacks.

All ships were told to set transmitters and receivers on 2902 kilocycles and to secure from all other frequencies.

2300: The 343 and 396 left for the Russells to dump their cargo. Their estimated time of arrival was 0400 love.

2340: LST 398 which had unloaded up the beach from the 340 was given orders to go alongside merchantman *Nathaniel Courier* off Tenaru Beach at 0700 and load 300 drums petroleum products. LST 397, which had not unloaded, was to get underway at 0500 (love) the 16th, proceed Tulagi, go alongside government wharf to pump diesel ballast. Use all existing facilities to expedite.

0020: LST 395 had unloaded and was having trouble with its scavenger blower. Required time to tear down, repair and reinstall approximately six to eight hours.

The new day started off all wrong, according to LST 340's "Guns" Tesori:

We began to move closer to the beach once again to unload our cargo of jeeps, trucks, communication equipment and the 250 army troops that manned that equipment. We barely got underway, when we were again put on "yellow alert". Once again it was reported that there was suspicious activity going on just north of us in the direction of Bougainville. Because of this, we delayed any further move toward the beach.

Just before noon, I decided to wash and clean up. I had been awake most of the night checking gun crews, and standing watch on the bridge. I was in my shorts, barefooted, my wristwatch and rosary were hanging from a hook under the mirror and my ring was on the shelf. I had just finished toweling when the "red alert" alarm sounded. I had just enough time to put on a shirt, pants, shoes (no socks), grab my gun, hat and helmet, put my binoculars around my neck, grab my kapok jacket and rush to my station on the bridge. My station was just forward of the conning tower.

I had all my gun crews check in with me that all was in readiness. All gun captains were ordered to keep a sharp eye out for planes. My stern gun crews were the first to spot the enemy planes coming toward us from the East in the direction of Tulagi. The sky seemed full of planes.

Captain Villella got the 340 underway quickly and began taking evasive action. The army troops were instructed to stay in their compartments and out of the way. This is a standard practice in such situations.

The Japs were determined that any plans to invade the Islands of New Georgia and Bougainville had to be stopped. They were very determined that was not going to happen. It is believed that is why they sent so many planes to attack our Flotilla that day.

The following entries in the Flot 5 War Diary, in combination with Tesori's observations, summarize the attack.

June 16 1943 Air Strike

Commander LST Flotilla FIVE in LST 340.

1337: LST 340 which had tried unsuccessfully to discharge cargo at Koli Beach got underway for Kukum Beach.

1345: Condition Red. [Ensign Tesori shifts position.]

As the Skipper continued with his evasive action, I shifted my position from directly in front of the conning tower to one behind it, so I could see the oncoming attack better. It was a good decision for two reasons. First I could give better directions to my gun crews. My experience in North Africa taught me that. Secondly, it did save my life.

1350: Nine planes high overhead. Nine bombs were released from three planes which attacked from port side. One bomb hit main deck and penetrated through to the tank deck where it exploded. The other two bombs missed amidships near starboard side. This plane was shot down.

Plane number two attacked from port bow scoring three near misses and strafed the bow. One man was killed and four injured of the ship's personnel, and nine Army troops were killed or missing. This plane was shot down.[40]

A Japanese Aichi "Val" dive bomber goes down smoking during the attack of 16 June 1943. Courtesy of National Archives.

Ensign "Guns" Tesori will never forget:

The second plane's two bombs hit us just forward of the conning tower, sending jeeps, trucks and other equipment straight up in the air in a huge ball of flame and smoke. We were soon ablaze from the bow to our superstructure. Debris was flying back and into our superstructure, and as well, onto our stern gun positions.

One other plane dropped bombs and six planes strafed the ship. LST-340 shot down two for sure, two more probables, and damaged four enemy craft. The explosion of the bomb created a terrific fire among trucks and gasoline aboard.

We lost all main engine power as well as auxiliary power, thus making it impossible to maneuver the ship or fight the fires. The third plane's bombs straddled us so close aboard that those of us on the bridge felt we could reach up and touch the one the came over us and landed close by on the starboard side. It was that bomb that caused all of us on the bridge and in the conning tower, to be blown around like bowling pins.

I was sent flying against the port side railing in a blanket of hot air. I found myself lying on top of Lt Jim Elliott, our Engineering Officer, who had been standing on the port side deck below, beside the galley door. Jim had apparently come up from the engine room to report his engine failure, since voice communication was gone, or to watch the air action taking place. I don't know which.

Japanese "Val" eludes antiaircraft fire during the battle of 16 June 1943. Courtesy of National Archives.

He was too stunned and surprised to see me lying across his body, as I was to be there. Neither of us said a word. I got up, went to the stern ladder and climbed back up to my station behind the conning tower.

My left hand was bleeding very badly, but I had felt no pain. Just a lot of blood was showing. I took out my handkerchief and wrapped the hand. The others on the bridge were still bewildered and shook up and collecting themselves: Commodore Carter, Capt Villella, Executive Officer, Chief Signalman and the enlisted men assigned to the bridge.

Not one of them knew what had happened to me. They never knew I was away and apparently never missed me in the confusion. I was too embarrassed to say anything.

Jim Elliott, for his own reasons, never mentioned the incident either. To this day, until this book is written, no one has known of my trip on a blanket of hot air and landing on top of Lt Jim Elliott. The heat from the blaze became so intense, and with the debris from the explosions flying through the air, Capt Villella ordered all of us off the bridge and conning tower and down to the stern section of the ship.

Commodore Carter and Captain Villella became concerned that the ship might be in danger of sinking, and ordered "abandon ship." As far as the Captain could determine all did abandon, except for the Commodore, the Skipper and me. Since we had lost all communications, we couldn't be sure. He had done what he could.

Our concern now was the ship's ammunition magazine. With no auxiliary engine, we had no way to flood the magazine and prevent it from blowing up. I offered to run a hose down to that area if we could get the "handy billy pump" to work, using sea water, it would pump into the area. The pump proved to be inoperable. So the Skipper ordered us off the ship. I went down the Jacobs ladder first, followed by the Commodore and then the Captain. The heat from the fire was now so intense, paint on the deck under our feet and on the 3"/50 gun tub was starting to peel off.

We were in the water for just a few minutes when we came under a strafing attack. We ducked under the water as best we could, but with a kapok life jacket on, it was very difficult. The planes not only strafed us in the water, but also our gun crews that were still in action. (They obviously did not hear the "abandon ship" order and stayed at their guns as long as possible.)

Fortunately, LST-340 was on a heading that took it toward the beach on Guadalcanal when we lost all power. There was just enough speed to enable the ship to beach itself. We were fortunate, also, to have members of a Naval Construction Battalion (Seabees) close by to come out with boats to pick us up.

Two of our sister ships, LSTs 353 and 398, came alongside to help fight the fires. LST-354 sent a fire-fighting party. The fire was brought under control in about four hours.

Japanese Air Raid, 16 June 1943, Guadalcanal. USS LST-340 burning after being hit by a Japanese bomb. LST-340 was run ashore off Lunga Beach after being hit, and her fires extinguished after doing considerable damage to her and to her cargo. A sister LST is assisting with firefighting. National Archives.

LST-340 continues to burn as LST-353 (right) moves alongside to assist in firefighting, 16 June 1943. Courtesy Ralph K. Brown.

LST-340 Army passengers and crew casualties are carried ashore at Lunga Point, 16 June 1943. Courtesy P.D. Clodfelter.

We were taken to air raid shelters, given dry clothes and coffee, and checked over by medical staff. LST-353 stayed close to the smoldering LST-340 to continue with the fire-fighting and to help remove the dead and wounded. It was a very sad sight for all of us, especially for me. I lost my gunner's mate, Salvatore Crivello, who had been with me from the first day I stepped foot on the ship in Norfolk. He had attended every gunnery school with me and had helped instruct every man on board on how to use and maintain those weapons. I lost others, of course, but Sal was special.

Our ship was credited with two enemy planes, but the damage to the ship and its personnel and troops was terrible. The troops were trapped in their compartments. They were either killed by the strafing or burned to death. Many were wounded and badly burned and in sad shape. Sal, when his body was recovered, had been cut in half by an enemy plane's shell.

Ensign Levi Wade, our Communications Officer who was in charge of our bow guns, suffered wounds to the head. Among the gun crews, 20-mm and 40-mm, all suffered shrapnel wounds. Sal killed; one lost an arm but yelled out, 'I still have one and can still fire!'

One of the men, James Stalp, picked Ensign Wade up bodily and carried him through the flames to the stern of the ship for medical help. He received the Silver Star for his act.

The price for those two enemy planes we shot down hardly seemed worth the price we paid. But as Commodore Carter said later, 'War always has a cost. That is why we are here, to make the Japs pay for what they did to us at Pearl Harbor.'

When the damage to the ship was examined, we learned we had sustained 122 holes in the port side hull. Our cargo which was destined for Rendova, was a total loss. The crew quarters and troop compartments were destroyed. All the ship's superstructure, Officer's Quarters, galley and everything below decks were completely destroyed by fire.

Commander LST Flotilla Five requested the LST 340 be salvaged. Tug *Pawnee* was designated to assist.

LSTs 343 and 396 were returning from the Russell Islands. The rest of the LSTs were scattered around the various beaches during the air raid. The Japs sent over 120 planes and American Forces knocked down more than 100 of them.[41]

The 340 crew and most of its officers spent the night aboard LST-353. The following day was spent putting out the still smoldering fire on LST-340 and salvaging as much equipment and personal gear as possible. There was very little to salvage. The officer's country

LST-340 salvage crew examines still smoldering aftermath on 17 June 1943. She was the first LST casualty in the Pacific. Naval Historical Center.

Admiral Nimitz summarized the June 16 air strike with these words:

On 16 June, the largest enemy force since 7 April attacked our shipping in the Guadalcanal area. Enemy forces consisted of at least 60 VB (bombers), screened by a like number of fighters.

One hundred four U.S. fighters were scrambled in defense, and 74 made contact with enemy. There were numerous U.S. ships in the transport areas off Lunga Point and in Tulagi. The attack lasted from 1315 to 1513 (-11).

ComSoPac credits his VFs (fighters) and ships' A/A with the destruction of 107 enemy planes. Six of our VFs were lost: two pilots being recovered.

During this attack the LST-340 received one hit which set fire to her cargo of trucks, gas, oil, etc., completely destroying [the cargo]. LST-340, though badly damaged, was beached and later salvaged.

At 1410 *Celeno* (AK-76) received 2 hits, and the resultant fire destroyed most of her cargo, though the ship was likewise beached and later salvaged.[42]

USS Celeno (AK-76) prior to Japanese attack. Naval Historical Center.

was completely gutted by fire. The publications and secret files were saved from burning, but were badly charred and wet.

The Flot 5 War Diary entries summarized the evening of 17 June:

2010: LST 354 was designated as temporary flagship for LST Flotilla Five. The flag staff moved aboard and began the job of transferring all the salvaged publications and gear aboard the new flagship. All supplies had been burned and the personnel had nothing but what could be begged, borrowed or stolen.

The officers and crew of LST 340 moved aboard LST 354 and remained there until the 354 shoved off for Purvis Bay several days later. LST 354 was a genial host to all the survivors; for what was theirs, was ours.

2039: Another Condition Red came by radio. Each one scrambled into his life jacket and helmet and made for his battle station. Those were tense moments. The blood in one's very veins turned cold. There were many scared people. It turned out to be a false alarm as no enemy planes appeared. The ship made preparations to get underway in case of attack. About 90 minutes later the personnel were secured form General Quarters.

The next two days were a real drag for the Flotilla staff as well as for the 340 crew and officers. The diary bottom-lines the challenges and tense moments of 18 June ending on a high note:

There were many problems to cope with: What will be done with the burned cargo aboard the 340? Where are all of the missing soldiers? Who could identify the dead that were carried out that day? What would happen to the crew of the 340? Then there was the problem which continually had to be answered: Send such and such a ship to load at such and such a beach to carry such and such a load to such and such a place.

Everyone worked like mad. In the meantime, the staff managed to get clothes enough to cover their naked bodies. All the clothing belonging to the crew and officer personnel was burned. All that they had to their names now was what they went over the side in. They were indeed happy to be able to go over the side.

1404: Condition Red. The ship went to GQ LST 354 was alongside the starboard side of 340.

1513: Secured from GQ. At each GQ ammunition clips and rounds were carried from the 354 to the 340 and all guns on the 340 were manned. Officers even crawled into the gun tubs and served as part of gun crews.

1516: Before we could crawl out of the gun tubs there sounded another Condition Red. Men remained at their posts. There was no action and no enemy planes appeared overhead.

1530: Both ships secured from GQ. In the evening there was a beer party staged just off the ramp of the burned ship to quiet the nerves of the bombed and fire-weary sailors and officers. It was for the personnel who participated in the disaster which befell the 340. A good time was had by all. It was certainly a good morale booster.

LST-354 moved alongside the 340 the morning of 19 June and a request was made for the salvage of LST-340, as well as temporary arrangements to quarter and subsist officers and crew pending salvage. Later, the officers and enlisted personnel of LST 340 were quartered and subsisted ashore at Tenaru Beach until they were transferred across the sound to Tulagi.

LSTs 339 and 396 checked in after arriving in the Russells to unload cargo. The 339 was to return to Purvis Bay for two days' availability and the 396 was to return to Koli Point. Word was received that another of Captain Carter's "Chicks," LST-472, was to arrive on the 26th. The Commodore began preparations to facilitate the unloading of LST-472 before any disaster could befall it. It was ordered to proceed to Tulagi and launch its LCT.

Guns Tesori shares a few more memories of the LST-340 with us:

When I finally had a chance to take a look at my normal battle station where I supervised all gun actions, I was shocked at what I saw. It was scarred with shrapnel marks. Had I been at that position when the bomb hit, I would have looked like swiss cheese, as one of our crew said. My move to the rear of the conning tower when the planes were first reported coming in off the Port stern, so as to get a better view and direct the guns more effectively, saved my life. It was my second close call, with the first being November 1942 during the North African invasion south of Casablanca. Someone was looking out for me.

Chaplain O'Neil, on LST-353, sent Capt Villella the message that burial for the casualties from our ship would be at 1330 at the Guadalcanal Cemetery. A number of our crew and several of our new-found friends among the Seabees attended the solemn ceremony. It is a scene I have not been able to erase from my memory.

It is easier today, or I would not have been able to write about it 51 years later.

Two of the soldiers among the dead had spent some time painting the Officer's Quarters on the trip up from New Caledonia, just for something to do. I had spoken to them as one is apt to do, asking about home, family and so forth. I felt I knew them. So I felt a special sadness for them as I did for Sal Crivello, my gunner's mate.

Because of the continuing air raids, and also there being no longer any need for our crew to remain on Guadalcanal, we were ordered to be moved to the nearby Island of Tulagi, just east of Guadalcanal. We had no idea what was there for us either. Regrettably, just before we were ready to leave, the crew asked to have one more look around on the 340, for old times sake. To our everlasting sorrow, one of our motor mechanics decided to go down to the engine room. Why, we will never know. On the way back up the escape hatch, we surmised, he slipped and fell, and broke his neck. When he didn't show up at departure time from the ship, a Chief went to look for him and found him at the bottom of the hatch. We buried him alongside the others.

Let's shift gears for a moment, because not all memories are so grim. Monty La Montagne (LST-448) has a couple of "Gold Braid" stories for you. The first one is on Roger Cutler, Cmdr LST Group 13. Listen up:

I watched Cutler come back from the Officer's Club one time while we were in Townsville, Australia. Keep in mind, he was the most dignified looking guy you've seen in your life. He had a big shock of white hair and was about 6'1". When I first saw him in Solomons, Maryland, he was wearing shorts and had two Irish Setters on a leash. Reminded me of Nimitz. Well, you get the picture.

There was nothing to do in that town except go into the bar. It was very nice and, of course, it was occupied by Australians as a rule, so we were interlopers. Cutler was a good drinker. He was all dressed up.

I happened to be over there talking to some of the officers. I knew them well, you know, the 446, 447, and 448... we were kind of inseparable and I was standing there by the ramp. The ramp was down on the beach and here comes Roger Cutler coming back and he was pretty high. Just forward of the ramp there was quite a deep hole and he didn't notice it or he thought it was maybe something very shallow. He made it into that damn hole right up to his waist!

The watch up on the ramp came rushing down to give him a hand and help him up onto the ramp. He thought he just had a short distance and he got himself really mired. He was soaking wet. If he was sober, he would never have done that. It was so funny to see this very dignified man looking like that.

Cutler's brother-in-law was Secretary of the Navy, Frank Knox, you know. Later in the war, he was a Flag on an LSD. I went aboard to see him. He had made Commodore by then.

Monty went on to tell me one of his favorite "Chick" Carter stories:

We were anchored off Florida Beach across the sound from Guadalcanal. We were drinking beer on the quarter-deck. We had a skipper who had been a Merchant Marine captain, a four-striper, and now that he was in the Navy he was only a two-striper. He had command at that point in time. The Gunner's Mate came up and said, 'I want permission to fire the 50-caliber machine guns,' and he said, 'Well sure, go ahead.' There wasn't another ship in the harbor. You couldn't see anybody anywhere, so they went up to the bow and fired away.

We're just sitting out on the quarter-deck drinking beer, all of the officers aboard. Pretty soon a radio message came in and the radioman came down and said, 'Hey, cease firing immediately because I just got a message some of the rounds are landing in an Army camp.' They were ricocheting all over the place and landing in the Army camp on the other side of the island.

'The hell with that,' said the Skipper. 'Keep on firing. It's okay. Just disregard that message.' He did, and the gunners, they just kept right on firing.

The next thing we saw was a small boat coming alongside with Captain Carter, a Commander and two or three other officers aboard. Boy did we disband in a hurry. Those beer cans disappeared.

Carter came aboard and said, 'Who's the Captain?' We were all two-stripers by this time. Jungerheld said, 'I am.' He was a very fine officer. We were great buddies. They said, 'We want to see you in your cabin right now.'

They were in there for about half an hour and when they came out, Jungerheld said, 'Guess what, I've just been relieved of my command,' with a big smile on his face. He wasn't upset by this at all because he was a very competent officer, a tremendous naviga-tor, and a four-striper in the Merchant Marines. The next time I saw him was when I had my own command. He came up the ladder to visit me and by the silver leaf on his shirt, I knew he was a full Commander. He had been spot promoted. He ended up on one of the flagships out there as navigator. He was that much of a whiz.

The 20 June War Diary entries included the following informa-tion on the movement of Flot 5 LSTs and other pertinent items:

LST-354 was still alongside the 340 as the day began. LST 343 and 397 departed Lunga for the Russells. LST 343 had rations and the 397 had fuel. They were to return to Purvis Bay for at anchor availability.

1215: Condition Red. [No enemy aircraft sighted.]

The Commodore requested that all LSTs leaving the Continen-tal United States be held until their complete allowances of spare parts were on board. There was also an urgent request for paint to camouflage the LSTs.

1354: LST-354 departed for Koli Point where Commodore made a final visit to Camp Crocodile before getting underway for Purvis Bay.

2115: Condition Red. GQ No bogeys sighted.

2215: Condition Red. GQ No shots fired.

"Washing Machine Charlie" paid the 'Canal/Tulagi area another nuisance visit at 0225 on 21 June requiring another scramble for battle stations. Later in the day, the diary described a significant request, plus more problems:

It is desired that a Medical Officer be put aboard each LST. These are available at Carter City and should go aboard by June 22nd.

The troubles never ended for the staff personnel of LST Flotilla FIVE. LST 353 which is anchored near LST 340 at Tenaru Beach may have to replace motor due to bent shaft... The 341 is having trouble retracting from the beach and requested the assistance of a tug. Escorted by *Trevor,* LST 343 departed Russells.

Tom Byrne (LST-488, and 460 short-timer) remembers his encoun-ter with an "educated native" this way:

When we first arrived in the Solomons, a canoe with 8 or 10

men in it pulled up alongside of us. An old guy with a derby hat on was up in the bow smoking a pipe. They had some hand-carved war clubs with them and we were making hand motions trying to tell them that we wanted to buy some of those war clubs.

After about 10 minutes...a young guy in the stern spoke up and guess what he said.'I say, old chaps, can I help you?' He was the son of the old guy in the bow who was the King. The son was going to take over when his old man died. He had graduated from Oxford University.

On 22 June, the First Lieutenants of all LSTs present were requested to report aboard the flagship and bring along an inventory of paint for use in camouflaging the LSTs.

The Commodore, who was very cautious, also issued the following instructions: "When swimming parties are allowed, each ship must have one manned boat standing by and keep a sharp watch with a rifle in an elevated position. The OOD will check all swimmers in and out. Provide recall in case of alert."

During the next four days (23-26 June 1943) the Flot 5 LSTs were kept busy effecting repairs, discharging fuel oil cargo and taking on water in Purvis Bay or the Hutchinson Creek anchorage. The weather was good so the ships got their new camouflaged coats. All things were made ready for the coming action.

The Commander South Pacific Force (Adm Halsey) issued Operation Orders for the movement on the New Georgia Island Group in the Central Solomons, code-named Operation TOENAILS. These orders called for the movement on Rendova, Segi, Viru Harbor, and Wickham Anchorage. The War Diary bottom-lined the command structure:

CTF 31 and CTG 31.1 was RAdm R. K. Turner, USN, in charge of the Western Movement to take Rendova and Munda.

CTG 31.3 was RAdm G. H. Fort, USN, in charge of the Eastern Movement to seize Wickham Anchorage, Segi, and Viru Harbor.

Operation TOENAILS Staging

With the help of the War Diary, let's follow the movements of the LST Flot 5 ships over the next few days as their officers and crews continue their get-ready for Operation TOENAILS.

27 JUNE 1943

Commander LST Flotilla FIVE in LST 354. LSTs 339, 341, 354 and 395 got underway at Purvis Bay for Guadalcanal. The first two started loading for the Eastern Movement to take place on June 30th. The rest of the LSTs were in Purvis Bay except LST 340 which was still on Tenaru Beach, Guadalcanal.

28 JUNE 1943

Commander LST Flotilla FIVE in LST 354. LSTs 339, 341, 354 and 395 loading at Guadalcanal.

LSTs 396 and 397 departed Purvis Bay for Guadalcanal to load.

LSTs 354, 395, 396 and 397 formed the ships of Task Unit 31.1.5, the Second Echelon to Rendova with Captain G. B. Carter in charge.

29 JUNE 1943

Commander LST Flotilla FIVE in LST 354. LSTs 354, 395, 396, and 397 continued loading at Guadalcanal. Got underway at 2358 for Russell Islands.

LSTs 342, 353, 398 and 399 with Commander P. S. Slawson, USN, in LST 342, departed Purvis Bay for Guadalcanal to load.

LSTs 339 and 341 departed Guadalcanal for Segi, New Georgia Island. (They would arrive on 'D' day which was June 30th.)

The Commander of LST Flotilla Five wrapped up the June 1943 War Diary with these words:

The future of LST 340 is dark. Two possibilities for it are: (1) to be stripped of all usable parts and converted into a Landing Craft Repair Ship; (2) tow the ship to the Continental United States for rehabilitation to return later as a re-born ship. [See End Notes.]

Finally LST Flotilla FIVE has reached its destination and is ready to carry guns, tanks, and men to further the fight to rid the South Pacific of the enemy.

That completes the first part of the LST Flotilla Five story except for the following "End Notes." We'll rejoin these pioneer LSTs for the invasion of New Georgia in our next book which will document the land, sea, and air operations in each Solomons campaign from Guadalcanal to Bougainville in 1942-43.

END NOTES

1. **LST Flotilla Five Solomons Campaign Scorecard** By the end of 1943, a total of 27 Flot 5 LSTs will have served in the Solomons as part of the THIRD Amphibious Force.[x]

- Twenty arrived prior to 30 June 1943. They were: LSTs 334, 339, 340, 341, 342, 343, 353, 354, 390~, 395, 396, 397, 398, 399, 446*, 447*, 448*, 449*, 460, and 472.

- Four arrived in September 1943. They were: LSTs 166*, 167*, 485, and 488.

- Three arrived in November 1943. They were: LSTs 70~, 71~, and 207~.

[x] Source: COMLSTFLOTFIVE War Diaries, 1 Jun–1 Dec 1943.
* Operated temporarily with ComSoWestPac during summer 1943.
~ U.S. Coast Guard-manned vessels.

All but the November arrivals earned the Navy Unit Commendation for their "gallant record of service" in transporting vital supplies to forces participating in the Solomons campaigns. The citations were identical, except for the vessel named. *(See following page.)*

2. **USS LST-340** was towed to Espiritu Santo, New Hebrides, for temporary repairs, then it left for California on 25 October 1943 under tow by a sea-going tug for a complete yard overhaul. Ensign Don Sterling, a 340 survivor, shed some light on this long, slow trip in our interview: "We had no power but we did manage to locate a Jap reefer and a Marine field range (cook stove), before leaving the Solomons. We had a cook, 10 men and 3 officers aboard the 340 hulk."

Lieutenant W. Villella, USN, was awarded the Silver Star for his skill and gallantry in fighting his ship against the 16 June 1943 enemy dive-bomber attack. Praise also came from Captain Grayson B. Carter for the commanding officers of LST-353, Lt L. E. Reynolds, USNR, and LST-398, Lt B. E. Blanchard, USNR, for their part in towing the 340 to shore and fighting her fire.

The battle-scarred ship arrived at San Francisco on 24 November 1943 and remained in the yard until April 1944.

Example of LST-398 Citation

> For outstanding heroism in action as a Unit of LST Flotilla Five during the Solomon Islands campaign, from March 1943 to May 1944. Arriving at Guadalcanal during a critical period for amphibious operations in the drive of the THIRD Amphibious Force up the Solomons, LST-398 played a major role in supplying our forces throughout a prolonged campaign. Operating in hostile and uncharted waters, and off difficult beaches, without adequate protection of surface escort and air coverage, she carried out a heavy operating schedule, constantly fighting the submarine menace to our supply train maneuvering up the Slot, and making every effort to get her vital cargo unloaded at combat destinations before the enemy could destroy her.
>
> In addition, LST-398 contributed to the development of this type of vessel as a hospital evacuation ship; helped to initiate the use of increased armament for all LSTs to repel Japanese air attacks; and assisted in the perfecting of loading and unloading techniques in order to facilitate the handling of her inflammable and explosive cargo during combat operations. An aggresive fighting ship, LST-398 along with her officers and men, achieved a gallant record of service which attests to the teamwork, courage, and skill of her entire company, and enhances the finest traditions of the United States Naval Service.

The above is an example of the LST citations—which were identical except for vessel name.

Seaworthy again, LST-340 stood out of San Francisco on 25 April 1944, bound for Hawaii. She arrived at Maalaea Bay on 4 May and was assigned to the northern attack force, Task Force 52, for the assault on the Mariana Islands.

The 340 was moored at West Loch, Pearl Harbor, on 21 May 1944, nested with other LSTs loading ammunition for the invasion. At approximately 1505 hours, LSTs 179 and 353 blew up. Both ships were moored immediately ahead of LST-340. The 340 was underway and backing down within five minutes, and, as she had lines to ships on either side, pulled them to safety as destruction spread among the closely-moored vessels. (LST-353 had helped save the 340 off Guadalcanal on 16 June 1943.)

By the time the explosions ceased and the fires were extinguished, six LSTs and three LCTs had been sunk with heavy casualties. Over 160 men had been killed and almost 400 had been wounded.

During the Marianas campaign, LST-340 stood off Tinian Island during the assault. On 21 July, while she was unloading trucks and embarking wounded at White Beach #2, heavy rains and typhoon-like winds whipped the water, and the sea rolled in extremely heavy swells. When the ship attempted to retract from the beach, she was caught by the wind and swells and broached on top of a coral reef, tearing holes in her hull and suffering heavy damage.

LST-340 was refloated on 13 August and towed to Tanapag harbor, Saipan. On 15 August, she was inspected and given temporary repairs, but the damage was such that plans were made to convert her into a barracks ship at Tanapag.

She was reclassified as IX-196 and named *Spark* on 20 October 1944. She was decommissioned on 24 October and struck from the Navy list on 1 September 1945.

LST-340 received three battle stars for World War II service.[43]

3.   **LST Update**   In 1992, the winter edition of *Naval History* magazine featured an excellent story on LSTs written by Cmdr Kendall King, USN, Captain of the USS *Fresno* (LST-1182), scheduled for decommissioning the following year. Here are a few bottom-line excerpts from his article on the number of LSTs built, LST conversions, and LST losses during WWII.[44]

LSTs performed other tasks throughout the war, extending their role well beyond Churchill's original concept.

Of the 1,152 LSTs contracted, 1,051 were actually built, although all received hull numbers. Of these, 113 LST hulls were converted to other types: some became motor torpedo boat tenders (AGP), battle damage repair ships (ARB), landing craft repair ships (ARL), salvage craft tenders (ARST), aircraft engine repair ships (ARVE), general store issue ships (AKs), and self-propelled floating barracks (LST(M) or APB).

LST-Hs were modified to provide immediate medical care and to evacuate the wounded: they transported more than 40,000 casualties during the Normandy Invasion alone.

Some LSTs became mini-aircraft carriers to support fixed-wing reconnaissance aircraft operations.

By war's end, 13 LSTs had been destroyed or sunk due to accident, grounding, or weather; 6 of them were lost on a single day in 1944 due to an ammunition explosion. Enemy action caused the loss of an additional 26. This relatively small ratio of losses to commissioned LSTs attests to the durability of the ships and the abilities of their crews in self-defense and damage control.

New wars and LST designs followed World War II. Although the vintage LSTs participated in Korea, the faster *Terrebone Parish* (LST-1156) class dominated the 1950s. It was followed by the *Desoto County* class in the late 1950s and eventually the *Newport* (LST-1179) class, the 20-knot LST. These ships earned names, and served in Vietnam, the Cold War, and Desert Storm.

Perhaps more than any other ship class, the tank landing ship remains linked to its World War II roots. The modern LST sailor would feel comfortable—or as comfortable as any LST will allow—on the original LST. He would still feel the excitement of turning toward shoal water to launch tracked vehicles or to ground a perfectly good ship on a beach. Certainly all sailors recognize that whether called by number or name, the LST that emerged 50 years ago was indeed a marvel.

CHAPTER 5

Biography of LCI Flotilla Five,
from Amphibious Training
to Guadalcanal

The written records of LCIs during WWII are few and far between. I consider myself fortunate to have, as primary sources
for this chapter, the War Diary of LCI-334 and personal interviews with plankowners[1] Alfred J. Ormston, LCdr USNR (Ret.), and
Thomas P. Mulligan, Lt (jg) USNR, commanding officer and engineering officer respectively.

I also interviewed more than two dozen other plankowners who
served in other Flot 5 LCIs in the Solomon Islands in 1943. Other key
sources of information include the LCI Flotilla Five War Diary for 1
June–31 December 1943; and the LCI National Association.

In this chapter, we'll track the adventures of an estimated 624
men who manned the first 26 Landing Craft, Infantry, or LCI(L), assigned to LCI Flotilla Five in the South Pacific. For the remainder of
this chapter, it will be understood that plain LCI means LCI(L), unless otherwise noted.[2]

First, I'll touch on the early training at Solomons, Maryland, such
as it was in 1942, then describe how the crews were selected, organized and assigned to the Flot 5 LCIs. The rest of the chapter will
follow our earlier landing craft chapter format: design and construction, shakedowns and sea trials, maiden voyages, and Southern
Solomons service and training—as Flot 5 prepares to invade hostile
shores for the first time.

USS LCI 334 is featured in this chapter because we can draw on
the dates, places, and actions in her War Diary. However, you'll find
excerpts from our personal interviews with many other flotilla crew
members who served in other LCIs during the same time frame.

Amphibious Training

The training facilities at the amphibious training bases at Solomons, Maryland, and Little Creek, Virginia, in 1942 were described in a previous chapter as "rushed to usable completion" in August by the Bureau of Yards and Docks. They weren't much better in October when Alfred Ormston, soon-to-be skipper of LCI-334, arrived at Solomons ATB.

Al Ormston: "We were sent up to Solomons, a whole squad of us, on an old ferry boat. It was rainy and the base was full of mud. It was nothing, and most of the sailors there had lost their pay records...it was a real mess. Cold weather. Miserable food. It was just a hell hole and everybody hated it, and wanted out...to change duties.

"There were only a few LCTs and no LCIs or LSTs, so what we did was practice on the LCTs. About half way through our time there our crew, No. 3038, was formed. One LCI showed up toward the end of our stay. It still had the wooden benches."

No one seems sure when the first LCI training ship arrived in the Chesapeake Bay area in 1942. It was probably sometime in October. So chances are the earliest trainees to go through Solomons ATB didn't even see their first LCI until they arrived at the builder's yard to pick up their ship.

Most new arrivals at Solomons ATB didn't have a clue as to what they were in for. Here's what Radioman Bill Bertsch (LCI-64) visualized: "No one knew what amphibious duty meant at the time. I, and others, thought it meant PBY airplanes [the Catalina flying boats employed for patrol, antisubmarine, and search-and-rescue during the war]. I was real happy with flight pay, etc., in mind. When we arrived in Little Creek and boarded the bus, the driver told us about the new landing ships."

Bertsch shared another Little Creek memory with me that I hadn't heard before: "There were Army Rangers training there, too. That surprised me. The first day I got in the chow line, I saw some of these guys that were dressed like commandos. I turned around to somebody and said, 'What the hell is this?' He said, 'They've got some Army Rangers training here.' They were doing things like making surprise attacks on one another. Hit and miss. It was amazing."

According to amphibian veteran and author Bob Weisser, when

the first landing craft arrived for training purposes, no training program had been established. Consequently, officers and crews alike simply looked the ship over, got to see what it was like on the inside, then watched as the skipper practiced handling her. In other words, training amounted to little more than a ride in the bay.

Quartermaster Don Brown (LCI-336) remembers his amphibious training this way: "Actual ship training consisted of a few days on an LCI in the Chesapeake. We went from Solomons, Maryland, down to Norfolk, Virginia. We laid around there and finally we got an opportunity to go out. We actually just went out in Chesapeake Bay. We really didn't do much there.

"The ship's regular crew didn't know much more than we did. Our biggest experience there was that all of us had to sleep in our hammocks. That was a big thing. Later we trained in Galveston for maybe two months."

Change came slowly, but change it did, commencing with the elevation of LCdr Camp to Base Commander, and the arrival of LCdr Barrett as executive officer on 7 December 1942.

Once organized, training would become quite comprehensive. Following classification testing, interviews and physical and psychological examinations, new arrivals were directed into classes in maintenance engineering, demolition, fire fighting, first aid, aircraft recognition, shakedown procedures and beachmaster operations. Schools were also conducted at ATB for cooks, bakers, administrative specialists and store specialists.

Tactical training included familiarization with mockups and practice in combat loading, boat lowering, beaching, assisting stranded vessels, docking and salvaging.[3]

It's a miracle that the early landing craft made it from the builders' yards to the open sea without more mishaps. But it wasn't long before ATB Solomons was processing thousands of transfers and reassignments monthly. In fact, according to Weisser, between 3 July 1942 and 1 April 1945 a total of 67,698 officers and men were trained at Solomons, Maryland.

Scuttlebutt has it that the women who were sunbathing along the beaches in Maryland and Virginia during the war still wonder why the landing craft had to pick their part of the beach for maneuvers.

Crew Formations

Crews for the first 26 Flotilla Five LCIs were formed up during the latter part of October 1942 at Solomons, ATB.

Al Ormston, the first C.O. of LCI-334, sent me a copy of the original 334 roster assembled at Solomons as Crew No. 3038. Al's comment with the roster was: "Note the predominance of apprentice seamen and lower ratings—talk about a green crew and officers...but we did learn!"

Crew No. 3038 consisted of 3 officers and 21 bluejackets. Only four of the enlisted men were petty officers: two Signalmen 3/c, one Electrician's Mate 3/c, and one Radioman 3/c. Missing expertise at this early stage had to include motor machinists mates as well as gunners, a bos'n and a cook.

Skipper Ormston explained:

Most of the sailors were just out of boot camp when we got them. On the Deck Gang, we had about seven. The Black Gang—the engineering gang, was about six. In the electrician's area, we had one electrician's mate and two strikers. Our radioman, Tom Litell, doubled as yeoman. Then we had quartermaster and ship's cook strikers.

Ensign Tom Mulligan was our engineering officer. Tom had been a practicing attorney out of Notre Dame University and Harvard Law School so, of course, they sent him to Diesel School. When we got him, they said he is very well-qualified to become an engineer officer. Tom was a great help on the ship and has been a great friend ever since.

Lt (jg) Sid Ussher, our executive officer, was a social worker in real life—a peaceful guy who our tough bos'n later said should have been a Chaplain.

They slipped up on me, of course, I was the third officer. I had done a lot of sailing in Tampa Bay. I guess, maybe I was the only one that had ever smelled salt water, so they designated me C.O. [Al was a Lt (jg) at this point.]

We split up the duties. I had navigation and communications. Tom Mulligan had engineering and the commissary. pThen Sid Ussher had the rest: deck gang, gunnery, training and everything else that was left over. That was about the extent of our original make-up.The average age of the Flotilla's enlisted personnel was under 20, and that of its officers, 26. Their youth, intelligence, courage, eagerness to win, and team spirit, were to make them one of the most outstanding amphibious outfits in the Pacific Theater.

C.O. Ormston, was not your typical 90-day wonder. He joined the Navy on 26 September 1941, before Pearl Harbor. I asked Al, "Were you interested in the Navy for some time or was it because you saw the war coming and wanted to pick your duty?" His reply: "All of the above. I was working for Florida Power at the time and one of my very close friends up in Yankee Town, who had just completed the V7 Program, came back with such glowing reports on the Navy and how glad he was he got in, and it inspired me."

Al went on to describe how, as a college graduate with a mechanical engineering degree, he applied for a commission, was accepted, and called up in September 1941 and sent to the Naval Station in Key West, Florida.

In Al's words:

The more you hang around a place like that—a good deep water port...a bunch of four-piper destroyers...old WWI submarine R-boats for underwater sound detection school...and, beginning in '42, the conversion/adding of .50-cal machine guns to beautiful yachts...and, of course, seeing the ships and subs going out—made you want to go to sea. I kept applying every chance I got...especially for PTs and destroyers.

Finally, around July 1, I was sent to Northwestern. They had a special indoctrination course for those who had already received commissions but had never had any Navy training. It was essentially the same course the 90-day wonders took. Only they didn't call it V7. A whole bunch of us at Tower Hall had gotten in and needed deck and navigation training.

I got out in early October and was sent down to Norfolk with a bunch of other reserve officers and sailors out of various training courses and then up to the Solomons ATB.

Harry Frey, the original skipper of LCI-70, was not your typical 90-day wonder either. For starters, he joined the Navy at age 37. Second, he received his commission without a college degree or one minute of indoctrination.

Here's Harry's bottom-line story for you:

I had a lot of small boat experience on Lake Michigan...but no college degree. Had a friend in the Officer Procurement office in Chicago...after hearing my story he said, 'Not much chance of your being accepted, but with your boating experience and business background (owner of a lumber yard in Michigan City) you can possibly pilot a desk and let some guy with qualifications go to sea. A month or so later...came that brown envelope telling me I was a Lt (jg) in the Administrative Command of the Atlantic Fleet.

I was sworn in at the Armory in Michigan City. They had never heard of this arm [amphibs] of the Navy, but it sounded like a desk job. My friend in Chicago, likewise, had never heard of this assignment. But on 22 October 1942 I reported to Norfolk and in a few days was aboard a cattle train headed for Solomons, Maryland...at that time a sea of mud.

As the crews arrived, they were given their assignments. Our cook was designated by his place in line...actually he was a machinist by trade (and cooked like one) but it was a great experience.

After six weeks, we went to Little Creek, Virginia, for assignment. We drew a ship being made in Orange, Texas...boarded a Pullman car that had been out of service for many years, with windows so dirty you had to go out on the platform to see out. Arrived in New Orleans, then to Orange, [Texas] a town of 8,000 pop... Consolidated Shipyard there was employing 20,000 men.

Our three [officers'] wives had come down, and finding a place to stay was virtually impossible but, by hook or crook, we finally each found lodging.

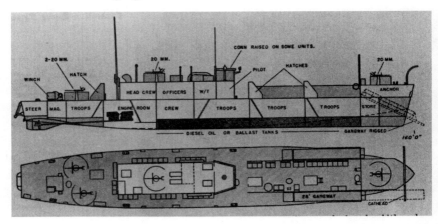

LCI(L) Landing Craft, Infantry (Large) I-350 Drawings. The ocean-going infantry carrier for direct unloading on beach. ONI/226.

Flotilla Five LCIs

The first 26 ships assigned to LCI Flotilla Five were built in four different shipyards and commissioned between 31 October and 17 December 1942. Here they are by yard and date of commissioning, all in 1942.

New York Shipbuilding Corp. Camden, NJ	George Lawley & Sons, Neponset, MA
USS LCI(L) 21...................8 December	USS LCI(L) 222.................3 December
USS LCI(L) 22...................8 December	USS LCI(L) 223.................8 December
USS LCI(L) 23...................8 December	
USS LCI(L) 24...................8 December	

Consolidated Steel Corp. Ltd., Orange, TX	Brown Shipbuilding Co., Houston, TX
USS LCI(L) 61.................12 November	USS LCI(L) 327...................31 October
USS LCI(L) 62.................13 November	USS LCI(L) 328...................31 October
USS LCI(L) 63.................16 November	USS LCI(L) 329.................8 November
USS LCI(L) 64.................12 December	USS LCI(L) 330.................9 November
USS LCI(L) 65.................14 December	USS LCI(L) 331...............16 November
USS LCI(L) 66.................14 December	USS LCI(L) 332.............17 November
USS LCI(L) 67.................17 December	USS LCI(L) 333.............24 November
USS LCI(L) 68.................17 December	USS LCI(L) 334.............24 November
USS LCI(L) 69.................24 December	USS LCI(L) 335.............27 November
USS LCI(L) 70.................24 December	USS LCI(L) 336.................3 December

(The East Coast-built ships would rendezvous with their Texas sisters on 25 February 1943 in the Panama Canal Zone.)

Design and Construction

Plans for the LCI(L) were developed by New York Shipbuilding at Camden, New Jersey, from preliminary designs drawn up by the Bureau of Ship's John Niedermair.

The British no doubt pressured the U.S. into developing a troop carrier landing ship, just as they had with LSTs and Liberty Ships. But they didn't design them.

John C. Niedermair, Technical Director of Preliminary Ship Design for the U.S. Navy's Bureau of Ships, described the preliminary design stages of the LCI in his 1975 oral history:[4]

> The next important landing craft [after completing preliminary designs of the LST]...was the LCI(L), landing craft, infantry. That was very interesting. Incidentally, I got the idea early in the game...that we would have to keep the number of pieces...plate thicknesses, and...shapes down in all these ships—not too many sizes. There would be a small inventory, see, because you didn't

want to go hunting around for this or that angle bar. I used to tell them that you couldn't have any more in shapes and plate thicknesses than you have fingers on your hands—five of each. Also, welding came in pretty good at that time...and diesel engines.

I must give credit to the...marine engineers in the Bureau of Ships, because they worked wholeheartedly in getting engines for these ships. And then there was Mike Robinson, Admiral Robinson later on, former engineering officer and head of the Bureau of Engineering, who came out of retirement when the war came on. He got into this business of organizing the production end of it.

There was also a Captain Irish involved in the production department. He worked in New York, up at Gibbs and Cox. [Gibbs and Cox had developed the detailed plans parallel with the contract plans for the LSTs to expedite construction.]

There was demand for this small infantry landing thing, so I got busy and studied it quite a bit. I used to work two days every day, you might say. I could do that because I only needed four or five hours' sleep.

One of the things we did here was to try to design the LCI in such a way that there would be very few parts, and the shape would be such that...you didn't have to furnace any plates you used.

I talked to Tom Bossett, manager of New York Shipbuilding Corp., about this boat that we were coming up with, and I suggested that he build the first one in his yard. This was going to be a steel ship and I wanted to test it out in a shipyard that had good naval architects and draftsmen. And Tom said, 'Oh, John, where would I put it?' 'Well,' I said, 'find a space in-between the cruisers. You've got plenty of room there. There must be plenty of room for this little fellow. Just build one. Build the first one and then somebody else will get it.'

I think they [the Bureau of Ships] already had the yard picked out—Lawley's [George Lawley and Sons] of Massachusetts as the prime yard.

So the hull form was developable. We developed the hull form, we sent the rough sketches. I got Captain Saunders in. He was head of the Taylor Model Basin. And Schoenherr came in. I wanted to talk to him about it. I wanted the self-propelled test run finished within a week. Could it be done? Towed tests and self-propelled tests.

They went away and we set up a paper model of it and tried to see whether we were getting it developable. We sent it down and the model basin finished all of their tests on the LCI in one week.

We ran into a considerable amount of trouble getting engines for these little LCIs. We also had trouble getting pipes and plumbing for them. The yards and the manufacturers were pretty well saturated in early 1942.

We were adding a bunch of new ships and they kept telling me the steel mills couldn't do it. The same way with the LST. We started using the steel that they rolled for automobiles...steel that was not considered very good because you could get folds in it...going through the mills.

The edges of this sheet steel were rather weak so they didn't think they could use it at first, but then they finally did use it [on the LSTs, LCIs and LSMs] by trimming the edges of all the plates that were rolled for this sheet stuff.

As far as the engines went, we had to use little Gray diesels. We put four of them on each shaft. They had two shafts. We packed them well together and geared them to a shaft, and that's the way we engined the LCIs...and it worked all right, and I was told later that anybody who had duty in an LCI engine room couldn't hear for the longest time afterwards.

It was this sort of short-cutting of red tape that made it possible for us to get all those ships put together.

Mr. Niedermair received many awards for his outstanding service as the U.S. Navy's Chief Naval Architect. He guided the designs from which some 8,000 combatant and auxiliary vessels were constructed.

Two of the most prestigious awards he received were the Career Service Award for outstanding public service from the National Civil Service League—the first Navy candidate to be so recognized—and the David Taylor Gold Medal from the Society of Naval Architects.

LCI Shipbuilding

In his article, "LCI Shipbuilding,"[5] Walter Kopacz described the accelerated plans for building LCIs starting at the Barber Yard in New Jersey.

Fabricated sections were made in a factory fourteen miles from the yard and moved on special trolleys to be loaded on flat railway trucks for the trip to the slipways. Here they were lifted into prepared cradles, each fabrication being numbered and marked for identification and positioning ready for welding.

After each fabrication had been inched into its exact place, the hull was welded at position 1, moved to position 2 for the deckhouse to be lowered into place and welded, then to position 3 for the combined pilot house and conning tower (square in the first models and round in the later ones) to be welded on top of the deckhouse.

Thus the craft moved from station to station much as a car moves down the assembly line. At position 4, the electrical and other installations were fitted and at 5, craftsmen completed the finishings.

The LCI(L) was then moved into a mobile floating dock which carried her into the river before being flooded to launch her. LCI(L)s were later built along many of the rivers by similar prefabrication methods.

The first LCIs came off the 'cookie cutter line' in late 1942 after the Joint Chiefs of Staff ordered full speed ahead for construction to coincide with an expected cross-channel invasion of France in 1943. That operation was postponed, but the priority for landing craft continued for both the Mediterranean and Pacific theaters.

LCI Profile and Specifications

Frankly, it's an anomaly to designate these 160-foot vessels "C" for Craft, instead of "S" for Ship, but it was originally planned to send them overseas in sections for assembly at each theater of operation.

LCI(L) Sea Trials. Courtesy ONI 226/1.

Operational Use: An ocean-going infantry carrier designed for direct unloading on the beach. Although living space, galley, and heads were provided for the troops, the space was limited to a practical operation time of 48 hours.

The LCI was 160 feet long, had a beam of 23 feet, and a full load displacement of 380 tons. They were the fastest of the large landing craft, with a designed maximum speed of 16 knots and a cruising speed of 12 to 14 knots in a generally calm sea.

The U.S. Navy further described the LCI in 1944-5 as follows:[6]

> *Crew*: 3 officers and 21 enlisted men.
> *Troops*: 6 officers and 182 men or 75 tons of cargo.
> *Armament*: 4 20-mm (1 forward, 1 amidships, and 2 aft).
> *Propulsion*: 2 sets of GM diesels; BHP 1,600; twin variable-pitch screws.
> *Fuel*: 130 tons fuel oil; 200 gallons lube oil.

The first 350 LCIs built to U.S. standards had designated hull numbers between 1-350. Later production carried hull numbers between 351-1098. LCIs numbered 1-350 were of the original "square bridge" type whereas numbers 351-1098 had a "round bridge."

A number of other design changes worth noting were made during construction. For example, the later group could travel twice the distance (8,000 miles at 12 knots) and carry an additional 17 troops.

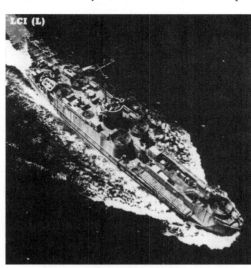

LCI(L) Landing Craft Infantry (Large) 351-1098. All production after 1 June 1944 incorporated a centerline ramp to expedite disembarking. ONI 226/1.

LCIs 402 and 354. Note 402 has the newer centerline bow ramp. All production after 1 June 1944 incorporated this new feature. ONI 226/1.

Troop spaces were rearranged and many of the later vessels were built with a center line bow ramp as opposed to the dual gangways hinged to fixed platforms on the bow. Other changes: heightened conning towers and mainmast moved forward.

A total of 912 LCI(L)s were built by U.S. shipyards: The U.K. and Russia received 220 and 30 respectively under Lend-Lease and the U.S. Navy and Coast Guard took delivery of the remaining 662.[7]

Ship's Tour

We have two LCI skippers standing by to give us a tour of an LCI. Let's start with Al Ormston:

First, the LCI was fabricated from pretty light (1/4") plate, which is not a lot of steel. But LCIs turned out to be very tough, despite the fact that the design was flat-bottomed with three skegs and two wheels, two propellers, in-between the three skegs. It pounded like a son-of-a-gun, went to leeward the minute you lost you power and skated around, so it was a very unusual type of ship to handle. The reason for that was the flat bottom design and very shallow draft so that it could be beached successfully.

You could trim the ship with the transfer of salt water ballast in the forward and after tanks, but you wanted to be very careful that you didn't put salt water into the one compartment that held fresh water.

The troops were assigned compartments below the weather deck. There were no bunks for the troops—strictly a short term deal. They were originally fitted out with benches. Ours was not.

One of the biggest problems...the heads provided in the troop compartments plugged up the first time that they were used. They were of an inadequate design, so we abandoned them and took 55 gallon steel drums and split them in two, then welded them with supports aft of the 20-mm guns and put toilet seats on them—a matter of practicality in the early days. The crew somehow managed to have heads that worked, but the others were just terrible.

All three officers shared one small cabin. We couldn't have breakfast until we got Mulligan out of the sack because the Ward Room table was underneath his bunk. There was a little pass-through from the galley, and they would pass the trays in our direction, and for the crew in the other direction. We all ate the general mess. That was the layout of the Ward Room. It did have a tiny toilet, wash basin and a shower.

The engine room was very cramped, of course. Everything was jammed into a little control station on the forward bulkhead. On each side you had a single shaft going back to a reversible pitch propeller. The quad engines gave you a lot of power and you could engage as many engines on each shaft as you needed. So if you were only cruising at 6 or 8 knots, you could cut out a couple of engines on each shaft.

The big hang-up on the reversible pitch props was that there was about a 14 or 15 second delay between all ahead and all astern,

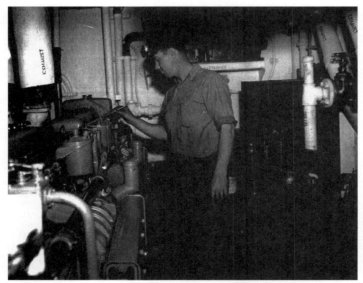

LCI engine room. Pictured: D. J. DeLaney, MoMM1/c. Courtesy Robert W. Kirsch.

and you could damn near die in between when you were coming up to a dock or some obstruction ahead of you, and you wanted to hear that thing roar and you had to wait. The bigger type of diesel engines, the LSTs for example, had a different type of reversing where it was a matter of just a few seconds.

We had no radar. We did have a gyro as well as a magnetic compass but, of course, the first time we stuck our nose out past the sea buoy at Galveston, all of the gyro mercury...splashed out and it was inoperative for the balance of the war. That was terrible, but everybody had the same deal.

Ensign Read Dunn, executive officer of LCI-335, will complete our little tour of an LCI with these words from his autobiography:[8]

On the ship, the three of us [officers] shared a single cabin about 6 x 9 feet. The captain had the single bunk and the engineering officer and I had the double bunks. Mine was on top. I hated that top bunk because I jumped up every time I heard the engines change or any strange sound and hit my head on the steel beam under the ceiling above. My forehead stayed bruised for three years.

On the main deck was the chart room, ward room, where crew and officers ate together, and the officers' quarters. Below the main deck were three compartments which were for the crew and the troops. Aft of the crew's quarters was the engine room.

LCI crew quarters. Pictured: RDM 2/c Sazpak and RDM 1/c
Henry Miller. Courtesy Robert W. Kirsch.

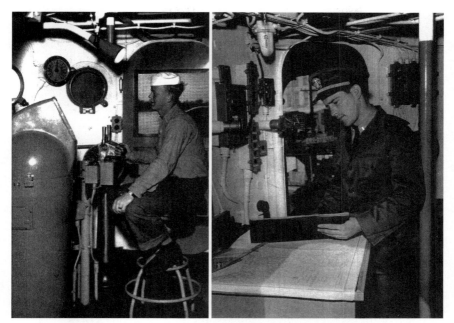

(At left) LCI conning tower. Pictured: QM 1/c Taylor. (At right) LCI chart room. Pictured: Lt (jg) William Ludes, C.O. Courtesy Robert W. Kirsch.

Above the main deck was the conning tower (the enclosed pilot's cabin from which the ship could be controlled).

There was an open bridge above the conning tower from which the ship could also be controlled in good weather or in restricted waters. The ship was steered by twin rudders controlled by a solenoid switch in the pilot's cabin which was operated by turning a handle. It had no steering wheel.

The speed was directed by an engine order telegraph in the conning tower which was connected to the engine room. Changes in speed were made manually in the engine room and reported by means of the telegraph. Changes in the pitch of the propellers and other engine changes, such as reducing the number of engines on a shaft, were made manually in the engine room on voice command from the officer of the deck through the speaking tube.

The big stern anchor windlass was powered by a gasoline engine which was always a concern in the war zone because of the explosive possibility if it was struck. Otherwise, the ship was all electric. The electric power was generated by two 250-horse power General Electric diesel engines which turned two large generators.

LCI galley with S 1/c (Cook Striker) Hershel Regeon. Courtesy Robert W. Kirsch.

Electricity not only powered the ship's lighting and heating but big pumps that moved water in and out of the eight large flotation tanks. The water in the tanks provided ballast underway. The tanks were emptied for landing. Some of the later ships had bow doors that were operated by electric motors; ours did not. The electric control panel was about 4 x 6 feet, with dozens of dials and switches.

The LCI was not a simple piece of equipment. We were told they were made with so many engines because those engines were standard stock items which could be taken from stock or reproduced quickly. A single large engine would have taken much longer to design and produce. The curious design was experimental. Ours was one of the first ships of its kind. The later models had better configuration, and were somewhat simplified and easier to operate.

LCI Conversions

Walter Kopacz described why, when, and how more than 100 LCIs were later converted into heavily armed rocket, gun, and mortar ships in his article on the "Number of LCIs Built":[9]

The birth of LCI (Rocket), LCI (Gun), and LCI (Mortar) ships was due to necessity.[10] It was observed that the last four minutes of the approach of the first wave of troops of an island invading force were sitting ducks. This was the most critical time of the whole operation. The Battleships and Cruisers laying out on the horizon and the Destroyers closer in had to stop firing due to the proximity of the first wave to the beach.

LCI(G) Landing Craft, Infantry (Gunboat). Many LCI(L)s were converted for close-in fire support in landing operations. ONI/226.

This also holds true for the air cover. The Japs in the Pacific knew this and simply went back in their caves and waited for the shelling and bombing to stop, then came out and raked the first wave with gun fire.

The first wave could get no support from the ships on the horizon, they were on their own. We needed a close-in support ship that could go in ahead of the first wave to cover the critical four minutes before the first wave hit the beach.

Two LCIs were outfitted with rockets and used for the first time at the Kwajalein Island Operation. Their success in this operation was so great that over 100 LCIs were soon converted to rocket, gun, and mortar ships. From then on, many of the LCIs were used only for close-in fire support for our landing forces. Thousands of soldiers' lives were saved by the support given by these ships.

Texas by Rail

Two contingents of Flot 5 LCI crews that took the train to Texas to pick up their ships: one to Orange and one to Houston.

John Barry (LCI-66) was in the Orange contingent:

I don't remember much about the train ride. Just that most people had never heard of Orange, Texas. We had visions of the wild west or something. So when we first got to Orange, there was nothing there for us. No place to sleep or anything else. We had to be put up in a hotel for probably a week or so before they got some barracks ready.

After we commissioned the 66, we sailed up what they called the ship channel, and then we went up through Port Arthur and out to Galveston. That was some trip. The only one who had ever been to sea before was the Captain. Everybody else was strictly new. I think we demolished everything...ran into every dock in Galveston, but anyway, that was one way to learn.

Don Brown (LCI-336) remembers the 336 crew's time in Texas:

We left Norfolk, just our crew, and headed for Houston. We stopped off in New Orleans for a few hours and then right over to Houston. They put us up in the YMCA. We went to the basement and stashed our stuff and then checked in and out on our own. Once in a while we would check in so they would know we were still around. We had a pretty free-wheeling time while we were in Houston.

About the first of January [1943] our ship was ready. Brown Ship-yards in Houston was the builder. After we picked it up, we went down river and tied up in Galveston. I do remember we practiced tying up to the dock a lot. We also learned how to control the ship by rudder and by changing engine speed or pitch of the props.

History of the USS LCI-334

As I said early on, the LCI-334 War Diary is a key information source for this chapter. For this reason, we'll be featuring the 334 a good deal more than the other Flot 5 ships. However, I will insert excerpts from my interviews with the crew members of other vessels whenever possible.[11]

The LCI-334 crew of enlisted men traveled to Houston with Radioman Thomas Littel in charge. The three officers flew home for brief leaves, then met up with the crew in Texas.

C.O. Alfred Ormston described the next few days:

The ship was still being fitted out when we arrived so the crew was quartered in the barracks and we [officers] stayed downtown at the Rice Hotel. The ship was covered with yard workers. There were welders all over everything, then about two days later we were commissioned. They did it so fast, we didn't even know what had happened. They came by with a truck load of ship's gear and dumped it off and we had to stow it. About 2 days after that we were under way down the Houston Ship Canal to Galveston.

The USS LCI(L) 334 (hereafter the LCI-334 or simply the 334) was officially commissioned at the Brown Shipbuilding Company in Houston, Texas, at 1525 on 24 November 1942. She remained moored to the quay until the afternoon of the 26th when a civilian crew and pilot came aboard to take her down the Houston Ship Canal into the Galveston Channel, and moored her to Galveston pier 38.

The 334 remained moored there until 30 November when her green amphib crew moved her to the Gulf Oil Dock where she took on 2,000 gallons of fuel oil. Finally at 1155, the crew moved her out into the Houston Ship Channel and the Trinity Bay area southwest of Houston where they got to practice shipboard drills and maneuvers for about six hours.

Skipper Ormston bottom-lined the initial shipboard training as follows:

> We reported to the LCI Flotilla 5 headquarters at the Cotton Docks there and were assigned to Division 28 under Group 14 headed by LCdr Alfred V. Janotta, a WWI vet and really fine man. He put a bunch of us green officers and men in a new type of ship. Nobody knew how to handle them but we went out and trained anyway.
>
> The flotilla staff consisted of about 15 people. A supply officer, an engineer officer, communications... They were presumably to train us but there wasn't a hell of a lot of training. Here we were a bunch of new folks just trying to learn our way. The Commander of the flotilla at that time was a retread Commander named Wolton.

Skipper Al Ormston's first command—LCI-334 at Guadalcanal. Courtesy of Al Ormston.

That was before Smith [James McD.] became involved later in the South Pacific.

The training that we did was primarily on our own out in Trinity Bay. We would also do tactical maneuvers with Janotta. We really stayed busy. We did drills and learned to work together. The ship handling, particularly in the canal and in the Galveston area, was just horrible. We also learned how to fuel, water and provision the ship.

The 334 (and several of her sisters) repeated these drills and maneuvers in the Trinity Bay area six out of the next thirteen days. She remained moored to pier 38 the rest of the time. Half the crew were given liberty each night. Galveston was a lively place then, as reported by a number of bluejackets.

The shakedown cruise, according to LCI-335 executive officer Read Dunn, really meant learning how to operate the ship.

The first day we had to learn how to dock the ships. Those flat bottom, shallow draft boats almost plane when underway, and without a keel they are difficult to keep on course. The engines have to be changed frequently and quickly, especially when coming into a dock in a wind. One of our skippers was a big, slow-moving football player who didn't seem to do anything quickly. Coming into the dock, he didn't reverse quickly enough to stop and went all the way through the dock.

The next day another one of the ships in our little group encountered a Mexican gunboat crossing its bow in the crowded harbor. The skipper could not remember who had the right-of-way or what to do about it. He crashed into the gunboat, and put it out of commission.

The third day, another of the ships had a similar problem when the ferry was crossing. That skipper was wrong about who had the right-of-way and crashed into the ferry. Fortunately, no one was hurt.

For the rest of the time we were ordered to take the ships into a little estuary off the main bay, which was quite shallow and, therefore, not used by commercial vessels. "The harbor master must have heaved a sigh of relief when our six LCIs left after all the grief we caused him.

On 14 December 1942, LCI-334 and her sister LCIs got underway at 0902 and proceeded through the channel to the Gulf of Mexico for training exercises. At 1746 they returned and anchored off the Bolivar Peninsula in Galveston Bay. This routine was repeated on the 15th and 16th before returning to pier 38 in Galveston.

On 17 and 18 December, the 334 underwent beaching practice for the first time at Bolivar Point in Galveston Bay, returning to pier 38 each evening about 1700. There were no further operations until 22 December when she got underway with several sister LCIs for various exercises and tactical maneuvers in the Gulf of Mexico. These maneuvers were repeated on 23 Dec. with the LCI Division 28 ships.

Christmas 1942 came and went with the 334 moored to pier 38 in Galveston. As Skipper Ormston remembers it, there was plenty of liberty for everyone. A few lucky crew members with families nearby got to go home for a few days. Commander Jannotta had a Christmas party and presented each one of the LCI skippers in his group with a ship's bell which the Navy Department had failed to put on the LCIs. It was 28 December before the 334 got underway again for tactical maneuvers in the Gulf—this time with Division 28 sisters 333 and 335.

Ship Alterations   On 29 December, LCI-334 returned to her maker, Brown Shipbuilding in Houston, for alterations in compliance with "Com LCI Group 4 order G/4010-42 dated 28 December, 1942" and moored to sister LCI-336 in Green Bayou. The following day she was unloaded and stripped of all gear in preparation for alterations.

The officers and crew were moved ashore and billeted at Brown's barracks in Green Bayou. The officers and some of the crew received leave while the ship was under alterations. Others hung out at the Balinese Room which was on a pier...a very popular place to have drinks and shoot a little craps, while scouting out the local talent.

The 334 remained moored at Brown Shipbuilding between 31 December 1942 and 18 January 1943 while undergoing conversion, alterations, and completion of unfinished work. One of the main changes was in the conning tower. The shipyard raised and modified the conning arrangement so that there was an enclosed pilot house with an open bridge above.

On 18 January 1943, the 334 was restowed with gear and the crew moved back aboard. On 20 January, she got underway for Galveston via Humble Oil's Baytown fuel dock. After fueling, she continued on to Galveston and moored to pier 39. On the 22nd, the 334 got underway at 0957, "swinging ship" to compensate its magnetic compass in Galveston Bay, then moored to pier 38.

Shakedown Cruise   The LCI-334 got underway on 23 January at 1325 for her shakedown cruise—the period of adjustment, clean-up, and training for a ship after commissioning or a major overhaul[12] —in compliance with Com LCI Flot 2's order.

At 1430 the LCIs formed column in order: LCI 332, (Lt William Nielson, USNR, Officer in Technical Command [OTC]), 331, 334, 336, and 69—all Flotilla 5 LCIs—plus the 343. Speed: 11 knots.

The six LCIs made numerous course changes in accordance with the operation order. By noon on 24 January, land was sighted in the Brownsville, Texas, area, about 300 miles southwest of Galveston. The night of 25/26 January, the weather turned thick with wind, rain squalls, and heavy seas making it difficult to maintain contact with the other ships. Consequently, the running lights were turned on at 2330.

Winds were now at gale force, with some seas breaking over the conning station. Only LCI-336 astern was visible to the 334 now. By 0445 on the 26th, speed was reduced to 5 to 6 knots due to heavy rolling and pitching.

According to Ormston, the shakedown cruise was a real test for the new LCIs:

> We got into two days of an almost hurricane proportion winter storm. It was cold. I thought it was cold back at Solomons [Maryland], but we had green water over the bridge and every piece of crockery on the ship was broken. The gyro compass, of course, went out and we lost contact with each other...we just could not see anybody.
>
> We finally turned our running lights on, despite the submarine threat, and went on dead reckoning...We found a sea buoy about two days later at Galveston. I think one of the other LCIs wound up in Brownsville, Texas, another up in Orange, Texas.

I asked LCI-332 radioman Ed Korpinen to describe their shakedown cruise in the Gulf. His response: "They wanted to see, I guess, how seaworthy these craft were. There was a hurricane brewing in the Gulf of Mexico. A bunch of us went out to sea and we hit that storm. We all survived but we were distressed. A couple of ships wound up in Louisiana, a couple off the Panhandle of Florida. They were scattered all over heck. The storm blew in there and took us over. We were completely out of control."

Radioman Steve Wiercinski (LCI-336) remembers the Texas weather and duty at the "Y": "I was surprised how rough it was down there. It was cold. I couldn't believe how cold it was going down through the Houston Ship Canal. After our shakedown, we had to go into Galveston to get our conning tower raised. They put an additional 6 feet on it...We spent our time in Houston at the YMCA. Duty there was great. We only had to report at 7 o'clock in the morning."

My interview with Radioman Bill Bertsch (LCI-64) confirmed something I had long suspected: lots of officers and bluejackets had cameras and kept personal diaries aboard ship, even though it was against Navy rules and regs. Here's Bill's story with a surprise ending: "Our 'Captain Queeg-type' executive officer took away our cameras in Galveston. He said, 'No cameras or diaries because we might be captured.' I think I was on one of the few ships that enforced the rules, because I stumble on guys all the time now that have all kinds of pictures. This guy [exec. officer] was a terror. He searched our lockers every once in a while and stuff like that. I found out later he had his own camera."

Top Off on GSK Read Dunn includes the following story in his autobiography: "One night, LCI-335 received orders to 'Top off on GSK and prepare to get under way at 0600.' We looked at each other. What was GSK? We learned that was Navy terminology for 'general ship's stores.' I never did learn what the K stood for.

"Supplies were the responsibility of the executive officer. I had to make out the order, but for how much? Where were we going and for how long? When would we next have an opportunity to draw supplies? What was the rate of consumption? No one knew the answers to any of these questions. I did the best I could. When I left the ship more than a year later there were still three cases of razor blades aboard."

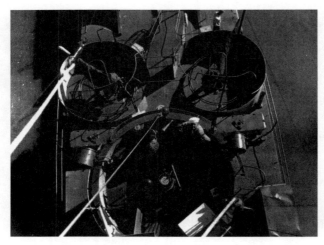

*LCI view from above.
Courtesy of Robert W.
Kirsch.*

Maiden Voyage of LCI Flot 5

On 4 Feb. 1943, LCI-334 got underway at 1217 to rendezvous with several other LCIs off the sea buoy at the Galveston Bay entrance.

The 334 officially departed Galveston, Texas at 1555 on 4 Feb. 1943 in company with LCI(L) Flotilla Five, formation "Baker," standard speed 12 knots, course 133 true, 127 PSC. The 334 was #2 ship in column astern the guide and flag, USS LCI-333.

Read Dunn, XO [Executive Officer] of the 335, hasn't forgotten those first days at sea:

> When we left Galveston that afternoon, we had no idea where we were going. We were simply following the leader. The only chart we had aboard was the chart of Galveston Bay. During the first night, the football-playing skipper who was a little slow lost sight of the other ships in the convoy. He was certain we were heading for the Mediterranean, so he turned due east. The planes found him about twelve hours later and headed him south.

> At noon the second day, the commander called for all ships to report their noon positions by flag hoist. When the flags were hoisted, the reported positions were all over the Gulf; no two were within ten miles of each other. That experience was a lesson for all of us. We knew that we had to learn navigation if we were going to survive.

> Navigation was the assigned responsibility of the executive officer on our ship. That meant me. Fortunately, we had aboard a couple of good text books on navigation and the necessary tables

Signalman's flag bag. Pictured: Left-unknown, Right-Al Redman S 1/c. Courtesy of Robert W. Kirsch.

for the conversions. In those days there were no computers and not even calculators; all the calculations had to be made by hand the old fashioned way. I was never very good with numbers, but Smitty, our quartermaster, was. He checked my math. After a great deal of hard study and months of practice, I managed to get a reasonably good star fix at night and a fair sun shot and noon position.

When we got to Panama we obtained a full set of charts of the Pacific. They were good until we got to the islands. There we encountered problems. Some of the charts of the islands obtained from the British Admiralty had been cartographed by Captain Bligh and had not been corrected since.

Coco Solo Sub Base Panama Canal   A week later on 11 February, the 334 and several of her Texas-built sisters arrived in the Coco Solo Submarine Base at 0912 after entering the gate at the north end of the Panama Canal.

The next eleven days at the Sub Base were uneventful. Al Ormston remembers awarding lots of liberty while in the Canal Zone. He particularly remembers blue moon cocktails: "You'd go into a bar and the girls would sidle up and say, 'Will you buy me a drink?' and you would. It was only blue-colored soda pop but we would pay for it."

Bill Brown (LCI-327) remembers the town of Colon as "...sort of odd. The Red Light houses were run like retail stores."

On 23 February at 0712, LCI-334 proceeded south in the Panama Canal at one-third speed in company with the other LCIs of Group 14.

The ship's log entries summarized the day's activities:

1105 Entered Gatun Lock (lower).
1155 Entered Intermediate Lock.
1245 Entered Upper Lock and proceeded through Gatun Lake.
1705 Entered Pedro Miguel Locks.
1930 Left Pedro Miguel Locks and proceeded through Miraflores Locks.
2100 Arrived at the US Naval Ammunition Depot (USNAD) in Balboa and moored to LCI-335.

Read Dunn summarized his memories of the Canal Zone: "Panama was disappointing. The towns were dirty and filled with bars and night clubs of sorts—hang-outs for the sailors of the world. But the trip through the canal was beautiful and exciting. When we docked on the Pacific side we quickly learned the importance of tide. There the difference in high and low tide is sometimes 15 or more feet. We had to tend the mooring line constantly."

LCI-334 got underway from USNAD at 0836 on 25 February 1943 and proceeded out the channel. At 1035 the 334 rendezvoused with the following ships:
LCIs **21**, **22**, **23**, **24**, 25, 26, 27, 30, 31, 34, **61**, **62**, **63**, **64**, **65**, **66**, **67**, **68**, **69**, **70**, **222**, **223**, 224, 225, 226, 227, **327**, **328**, **330**, **331**, **332**, **333**, **335**, **336**, and last, but not least, the **334**.*

LSTs 334 (guide and OTC) and 390.

SCs (Submarine Chasers) 481, 637, 699, 702, 731, 732 and 741.

* The 25 bold-faced LCIs were the first Flot 5 LCIs assigned to the Pacific. Other LCIs, including the 329, would report later on.

The 44-ship convoy got underway in LCI cruising formation "Baker" with the 334 as division leader of the column on the starboard side of the 328, the LCI Group guide, and proceeded southward in the Gulf of Panama at 9 knots. The next ten days were relatively uneventful—"underway as before, same formation and speed"—with occasional course changes.

Earl Fincham (LCI-223) describes how not to get lost at sea: "Between the Canal Zone and Bora Bora, one ship got a little out of

LCI stern view. Courtesy of Robert W. Kirsch.

line and the officer on the bridge told the kid to give it five degrees left rudder. About an hour later, the officer couldn't see any ships anywhere. Finally, the kid in the wheelhouse says, 'We still got 5 degrees left rudder.' He was going in circles. It took them two or three days before they got back where they belonged."

John Barry described two challenging problems they experienced between Panama and Noumea: "We lost our steering and had to hand steer. We somehow lost power to the drive or something, and so that meant an arrangement with some pulleys...right screw and left screw. We had to receive orders from the conn down there as to which way to steer the darn thing. We lost an engine, too. Fortunately, we carried two spare engines. "Oh, and we also carried a load of canned vegetables, canned stuff for the Army, in the holds where we would normally have troops. We hauled that all the way to Noumea."

On 8 March 1943, Division 28 fell back for some 20-mm antiaircraft practice shooting at a kite target towed by the 328, LCI group guide. LST-390 was apparently experiencing mechanical difficulties because on 16 March she was continually dropping back out of station and slowing down the convoy.

Bora Bora On 19 March at 0640 the aircraft alarm pennant was hoisted; however, the plane was quickly identified as a "friendly." At 0646 the convoy headed toward the northeast side of beautiful Bora Bora Island, one of the Society Islands, and proceeded into Teavanui Harbor and moored alongside LCI-332; it was the end of the second and longest leg (22 days) of the maiden voyage.

Most sailors would quickly call six days in Bora Bora good duty. Between 19-25 March, the 334 remained "moored as before" except for two interruptions: to take on water and to "swing the ship."

Al Ormston remembers Bora Bora and its natives: "We just happened to be on liberty at a time when an Air Force general was having a farewell luau. There was a big celebration, hula dancers and whatnot. All the natives were out there on the dance floor... Tom Mulligan was in on it, I remember. They had a steel band using old pots and pans and so forth. I never heard anything like it. Damn if they didn't start playing the 'Notre Dame Victory March' and there goes Mulligan out in the middle of the floor dancing with the natives. We had a real good time. The natives were very friendly and, of course, they love to sell you things like cat's-eye shells. I got a beautiful cloth with beautiful designs."

On 25 March 1943, the 334 and several sister ships got underway at 1646 and proceeded out the Bora Bora channel in the following order: SC-637 and LCIs **328**, **332**, **327**, **331**, **334**, **330**, and **336**. The LCIs and the sub-chaser rendezvoused off the entrance and formed a double column cruising plan with the 328 as guide and flag with the 334 leading the starboard column.

The 44-ship convoy that had left the Canal Zone was disbanded in Bora Bora. Some vessels were diverted to other destinations; others were simply awaiting orders or in line for repairs.

The third leg of the 334's maiden voyage only took five days. The sea routine was much the same, except zigzag practice commenced on 27 March and speed changes were inaugurated on the 29 March: 12 knots in daylight, 10 knots at night.

Pago Pago The night of 29/30 March, land was sighted on the starboard bow at 0300, identified as Manua Island. The convoy proceeded to the swept channel entrance to Pago Pago. A course correction was made after a warning by station's mine sweep and the

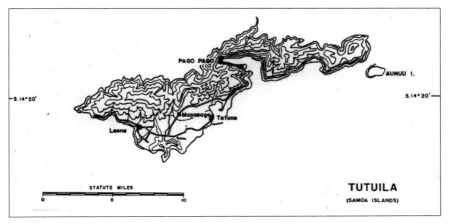

Tutuila, Samoa Islands.

ships proceeded west and into the channel on proper bearing.

On 30 March 1943 at 1327, the 334 moored alongside LCI-331 in Tutuila, Pago Pago in American Samoa. I asked Captain Ormston if he had had liberty in Pago Pago. His response: "Yeah. But there wasn't much, just to walk around the beach, but they did have an officer's club that I helped close down one night. I got acquainted with one of the other LCI skippers. I don't know how it happened but we wound up in the damn hills way back up where the natives were friendly. We drank some of this...I don't know what the hell it was. You talk about hangovers. I had the granddaddy of them all the next day.

"But the thing that was kind of unhappy about Pago Pago was the damn small boats. The little canoes came out and started swarming around our 334 while we were still anchored there...and someone came and shook me and said, 'They're here, captain.' Apparently during the evening of the celebration back in the hills, one of us, and I think it might have been me, had promised that we would give them a Victrola. Anyhow, I think what we finally settled for was giving them some records, but that was rather embarrassing."

The 334 took on fuel and water during her three-day stay in Pago Pago. On 2 April the 334 stood out from Pago Pago Harbor at 0805 in company with the following ships: LSTs 334 and 390; LCIs 330, 331, 332, 327, 328, and 336. The 334 was the LCI guide ship astern the LST-334. Destination: Noumea, New Caledonia.

Though LCI(L)s roll and pitch, they are nonetheless seaworthy boats. U.S. Navy.

On 3 April, the convoy formation was changed to allow LCIs 334, 336, 328, and 332 to take position as submarine screen through the area northwest of the Fiji Islands to New Caledonia. The balance of the trip to Noumea was more or less uneventful. The convoy crossed the International Dateline on 5 April at 0800, advancing the date to 0800 6 April. Later that day, squalls were encountered with strong southerly winds accompanied by heavy swells. Net result: the 334 rolled a maximum of 45 degrees to starboard. The weather continued to be rough with visibility hampered by rain squalls on 7 April, then subsided.

Elmo Pucci (LCI-329) explained why the 329 was not part of the convoy that left Panama. He then went on to depict the lonely (and largely unappreciated) role of a ship's cook: "We got stuck at the Panama Canal. We got caught in some wind there and fouled up a screw. Had to go back to Coco Solo and go into dry-dock. Next thing you know, we were all by ourselves. All the other LCIs had continued on. We went the rest of the way to New Caledonia all by ourselves cruising at 12 to 14 knots tops."

I asked Elmo if he enjoyed his job as ship's cook. His response: "No, not really. It was a lot of work. There was nobody else. You're the only cook—so you gotta be the cook, you gotta be the baker, you gotta be the commissary steward and the storekeeper—the whole kit and caboodle! It was a tough job; you went to work 7 days a week. I was glad to get off that thing in 15 months."

Noumea, New Caledonia

On 10 April the convoy made landfall at Bulari Passage at 1021 and proceeded in column through the swept channel mooring off

Noumea, New Caledonia, in Great Road Anchorage with the other ships of LCI Flotilla Five at 1651.

The 334's log entries read, "Moored as before Noumea, New Caledonia, No operations" for the next six days. (The old "hurry up and wait" war game had started.)

Pharmacist mate Homer Reighard joined the crew of the LCI-62 in New Caledonia. (He also served on LCIs 23 and 223 later on.) He had shipped out of San Pedro in mid-1942 with a crew of men tasked to build MOB-7 in Noumea. When the hospital was completed, the crew (all plankowners) took examinations. Homer made Pharmacist Mate third-class and was assigned to independent duty on the 62. I asked him to explain what that meant: "That's duty without a doctor. We were the sole medical on an LCI. We only had one doctor in the flotilla."

Serious Training Gets Underway

On 19 April, shipboard training to prepare for war began:

19 April - Tactical maneuvers and towing practice.

20 April - Practice coming alongside and clearing a large ship.

21 April - Practice mooring and taking on water.

On 22 April at 0515, the 334 proceeded with LCI Flot 5 around the South Reef to Alomeve Passage, Isle of Pines, and anchored near Kuto Bay. More training followed:

23 April - Tactical maneuvers off Isle of Pines.

24 April - Exercising at drills and maneuvers.

25 April - Beaching practice.

26 April - Tactical maneuvers in morning, 20-mm gunnery practice in afternoon. Target: Infernal Island beach. (Observation: when guns depressed low enough for surface target, life-line stanchions interfere with line of fire creating a dangerous situation.)

27 April - Repeat April 26 practice plus beaching operations.

On 28 April at 0530, LCI Flot 5 proceeded to Noumea via outer passage clearing southwestern reefs and entering Bulari Pass to anchor seaward of Isle Nou at Ause aux Boefus at 1926. The next few days were reasonably free of activities.

On 5 May, LCI Flot 5 returned in formation to Isle of Pines via the Inside Passage for some concentrated beaching practice.

6 May - Day and night beaching practice.

7 May - Beaching and target practice.
8 May - Towing and being towed as a disabled vessel, and beaching as such, plus night maneuvers.
9 May- Repeat of May 8 practices. (The 334 beached a total of 9 times off Kuto Beach.)

On 10 May, the General Quarters (GQ) alarm was sounded at 0545. GQ was secured at 0620. At 0739 the LCIs beached at Kuto Cove, then retracted at 0926 and proceeded in column with LCI-328 as guide for maneuvers. Ships in order: 328, 330, 333, 334.

At 1039, LCIs 328 and 330 collided on a turn movement southeast of the Isle of Pines without serious consequences. All ships returned to Kuto Bay for several more practice sessions of beaching and retracting between 1840 and 2025.

The Flot 5 ships departed Kuto Bay at 0720 on 11 May for Aux Boeuf Anchorage, Isle Nou, Noumea, arriving at destination at 1311. Ormston: "The time down at the Isle of Pines was really something. It was intense training and the sailors and the officers loved it. We were learning the ship and how to handle it and how to maneuver while still out of range of the air raids. You couldn't do that kind of training on the Chesapeake."

On 13 May the 334 proceeded to the Great Road Anchorage and entered dry dock ARD-2 at 1100 for bottom cleaning, scraping, zinc renewal and inspection. She left dry dock the following afternoon at 1500 and returned to Anse Aux Boeufs where Navy Yard welders came aboard to repair stanchions and ramp rollers.

On 15 May she moved alongside LCT-482 to load and stow LCI Flotilla spare engines, anchors, and parts. The following morning at 0900 the 334 moored alongside LCI-23 for supply transfers. Later that same morning, she took on 14,310 gallons of diesel oil.

Read Dunn, the 335 XO, has another story for you. Listen up:
While in New Caledonia awaiting orders to proceed to the Solomon Islands...we received notice to transfer three or four of our younger men and receive replacements.

The high command was concerned about sending us into the war zone with no experienced personnel. We were sent a chief boatswain, a boatswain and a gunner. To obtain these men the command had sent a cadre order to the large naval vessels in the harbor. Of course, what we were sent was what those large ships didn't want.

The chief was the biggest surprise. After posting orders of the day dutifully for a couple of days and finding none of the orders carried out, I became suspicious and investigated. Our new chief could not read or write. How did he get in the Navy, and how did he get to be a chief, if he could not read? The answer was that he had been in the tuna fleet in the Pacific and had been blanketed into service with the fleet. The Navy had commandeered the entire fleet—boats and crews. He knew how to handle lines and perform the usual seaman's duties but little else. We transferred him the first chance we had.

The gunner had spent his entire Navy career on battleships. When our little flat-bottom ship rolled, rocked and yawed, he turned 'green'—the Navy word for seasick. He was of no use as a gunner in his bunk. We had to transfer him.

The third man was good. He was able and personable. Everybody liked him. Unfortunately, the first week out of New Caledonia, he was washed overboard trying to secure the ramps during a storm. We were in the war zone in submarine-infested waters and were not allowed to stop to look for him. That was our first understanding of war.

The tension was beginning to build. Everyone knew preparations were being made to move up to the combat zone. It was just a question of when.

On 18 May, the 334 moored alongside LCI-327 at 0843 to pick up decontamination material—then delivered it to LST-396 in Port Noumea. Later that same day she moored alongside LST-339 at the Nickel Docks to take on water overnight.

Southern Solomons Training and Service

The day everyone had been anxiously anticipating finally arrived! On 20 May 1943 at 1051, six "early bird" Flot 5 LCIs stood out from Noumea and proceeded toward Guadalcanal. Commander James M. Smith, USN, OTC in LCI-222. Order of ships: 222, 223, 332, 333, 334, and 336.

At 1219 the small task unit passed the Amadeo light abeam to starboard and proceeded northwest along the southwest coast of New Caledonia, speed 12 knots, cruising formation, two columns:

port column led by 222 (flag and guide), 223, 332; starboard column 333, 334, 336.

On 23 May two bogeys were sighted at 0630 near task unit disappearing into clouds. At 1410 a large yellow cloud of smoke was observed on the horizon bearing 325 true. LCI-222 temporarily left formation to investigate. (Ormston never did learn what ship got hit, if any, before they got there.)

At 2200 the formation was challenged by a friendly destroyer. At 2300, land was sighted bearing 275 true, identified as the southeast coast of San Cristobal Island in the Solomons.

The morning of 24 May, the LCI task unit proceeded along the northwest coast of Guadalcanal Island and at 1450 anchored off Lunga Point and secured.

The Flot 5 LCIs had a rude welcome that first night, according to Skipper Ormston: "We got shot at the first night. A lot of [our] people thought we were surfaced submarines because the LCI profile looked like a submarine, so a lot of 20-mms and 40s came at us and, of course, we got on the horn. We also had an air raid that first night and we thought, 'My gosh, what are we getting into?'"

The following morning at 1117 the LCIs got underway for the Amphibious base in the Florida Islands about 19 miles north of the 'Canal across Ironbottom Sound.

The 334 entered Tulagi Harbor at 1254 and moored alongside LCI-222. Later that evening at 1841 she moved alongside LCI-333 at the LCI unloading barge to offload base spares. (A Condition Red interrupted this project at 1916 for about 30 minutes.)

With offloading completed, the 334 proceeded to Makambo Island between Tulagi and Florida Islands and anchored offshore. The LCI Flotilla Five staff personnel who had accompanied the earlybird LCIs to the South Pacific would continue to live on the ships for some time as there was not yet much in the way of facilities on the beach.

Russell Islands Visit The afternoon of 26 May, the 334 returned to the 'Canal and anchored off Lunga Point. At 2333 that night LCI Flot 5 vessels 222, 223, 332, 333, 334 and 336 got underway for the Russell Islands in column formation. Shortly thereafter at 0021, the guide ship collided with an unidentified vessel. The damage was only slight, so the formation continued.

A few minutes later, two LCIs ahead commenced firing their 20-mm guns at an object abeam to starboard which resembled a submarine resulting in a GQ alarm. Firing ceased at 0051 and all hands secured from GQ.

At 0647 on 27 May, the LCIs entered Renard Sound and anchored. The 334 was underway again at 1125; beached at Blue Beach at 1203 and took aboard 150 U.S. Army troops; retracted at 1447; and anchored in Renard Sound at 1458.

At 1547, the 334 got underway for Yellow Beach; beached at Wernham Cove at 1708 (still in the Russells); then disembarked and reembarked the troops and equipment by 1730; retracted and returned to Renard Sound and anchored at 1840. Talk about on-the-job training!

On 28 May 1943, the LCIs shoved off for Kokumbona Beach, Guadalcanal at 0030. At 0440 while passing Savo Island, the formation was fired upon from the port beam by an unidentified source, and as a result, GQ was sounded. At 0645 LCI-334 beached on Kokumbona Beach and disembarked, then reembarked troops. She retracted at 1005; rebeached at 1059 with troops off, then on again; retracted at 1114 with troops aboard and practiced landings again at 1150 and 1330. Finally at 1851 she anchored off Kokumbona Beach.

The June 1943 War Diary of Commander LCI Flotilla Five summarized the U.S. Navy's chain of command in the South Pacific:[13]

Commander in Chief, US Navy	Adm Ernest J. King, USN
Commander in Chief, Pacific Fleet	Adm Chester W. Nimitz, USN
Commander South Pacific Force	Adm William F. Halsey, Jr., USN
Commander Amphibious Force, SoPAC	RAdm R.K. Turner, USN
Commander Landing Craft Flotillas, SoPAC	RAdm G.K. Fort, USN
Commander LCI Flotilla Five	Cdr C.L. Walton, USN

All operation orders were generated by Admirals Turner or Halsey. Commander Walton spelled out the status/location of the LCI Flot illa Five organization as of 1 June 1943 in the War Diary as follows:

LCI Flotilla Five Organization [14]

Commander LCI Flotilla Five   Cdr C.L. Walton
  Group Thirteen: LCdr M.M. Byrd, USN.
   LCIs 21, 22, 61, 62, 63, 64, 65, 66, 67, 68, 69, 70.
  Group Fourteen: LCdr A.V. Jannotta, USNR.
   LCIs 23, 24, 327, 328, 329, 330, 331, 332, 333, 334, 335, 336.
  Group Fifteen: Cdr J. McDonald Smith, USN.
   LCIs 222, 223.

LCIs 328 (Temporary Flagship), 329, 331, 335, 21, 22, 24, and 66 operating in Noumea area under LCdr A.V. Jannotta, USNR, Commander Group Fourteen, (CTU 32.5.1). Training and upkeep.
LCIs 61, 62, 67, 68, 70, and 327 operating in Espiritu Santo area under LCdr M.M. Byrd, USN, Commander Group Thirteen (CTU 32.5.2). Training and upkeep.
LCIs 23, 63, 64, 65, 69, 222, 223, 330, 332, 333, 334, and 336 operating in Guadalcanal-Russells area under Cdr McDonald Smith, USN, Commander Group Fifteen (CTU 32.6.3). Training and upkeep.

Beaching Exercises This repetitive beaching, loading and un-loading of troops training continued for another three days on Kokumbona Beach. On 1 June the exercises continued with new troops after an early morning run to the Russell Islands. On 2 June, it was back to the 'Canal for more of the same.

Ensign Tom Mulligan, the 334's engineering officer, described his visits to the Guadalcanal beaches during breaks in troop training this way: "We were able to get ashore often and see first hand evidence of the ferocity of the battle for Guadalcanal. Bones, helmets, implements of war, shell holes, shattered trees and so forth. We climbed a hill one day and saw how dug-in the Japs had been with machine gun nests and emplacements so cleverly concealed."

On 3 June, the only break in the beaching exercises came at 0752 when, after the troops came aboard with their gear, Skipper Ormston discovered the 334 was hard aground forward and had to be towed clear of the beach by LCI-333.

June 4-8 was spent in much the same way beaching and retracting time after time with Army troops on either Kokumbona or Doma Cove beaches, Guadalcanal or in Renard Sound in the Russells. One break, in what was fast becoming a dull routine for the 334 crew, was a trip to Paddy Bay off Botata Island in the Russells on 6 June, where troops were taken aboard from lighters.

I questioned Skipper Ormston about the boring routine of so many beaching reps. His reply: "We were still learning, too...how to get the ramps down and the troops off more quickly without fouling the ramps or dropping them prematurely. We used the manual cranks at first but then learned to rig them so that our forward anchor winch could pick the ramps back up again and get us the hell out of there faster. That little modification was very helpful."

On 9 June, the LCIs returned to their home base in Carter City on Florida Island. The 334 beached at Carter City at 1455 to undergo repairs. Later that evening a Condition Red alert called all hands to battle stations so the 334 retracted and got underway. (It was to be the first of 17 air raid alerts LCI-334 would experience over the next 19 days.)

Bill Bertsch, LCI-64 radioman, remembers a practical joke played on one of their crew replacements while tied up at the Amphib repair base in Carter City on Florida Island: "Some of us ol' salts told this guy about the great liberty in Carter City...saying there was one Quonset hut building that had a bar and some good-looking native girls that really liked to take care of LCI crewmen.

"The next day he was told he won the daily lottery to go ashore. He dressed in full whites and took the shoreboat trip. This shoreboat took passengers from all the LCIs, LSTs and LCTs in the Tulagi/Florida Islands area to Carter City. When he returned hours later he was mad and embarrassed to be taken in so easily. However, we all became a tight group of friends."

On 10 June, Commander C. L. Walton, Commander LCI Flot 5 departed Noumea in LST-395 enroute to Guadalcanal.

The Flot 5 LCIs enjoyed a break in their training exercises for several days as they marked time beached or anchored off Carter City or in Hutchinson Creek. The name Hutchinson Creek is somewhat misleading according to Al Ormston: "It was a big long creek. The water hole was up in Hutchinson Creek...and it was long enough that we could make sea trial runs to check our speed. It was a big bay is what it was."

There were five GQs over the next six days. Three were night

Crew of LCI-222 in Carter City, Florida Island Amphibs Repair Base near Tulagi, circa 1943. Front Row (L to R): Lige Loar Y2/c, Robert Williams Y2/c, Alfred Warm Y3/c. Back Row (L to R): Lt J.G. Donald Loban, Marvin Williams Y3/c, Lt Dittman. Courtesy of Alfred Warm.

raids of the "Washing Machine Charlie" variety. One was early, another mid-morning, but the 334 was not attacked. The only AA fire observed was over the 'Canal at 0530 on the 15th.

On 15 June Flotilla Commander Walton arrived at Guadalcanal in LST-395 and transferred to the LCI-333 (Temporary Flagship) and anchored in Kokumbona Bay in company with LCIs 222, 223, 332, 334, and 336.

LCIs 23, 63, 64, 65, 69, and 70 were operating in the Russells area carrying out training operations with units of the U.S. Army.

June 16 Air Raid

June 16, however, was another story. The Flot 5 LCIs got underway at 0440 for the 'Canal and beached at Kokum to take on troops and gear at 0700. The 334 retracted and got underway for Kokumbona where she beached at 1005. The ship had just retracted when the skipper received a Condition Red from Cactus Radio at 1350.

The 334 "Log and War Diary" for 16 June 1943 summed up the next 90 minutes as follows:

> *1350:* Air raid warning, General Quarters. Many airplanes observed in combat. Formation of Japanese bombers observed dropping bombs near Lunga Point. Great clouds of black smoke seen at Lunga. Approximately ten planes seen shot

down, four in flames. Two parachutes seen.
1500: Beached at Kokumbona.
1520: Secured from battle stations.

Thomas Littel, the 334's radioman, remembers the big Japanese raid as if it was only yesterday: "We were among four or six LCIs loaded with troops practicing landings on Guadalcanal. We stayed between Guadalcanal and Tulagi, and in formation steamed in an elliptical pattern until the raid concluded, with soldiers aboard throughout.

"An Australian P-40 flew by at low level. He was peppered with 20-mm fire because he looked like a Zero and the oval paintings made the gunners think it was Japanese. Henderson Field called and raised hell about it."

In his June 1943 summary for the Joint Chiefs, Admiral Chester W. Nimitz, CinCPOA, bottom-lined the 16 June attack as follows:

On 16 June, the largest enemy force since 7 April attacked our shipping in the Guadalcanal area. Enemy forces consisted of at least 60 VB (bombers), screened by a like number of fighters.

One hundred four U.S. fighters were scrambled in defense, and 74 made contact with enemy. There were numerous U.S. ships in the transport areas off Lunga Point and in Tulagi. The attack lasted from 1315 to 1513 (-11).

ComSoPac credits his VFs (fighters) and ships' A/A with the destruction of 107 enemy planes. Six of our VFs were lost, two pilots being recovered.

During this attack the **LST-340** received one hit which set fire to her cargo of trucks, gas, oil, etc., completely destroying it [the cargo]. LST-340, itself, though badly damaged, was beached and later salvaged.

At 1410 ***Celeno*** (AK) received 2 hits, and the resultant fire destroyed most of her cargo, though the ship was likewise beached and later salvaged."[15]

Obviously no one participant observed all of the action that day since the air-to-air combat ranged over a fairly wide area, from south of Guadalcanal Island to the northern Russells.

The Flot 5 LCIs resumed beaching exercises with different troops on 17 June. At 1951 that evening LCI-336 collided with LCI-65, which was proceeding at 2/3 speed towards the West Beach. The 334 took over as guide ship after the collision and beached at Kokumbona at 2036. Ten minutes later, the GQ alarm went off, and the ships retracted from the beach. Heavy antiaircraft fire was observed over Tulagi Harbor during the alert.

The ships secured from GQ at 2230, beached at 2240, retracted and anchored off the beach at 2325...another day on the job in the Southern Solomons. Now, let's break for a little story.

In my pre-interview questionnaire for amphibian vets, one of my questions was: "Do you recall any heroic and/or humorous memories based on your Solomons experiences you would like to share?" I was amused by Mike Scalpi's (LCI-66) answer: "I think the most heroic thing was eating Spam month after month without puking. Also drinking some of the water we had to suck up from different streams on the islands we raided. We did not have the capability of making fresh water (distillation). We had to put so much chlorine in it, you couldn't even drink it. It smelled."

The next three days were much the same. Beach at Kokum and retract with new troops and continue the drills at Kokumbona. Training on the 18th and 20th was interrupted by four red alerts: one on the 18th at 1407; and three on the 20th at 0220, 1215, and 2110. Still no direct attacks on LCI Flotilla Five. It was now quite obvious the Japanese knew something big was about to happen. The only questions: "When and where?"

Early on the 21st, the LCIs deposited their troops on Kokum Beach and returned to Tulagi Harbor, then to Hutchinson Creek where the 334 moored alongside LCI-332. The ships remained there until 25 June when they got a wake up GQ call at 0420. The LCIs got underway at 0757 to conduct speed trials in Purvis Bay. These speed runs were interrupted by another GQ between 1335-1455. While returning to Hutchinson Creek, the 334 grounded on a reef while approaching to moor alongside LCI-69, causing slight damage to the starboard screw.

The GQ alarm rudely awakened the 334 crew at 0450 on 26 June but no enemy planes came into sight. At 0610 the 334 provided transportation for several officers from Purvis Bay to Koli Point on the 'Canal.

At 1340 she got underway again with a Marine Reconnaissance Party and disembarked them at Halavo Seaplane Base; then moved on to Purvis Bay to disembark several officers into small boats; and finally, returned to anchor at Carter City— a regular Ironbottom Sound ferry!

On the 27 June, the 334 remained within the confines of Tulagi Harbor. She got underway once during a red alert between 1515 and 1549 but no enemy planes showed up.

Bill Bertsch (LCI-64) told me one of my favorite war stories— a personal experience of his with a very happy ending! It's out of context here, so we'll have to fast-forward to 1944. Here's Bill:

When I came back from the South Pacific after the Leyte [Philippines] invasion, I got home on Christmas Eve and had my 30-day leave. Then I checked in at the Little Creek ATB for another assignment.

One day, I was asked to report to the Executive Office. I was sure I was in trouble but I went over there and he looked at me and said, 'Bertsch, you were on an LCI gunboat, right?' They had changed our classification from an LCI(L) to an LCI(G). So I said 'Yes, sir' and he said, 'Okay.' He said 'I've looked at your service record. Go back and get your dress blues on, you're going over to Washington, D.C. There will be another LCI fellow joining you; he's a gunner's mate.'

So, when we get to Washington, we were met by a guy who takes us to the Office of Industrial Incentive, a Navy organization trying to increase factory production. It turns out they especially wanted us to visit factories where they make rockets, because rockets were a big thing then. They wanted veterans' stories to inspire the workers.

So I was teamed up with the gunner's mate, a Marine, a Navy Ensign, and an aviation machinist mate. We had all been in combat.

They just assumed I had been on a rocket boat [LCI(R)] but I was really on a gunboat [LCI(G)]. The LCIs listed as 'G' at the time sometimes included both rocket and gun boats. I wasn't asked, nor did I volunteer, that I wasn't a rocket sailor.

To make a long story short, they had us memorize these little speeches and we were given trucks. The Marine and I had one truck. It had fold-down sides and we had pictures of invasions with ships hitting the beach and all that. We also had the wing of an airplane with rockets underneath and a German V1 buzzbomb to show them the terror that had hit England. That was really an eye catcher—people really liked to see that buzzbomb.

They sent our pictures out to various factories in the northeast and then we started on a tour. We visited all kinds of defense industries including munitions factories in Pennsylvania and the northeast. As we were driving into Bridgeport, Connecticut, the Marine and I, we had to go by a beach. The beach was like 8 to 1 women and we said, 'Oh my God, we gotta get back here.' So we checked into the hotel, put our dungarees on over our bathing suits, and went out to the policeman on the corner and asked, 'How do we get a bus to that beach?' 'Well,' he told us, 'take the number 5 or whatever.' We didn't know that there were five beaches around those parts.

Anyhow, the bus took us to a place called Pleasure Beach where they had like a little Coney Island beside the beach. We almost didn't get off the bus because we were pretty sure it was the wrong beach, but we says, hey, as long as we're here, let's go to this beach.

We stumble out onto the beach and put our towels down, and I looked across 10 to 20 yards of sand and I see this girl over there. She's with a guy and it was just one of those things, you know, when you get hit by a...there used to be a fighter called Johanson who said he could hit like a thunderbolt and well...I was hit by a thunderbolt.

I looked at her and it was just one of those things...and I kept doing all kinds of things trying to catch her attention. The next day, she came down again and she's with this guy, but the third day, she's not. She's with her nephew. I talked to her and learned she already had a ticket and was moving to California. She was gonna leave the next Tuesday.

We had a date that Friday night and as fate would have it, I convinced her not to take the train, and we got married—3 weeks later! We're still married and just celebrated our 50th wedding anniversary.

You had to get permission from the commanding officer to get married in those days, you know. He wasn't going to give permission. He said, 'You don't know this girl. She's Italian-Catholic and you're German-American and a Methodist. You have nothing in common. You don't have anything in common other than you met at the beach. What the hell is that?' He went on to say, 'She wants to get on the pension roll in case you go overseas and get killed.' So anyway, we finally convinced him that even though he had already been divorced, why not let us get married.

So we got married in July 1945. I had her follow me on the trip after that because she couldn't ride in the truck. We were up in Boston on VJ-day. The trip lasted about five months and...gave me a lifetime of happiness. I'm sure glad I didn't explain to that officer that he had made a mistake in thinking I was on a rocket LCI!"

Operation TOENAILS Staging [16]

On 27 June 1943 at 1700, LCIs 23, 329, 330, and 331 departed for Wernham Cove to embark personnel of 43rd Division in compliance CTG 31.3, 260109.

On 28 June 1943 at 1600, LCIs 21, 22, 67, 68, and 69 departed for Renard Sound in compliance CTG 31.3, 270332 and CTF 31 Secret Operation Order AL10-43.

At 1700 same date, LCIs 24, 223, 332, 333 (Temporary Flagship), 334, 335, and 336 departed for Wernham Cove in compliance CTG 31.3, 270328 and Commander Eastern Force, Secret Operation Order AL10-43. Commander Walton, USN, OTC in LCI-333.

At 2320 on 28 June, LCIs 24, 223, and 332 anchored in lee of Alokum Isle in the Russells area.

To Be Continued

Due to space limitations, we must continue the LCI Flot 5 story in our next book— starting with the invasion of the New Georgia group of islands in the central Solomons. It will also provide complete land, sea, and air coverage of all Solomons campaigns, from Guadalcanal to Bougainville during 1942-1943. Please stay tuned.

An amphibious operation, in order to succeed, you've got to roll; it's got to grow. If you get sealed off on your beachhead, you may be safely ashore all right, but you're not going anywhere.

—Vice Admiral Richard Conolly

CHAPTER 6

Looking Ahead

That completes our biographies of the APD destroyer transports and the new shore-to-shore LCT, LST, and LCI landing ships and craft. Now for a sneak preview of my next volume, the second in a trilogy covering South Pacific amphibious operations during World War II.

The Solomons Campaigns 1942-1943
From Guadalcanal to Bougainville

We lead off with a brief review of where things stand in the Pacific just prior to the Guadalcanal-Tulagi landings in the southern Solomons, dubbed "Operation SHOESTRING." First, we examine Japan's empire expansion and armed forces buildup, as well as America's war plans and buildup prior to the sneak attack on Pearl Harbor.

We then recap the Battle of the Coral Sea (7-8 May 1942), the first naval clash fought entirely with carrier aircraft—and Admiral Yamamoto's first taste of defeat—when Allied forces intercept the Japanese Port Moresby, New Guinea, invasion forces.

We recount how Yamamoto suffered a decisive second defeat, thanks to some code-breaking, luck and skill on the American side —in the Battle of Midway (4-6 June 1942). U.S. Dauntless dive bombers sink four large carriers, all veterans of the Pearl Harbor attack, along with hundreds of their experienced pilots, skilled mechanics and all of their aircraft. The U.S. Navy lost one carrier, the *Yorktown*, plus many valiant pilots and their aircraft.

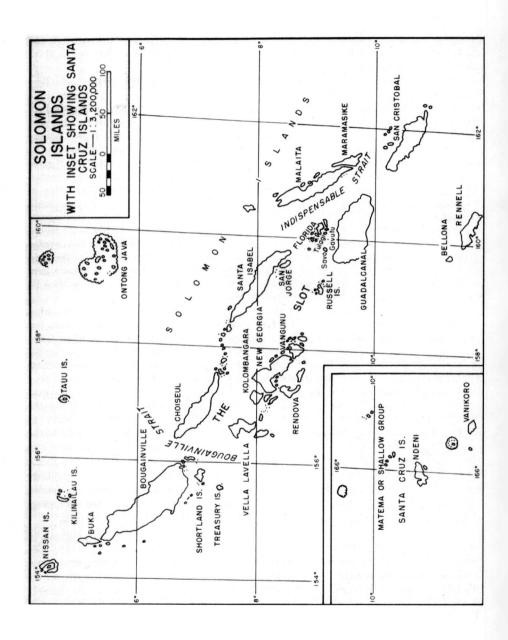

Solomon Islands Map. Courtesy U.S. Marine Corps.

Chapter 1. The Struggle for Guadalcanal, 7 Aug 1942 – 9 Feb 1943

Since I don't believe in "reinventing the wheel," this is an abridged version of Volume V of *History of United States Naval Operations in World War II* by distinguished historian RAdm Samuel Eliot Morison. It has been condensed and edited by the author's grandson, Samuel Loring Morison. The U.S. Navy experiences more fighting in the six-month campaign code-named "Operation WATCHTOWER," than in any three previous wars. Major naval actions covered include the severe defeat of the U.S. in the Battle of Savo Island, and the three-day Naval Battle of Guadalcanal in which two rear admirals were lost. The relation between the ground fighting and the naval warfare, which was a significant feature of this campaign, is described in considerable detail. In addition, numerous naval actions are recorded as well as the sufferings of the supply train and the almost daily air fighting.

Historian Morison summarized the "cost and return" of the Guadalcanal campaign with these words:

> In war's brutal scale of lives lost against lives risked, the bloodletting from 60,000 Army and Marine Corps troops committed to Guadalcanal, had not been excessive; 1592 killed in action. Navy losses, never to this day compiled, were certainly in excess of that figure, and several score fliers of all three air forces had given their lives. But the Japanese had lost about two thirds of the 36,000 men who fought on Guadalcanal—14,800 killed or missing, 9,000 dead of disease and 1,000 taken prisoner. Many thousand more soldiers went down in blasted transports or barges, and the number of Japanese sailors lost in the vicious sea battles will never be known, because such matters do not interest the Japanese...
>
> Tactically—in the sense of coming to grips with the enemy—Guadalcanal was a profitable lesson book. The recommendations of Guadalcanal commanders became doctrine for Allied fighting men the world over. And it was the veteran from "the 'Canal" who went back to man the new ship or form the cornerstone for the new regiment...
>
> Strategically, as seen from Pearl Harbor or Constitution Avenue, Guadalcanal was worth every ship, plane and life that it cost. The enemy was stopped in his many-taloned reach for the antipodes...
>
> There were more subtle implications to Guadalcanal. The lordly

Samurai, with his nose rubbed in the mud and his sword rusted by the salt of Ironbottom Sound, was forced to revise his theory of invincibility...

For us who were there, or whose friends were there, Guadalcanal is not a name but an emotion, recalling desperate fights in the air, furious night naval battles, frantic work at supply or construction, savage fighting in the sodden jungle, nights broken by screaming bombs and deafening explosions of naval shells.

Chapter 2. Amphibious Rehearsals in the Russells, 21 Feb 1943

Operation CLEANSLATE provided the opportunity to test the dozens of suggestions arising out of WATCHTOWER as well as the second use of the new tank landing craft (LCTs) in a shore-to-shore amphibious assault movement of troops and materiel.

This landing, if it did nothing else, fulfilled Marine MajGen Vandegrift's requirement that "...landings should not be attempted in the face of organized resistance if, by any combinations of march or maneuver, it is possible to land unopposed and undetected..."

Chapter 3. Lull Between Storms, Feb – Jun 1943

This so-called "lull" saw the U.S. buildup of supplies, aircraft, and the new landing ships and craft, as well as Admiral Yamamoto's last major air offensive against Guadalcanal—promised to the Emperor as compensation for losing the island. The largest enemy air raids since Pearl Harbor, occurring on April 7 and June 16, are depicted.

Chapter 4. The New Georgia Campaign, 21 Jun – 20 Sept 1943

The five separate TOENAIL operations in the central Solomons at Rendova, Segi Point, Viru Harbor, Wickham Anchorage, and Rice Anchorage are recorded, as well as the naval battles of Kula Gulf, Kolombangara, and Vella Gulf.

The Guadalcanal-Tulagi operation, which stopped the enemy advances in the Pacific, has been described as a defensive-offensive campaign, and arguably the key turning point in the Pacific war. But the New Georgia operation, culminating in the capture of the strategically important Munda Airfield, was the first large-scale land, sea, and air offensive in the Pacific. It was also the first U.S. amphibious operation to deploy the new LCTs, LSTs, and LCIs.

Strategically, as long as Japan held Munda and had the planes, she could stop the Allies at the Russells. If, on the other hand, the Allies could base planes at Munda, they could deny everything below Bougainville to the enemy, and would have another leg-up toward Rabaul.

Japanese air strength in the Solomons area was estimated at approximately 380 planes for combat purposes. In addition to the airfield at Munda, the enemy had fields at Buka, Kahili, Ballale, and Kieta, as well as seaplane bases at Shortland-Faisi, Rekata Bay, and Soraken.

The primary objective: to capture the Munda airfield on the island of New Georgia. Preliminary landings to support the main effort were to be made at:

- Rendova, the island separated from New Georgia by a narrow channel and within artillery range of Munda airfield.
- Segi Point, at the extreme southeast end of New Georgia. (The 47th NCB would immediately set to work constructing an airstrip.)
- Viru Harbor, on New Georgia's southern coast. (The 20th NCB would build a PT-boat base.)
- Wickham Anchorage on Vangunu Island.
(Possession of Viru and Wickham will protect supply lines and provide staging areas for the New Georgia operations.)

The second phase of the operation consisted of invading New Georgia proper to seize Munda while a Northern force secured the Bairoko-Enogai area, in order to prevent the Munda garrison from being reinforced from the north.

Task Force 31, under the command of RAdm R.K. Turner, was subdivided into two groups:

- **TG 31.1**, the Western Force under the direct command of RAdm Turner, would conduct the operations in the Rendova-Munda area.
- **TG 31.3**, the Eastern Force, under the command of RAdm G.H. Fort, would be responsible for landings and subsequent operations at Viru, Segi, and Wickham Anchorage.

Task Force 36, the covering force, acting under direct command of Adm Halsey, covered the operation and furnished fire support.

Task Force 33, the main air support, operated under the command of VAdm A.W. Fitch (South Pacific Air Force). Its principal duties were to conduct reconnaissance and striking missions and provide direct air support during landings. RAdm Marc A. Mitscher, as commander of aircraft in the Solomons (Airsols), had tactical command initially of that portion of the task force which operated from Henderson Field and other bases in the Solomons.

The ground troops for all TOENAILS attack forces were designated the New Georgia Occupation Force (NGOF) under the command of MGen John H. Hester, U.S.A. NGOF was comprised of the 43rd Infantry Division; Marine 9th Defense Battalion; the 136th Field Artillery Battalion from the 37th Infantry Division; the 24th Naval Construction Battalion(NCB); Company O of the 4th Marine Raider Battalion; the 1st Commando, Fiji Guerrillas and assigned service troops.

Space limitations simply won't permit me to detail all of the amphibious components of the five TOENAIL operations here. However, the following landing ships and craft (listed in this book) participated in one or more of the landings:

APDs: *Crosby, Dent, Kilty, McKean, Schley, Talbot,* and *Waters.*
LCTs: 60, 63, 66, 67, 127, 128, 132, 133, 134, 139, 144, 145, 146, 156, 158, 159, 180, 322, 324, 325, 326, 327, 330, 351, 352, 367, 369, 377, 461 and 482.

LSTs: 341, 342(F), 343(F), 353, 354, 395, 396, 397, 398, 399, 472.
LCIs: 21, 22, 24, 58, 61, 62, 64, 65, 66, 67, 68, 69, 70, 129, 222, 223, 323, 332, 333, 334, 335 and 336.

The main landings began on June 30 when Marine and Army forces went ashore on Rendova Island, across the lagoon from the Japanese air base at Munda Point on New Georgia Island.

On July 5, the 43rd Infantry Division hit New Georgia. Ashore, the Americans met fierce resistance but were aided by close support from Marine air squadrons based on Guadalcanal. The Munda airfield was finally taken on August 5.

We've hardly scratched the surface of this multi-faceted story, but that's going to have to do for our sneak preview. The new shore-to-shore landing ships and craft had turned in better than satisfactory performance. According to RAdm Fort:

- Some LSTs transported 400 men each for short periods...LCTs carried as many as 250 men overnight, but in exposed positions...
- The LCIs carry about 170 combat troops...For unopposed short runs of a few hours, 350 men have been transported on a single LCI...They are ideal for night landings on good beaches.
- The LCTs had been the most useful of all types. However, low speed (6 knots) limits their daily staging in combat areas to about 100 miles per night...It is still advisable to have them underway only at night. Against a head sea, their speed is greatly reduced, sometimes to two knots...The crews and officers have been standing up well in spite of operating two out of every three days.

Chapter 5. The Occupation of Vella Lavella, 15 Aug – 9 Oct 1943

Bypassing heavily defended Kolombangara, U.S. and New Zealand forces took Vella Lavella. The landings at Barakoma and later resupply runs are covered—including the loss of LSTs 396 and 448. The naval Battle of Vella Lavella is also covered.

The principle of seizing unoccupied territory for the development of an airfield—soon to be repeated in the Bougainville operation—was worked out in this campaign.

The success of the operation clearly demonstrated the soundness of the strategy of bypassing enemy strongholds, then blockading and starving them out. This operational pattern, frequently repeated later in the Central and Southwest Pacific, was rehearsed successfully for the first time in the Central Solomons.

Chapter 6. The Bougainville Campaign, 27 Oct – 25 Nov 1943

The Marine landings on Bougainville were preceded by the seizure of the nearby Treasury, Shortland and Choiseul Islands. Code-named GOODTIME, the Bougainville operation was part of the Allied plan, Operation CARTWHEEL—to get rid of Rabaul, the massive, heavily-defended Japanese base on the eastern end of New Britain Island. From an airfield on Bougainville, U.S. fighters would be close enough to the Japanese base, about 200 miles, to provide escort for Rabaul-bound bombers.

Debate about dealing with Rabaul split U.S. strategists. General Douglas MacArthur wanted to invade and overpower Rabaul. The Joint Chiefs of Staff (JCS), believing that too many U.S. troops would die in an amphibious landing, wanted to neutralize the base with continual bombing raids.

At the Quebec Conference of August 1943, President Roosevelt and Prime Minister Churchill established the strategy for the U.S. Central Pacific Campaign and made the decision about Rabaul by siding with the JCS.

In his operation plan of 12 October 1943, Adm Halsey, ComSoPac, set 1 November as D-day. RAdm Wilkinson, who was placed in command of the operation was to seize and hold a suitable site in the northern Empress Augusta Bay area. There he was to establish facilities for small craft and construct such airfields as might be directed by ComSoPac.

In the same operation plan, Admiral Halsey directed Commander Aircraft, South Pacific to support the operation with land-based planes by providing defensive reconnaissance, air cover, and air support for forces engaged. He was also to provide support by strikes against airfields on Bougainville and against any enemy units threatening the attack force.

RAdm Frederick C. Sherman, commander of a carrier task force, was directed to support operations of the land-based planes by strikes against enemy bases and also to base aircraft ashore when directed.

RAdm Aaron S. Merrill, in command of a task force of cruisers and destroyers, was directed to destroy enemy surface vessels which might threaten RAdm Wilkinson's operations. Submarines under command of Capt James Fife, Jr., were to attack enemy shipping and surface units.

The Third Marine Division, reinforced, MajGen Allen H. Turnage commanding, was assigned the northern Empress Augusta Bay mission. For this operation, the 2nd and 3rd Raider Battalions were organized as the 2nd Raider Regiment. LtCol Joseph P. McCaffery took over the 2nd Raider Battalion.

The Eighth New Zealand Brigade Group, reinforced, commanded by Brigadier R.A. Row, NZEF, was assigned the Treasury Islands operation. The force for the Choiseul diversion was the 2nd Marine Parachute Battalion, commanded by LtCol Victor H. Krulak.

Admiral Wilkinson, Commander Third Amphibious Force, had the responsibility for the detailed planning of the naval operations. His operation plan included plans for logistics, naval gunfire, minesweeping, minelaying, communications, and boat pools. The ships for the two landings were divided into the Northern Force, for Empress Augusta Bay, and the Southern Force, for the Treasury Islands. Admiral Wilkinson designated RAdm George H. Fort commander of the latter force, and retained command of the Northern Force himself.

Seizure of Treasury Islands, 27 Oct – 6 Nov 1943

The Treasuries, 28 miles south of Bougainville were chosen as the site of an advance air and naval base to neutralize Japanese strongholds on New Britain, New Ireland, and Bougainville.

PT-boats based at Lambu Lambu, Vella Lavella, and at Lever Harbor on northern New Georgia were to screen the approach by a picket line from the Shortlands to Choiseul. Wilkinson also made various ground units, under command of Brigadier Row, NZEF, available for the operation. The New Zealanders were seasoned veterans who had participated in the campaigns of North Africa, Greece and Crete.

Admiral Halsey directed shore-based aircraft to support the operation by furnishing air cover and support, and to neutralize enemy airfields in the Bougainville area.

Transport units under Admiral Fort were divided into five groups, each with its tactical commander.

Choiseul Diversions, 27 Oct – 4 Nov 1943

As a diversion for the Treasury landings and for the Bougainville operation to come, a Choiseul Island landing by the 2nd Marine Parachute Battalion, under command of LtCol Victor H. Krulak, was planned for midnight of D-5 day. The operation was to be carried out by some of the same ships that participated in the Treasury landings during the day.

TransDiv 22 and TransDiv 12 completed unloading at Treasury Islands at 0800 on 27 October and began the return to Guadalcanal. A short time later, TransDiv 22 left the convoy and set course for Vella Lavella Island, via Gizo Strait and lay to off Juno River at 1830 on 27 October. So smooth was the planning that a large number of loaded boats were off the beach and ready to come alongside as soon as the APDs stopped. The 800 men of the 2nd Marine Parachute Battalion, acting as infantry, were embarked expeditiously.

TransDiv 22, in column, then fell in astern of the *Conway* as guide and proceeded across the Slot at a speed of 15 knots. At about 2352, a boat with a scouting party left the APDs, and at 0019 the first wave of boats followed.

The Marines' swift and vigorous activity surprised the enemy and created the impression that a larger force was at work. Its mission completed, the battalion was withdrawn in LCIs at 0150 on 4 Nov.

Bougainville Landing, 1 Nov 1943

The Amphibious Force for the first echelon consisted of eight transports, four cargo ships, seven destroyers, four destroyer/mine-sweepers, and two fleet tugs.

These forces, called the Main Body, Northern Force, were organized around three divisions of the Transport Group, under command of Commodore Lawrence F. Reifsnider. Many subsequent echelons would be transported in LSTs.

The initial landing force for the Cape Torokina landing at Empress Augusta Bay was the 3rd Marine Division, reinforced (less 21st RCT and a few other troops reserved for later echelons). The 3rd Marine Division was commanded by MGen A.H. Turnage, USMC.

Other components of the landing force included: 2nd Provisional Raider Regiment; 3rd Defense Bn. (less detachments); Detachment Naval Base Unit No. 7; and Boat Pool No. 11. Total Personnel: 14,321.

The Approach   During the evening of 30 October, RAdm Wilkinson, commander of the task force, and Gen Vandegrift, Commanding General, First Marine Amphibious Corps, embarked in the *Clymer* off Koli Point and joined the three transport divisions at the rendezvous point the following morning at 0740.

Final arrival in the Cape Torokina transport area was set for daylight to permit visual detection of uncharted shoals believed to be offshore. During entry to the area, the transports were to fire ranging shots on Cape Torokina and to spray Puruata Island with 20-mm gunfire.

Landing and Beach Conditions   By 0645 all transports were in the transport area, and the signal "land the landing force" was executed. Ships dropped anchor underfoot and the Marines were "rail-loaded," before the boats were lowered. Between 7,000 and 8,000 troops were landed in the first wave at 0726, H-hour minus 4 minutes.

Admiral Halsey pronounced the beach and terrain conditions "worse than anything ever encountered before in the South Pacific." For more than a mile inland the terrain consisted of swamp except for two narrow corridors of land raised a few inches above swamp level. The beaches were so narrow that in most places two bulldozers could not pass abreast between jungle and sea.

What followed, according to one officer, was "almost a disaster." Bottom line: eighty-six boats from the entire transport group (64 LCVPs and 22 LCMs) were broached and stranded during the landing operations. Machine-gun fire from the northern side of Puruata Island was encountered on the way in to the beach. Shore batteries on Torokina Point held their fire until our boats were only 50 yards offshore, then opened up with deadly accuracy.

Later examination of the defenses on Beach Blue One revealed two 77-mm guns, two 90-mm mortars, and fifteen machine guns located about ten yards from the water's edge, all well-emplaced in pillboxes.

Of the eight boats in the first wave from the *President Adams,* three received direct hits. Ten other boats were damaged by gunfire to such an extent that they had to be hoisted for repair. Salvage boats operated throughout the landing period of nine hours within easy range of enemy guns, and officers and men of the beach party repeatedly risked their lives to rescue wounded men from the water. Some 500 tons of cargo and vehicles were unloaded from the boats under the most difficult conditions.

Unloading and Retirement   Each ship provided its own shore party, except that the naval platoons for AKAs were formed from embarked personnel of the Naval base unit. The AKAs had a shore service platoon of 200, plus ship details of 20 men per hatch and boat details of three men per LCM and two men per LCVP. The APAs had a similar complement. The total number of troops employed in the shore party for the division landed was roughly 5,700, or somewhat over one-third of the total embarked.

There were numerous causes for delay in unloading: two air attacks, during which all ships had to suspend unloading and remain underway for maneuvering; poor beaches at the northern area which necessitated the shifting of five ships to new beaches; the loss of 86 landing craft by stranding, and others by enemy gunfire; and interference by enemy snipers.

These and additional deterrents made it impossible to complete the unloading before dark. Consequently, CTF RAdm Wilkinson ordered the entire transport group to get underway at 1800 and retire toward Guadalcanal along the track of the approach.

The Marines Attack   The 3rd and 9th Marines, assisted by the 2nd Raider Battalion, began slogging inland through swamp and jungle soon after landing, to press their attack against the enemy by seizing a swath of the coast from Cape Torokina to the northwest. At the same time, the 3rd Raider Battalion (less company M) assaulted Puruata island off Cape Torokina, silenced the machine gun, and destroyed the last defenders on that island by late afternoon 2 Nov.

Over the next several days the Marines advanced inland to extend their perimeter. There were occasional engagements with small enemy patrols, but the greatest resistance during this period came from the terrain, which consisted largely of swampland and dense jungle once one moved beyond the beach. The thing most Marines would remember about Bougainville would be the deep, sucking mud that seemed to cover everything not already underwater.

Meanwhile, the "Pacific Express" reinforcement/replenishment operation was just beginning. The following landing craft, listed elsewhere in this book, would play an important role in one or more of the Solomons campaigns.

APDs: *Manley, McKean, Stringham, Talbot, Waters, Dent, Humphreys, Sands, Schley, Kilty, Ward,* and *Crosby.*
LCTs: 58, 60, 62, 63, 66, 67, 127,128, 129, 132, 133, 134, 139, 144, 145, 146, 156, 158, 159, 180, 181, 322, 323, 324, 325, 326, 327, 330, 351, 352, 367, 369, 377, 461 and 482.

LSTs: 70, 207, 334, 339, 341, 342, 343, 344, 353, 354, 390, 395, 396, 397, 398, 399, 446, 447, 448, 449, 460, 472, 485 and 488.

LCIs: 21, 22(G), 23(G), 24, 61, 62, 63, 64, 65, 66, 67, 68, 69, 70, 222, 223, 322, 330, 331, 332, 333, 334, 335 and 336.

Army's 37th Division Arrives   The 37th Division began arriving in early November to reinforce the perimeter. On 23 November the 1st Parachute Battalion came ashore and temporarily joined the Marine Raiders, now acting as corps reserve. On 15 December, control of the landing force passed from I Marine Amphibious Corps (IMAC) to the Army's XIV Corps. The American Division gradually replaced the 3rd Marine Division, which had borne the brunt of the fighting. The 3rd Marines remained on Bougainville until 11 January 1944, when the Army relieved them.

General Griswold's XIV Corps was manning the perimeter in March 1944 when the Japanese assembled a counterattack force some 15,000 to 19,000 strong. But by this time, with a strength of approximately 62,000 men, including the American (Gen Hodge) and 37th (MajGen Robert S. Beightler) Divisions, XIV Corps was a powerful force. Nevertheless, for two weeks, again and again the Japanese troops charged only to be hurled back, each time suffering large losses.

Almost every weapon the Japs have got can reach us on the beaches. We have to take high casualties on the beaches—maybe 40 percent of the assault troops. We have taken such losses before.

—LtGen Holland Smith

APPENDIX A
Amphibious Force Ships and Craft [1]

	DISPL.[2]	TOTAL VESSELS[3]	TOTAL LOST[4]	COMM. or CONV.[5]
Ship-to-shore Cargo Ships & Transports				
AK Cargo Ships	1600-8900	160	3	'41-'45
AKA Attack Cargo Ships	4087-8045	108		'43-'45
AP Transports	1745-43,407	129	8	'21-'45
APA Attack Transports	4247-13,529	227	2	'43-'45
APc Coastal Transports	147-186	69		'42-'43
APD High Speed Transports				
-Converted Destroyers or Seaplane Tenders	1020-1190	32	8	'40-44
-Converted Destroyer Escorts	1400-1450	95		'44-'45
Shore-to-shore Amphibious Landing Ships & Craft				
LCT Landing Craft, Tank (Mark V & VI)	123-143	1,435	75	'42-'45
LST Landing Ship, Tank	1490	913	41	'42-'45
LCI(L) Landing Craft, Infantry (Large)	178-209	905	16	'42-'44
LCI(G) Landing Craft, Infantry (Gunboat)	210-230	218	8	'44-'45
LCI(M) Landing Craft, Infantry (Mortar)	235	60		'45
LCI(R) Landing Craft, Infantry (Rocket)	215	52		'45
LSM Landing Ships, Medium	513-520	474	9	'44-'45
LSM(R) Landing Ships, Medium (Rocket)	760-1187	50	3	'44-'45
LC(FF) Landing Craft, Flotilla Flagship	234	49		'43-'44
LCS(L) Landing Craft, Support (Large)	123	130	6	'44
LSV Landing Ships, Vehicle	4626-5177	6		'44-'45
LSD Landing Ships, Dock	4490-4546	18		'43-'45

[1] Morison, *History of United States Naval Operations in World War II,* Vol. XV, pp. 79-109; Principal reference works cited include: *Ships Data US Naval Vessels,* editions of 1943, 1945 and 1949; *United States Naval Vessels* (ONI 222-US) 1 Sept. 1945; Comairpac *Index of United States Fleet,* 1 Dec. 1944; and K. Jack Bauer's manuscript, "Ships of the United States Navy, 1775-1945."
[2] DISPL. - Light displacement, i.e., ready for sea but without consumable or variable items or crew.
[3] Ship counts will vary somewhat due to ship conversions and/or transfers under Lend-Lease.
Note: ship losses have not been deducted from ship totals.
[4] Number of ships or craft lost in combat or by accident, 27 Jun.1940–2 Sept.1945 when data available.
[5] Year commissioned or converted.

LST (3) Landing Ship, Tank (class 3). A British adaption of the American design shown with LCT and Army MTLs carried on deck. ONI/226.

LSM Landing Ship, Medium. An oceangoing tank landing ship designed to operate with LCI(L) convoys. ONI/226.

LSM(R) Landing Ship, Medium (Rocket). Converted LSMs serve as rocket support ships in amphibious operations preparatory to landings. ONI/226.

LCS(L)(3) Landing Craft, Support (Large)(Mark 3), designed to provide close-in fire support for landing operations and to intercept and destroy inter-island barge traffic. ONI/226.

LSV Landing Ship, Vehicle designed to transport large numbers of LVTs, DUKWs, and troops in a fast amphibious task force to the landing area; disembarking vehicles over a stern ramp. ONI/226.

Amphibious Force Ships and Craft [1]

	LENGTH	DISPL.[2]	TOTAL VESSELS[3]
Small Ship-to-shore Landing Craft			
LCC Landing Craft, Control	56'	30-50	99
LCM Landing Craft, Mechanized (Mks II-IV)	45'-56'	23-26	11,496
LCP(L) Landing Craft, Personnel (Large)	36'8"	5.8	2,193
LCP(R) Landing Craft, Personnel (Ramp)	35'10"	5.8	2,631
LCR(L) Landing Craft, Rubber (Large)	16'	395 lb.	10,123
LCR(S) Landing Craft, Rubber (Small)	12'5"	210 lb.	8,150
LCS(S) Landing Craft, Support (Small)(Mks I-II)	36'8"	9-10	558
LCV Landing Craft, Vehicle	36'3"	7	2,366
LCVP Landing Craft Vehicle, Personnel	36'3"	9	23,358
LVT Landing Vehicle, Tracked (Mks I-IV)	21'6"-26'1"	7.5-12.5	15,501
LVT(A) Landing Vehicle, Tracked (Armored)(Mks I-IV)	26'1"	11.4-17.0	2,850
TOTAL:			**79,325**
Amphibious Trucks			
DUKW	31'8"	5.8	NA[4]
Jeep	15'7"	1.6	NA

[1], [2], [3] *(Footnote information is given below chart on p. 247.)*
[4] NA - Not Available

LVT(A)(4) Landing Vehicle, Tracked (armored) (Mark 4) with an army 75-mm Howitzer. Capacity:5,000 lbs ammunition and gear. ONI/226.

LCC(1) Landing Craft, Control (Mark 1) Lead-in navigational craft for landing boats; to mark line of departure; for traffic control; for preliminary hydrographic surveys. Not intended to beach. ONI/226.

LCR(L) Landing Craft, Rubber (Large). A BAR man in the bow of the rubber landing craft provides covering fire as the 10-man boat crew reaches the undefended beach of Pavuvu in the Russell Islands. U.S. Marine Corps Photo.

LVT(3) Landing Vehicle, Tracked (Mark 3) capable of landing 24 fully equipped troops or 8,000 lbs of cargo. ONI/226.

DUKW 21/2-ton, 6x6 amphibious army truck for ship-to-shore transport. ONI/226.

LSD Landing Ship, Dock. Transports loaded landing craft to the landing area, where the hold is flooded and the small craft move out under their own power. ONI/226.

APPENDIX B
Sources

I have drawn on numerous sources for this volume. The primary sources are listed below. If a reader wishes to research his career and any ships he might have served on, a complete story can be obtained by visiting or writing the places listed below. If by chance the data desired are not at these places, the capable personnel there will be able to direct you to where to look.

A. U.S. Government

1. Archives and Records Sources

a) *National Personnel Records Center (Military Personnel Records) 9700 Page Blvd., St. Louis, MO 63132-5100;* TEL: 314-538-4141 (Navy/ MarineCorps/Coast Guard).

When phoning the above number you will receive a taped message. You can leave your name and address and the center will send you the proper form to fill out. You can also fax your request to 314-538-4175. Response will be made by U.S. Mail.

This Center maintains individual Personnel Records ("service records") and Medical Records (only to 16 October 1992) of Navy Commissioned officers and enlisted personnel, Marine Corps officers and enlisted personnel, U.S. Air Force Commissioned Officers and enlisted personnel and Army Commissioned Officers and enlisted personnel. The Center honors requests for information at no charge for veterans and members of their immediate families. Write and request Standard Form 180 to submit inquiry.

Author's note: If you plan to research your own story or that of an immediate relative, start here. It will give you important leads; specific dates when/where you served, on ships or shore duty.

b) *National Archives, Textual Reference Branch, 700 Pennsylvania Avenue, NW, Washington, D.C. 20408;* TEL: 202-501-5305.

This branch holds all records prior to 1 January 1941 and has no World War II material on file.

c) *National Archives II, Textual Reference Branch, 8601 Adelphi Road, College Park, MD 20740;* TEL: 301-713-7230 (textual material) or 301-713-6795 (photographic material).

The Textual Reference Branch in National Archives II maintains the deck logs of navy ships dating from 1 January 1941 through 31 December 1961.

A very large majority of all World War II War Diaries, Operational Plans, Action Reports, Damage Reports, etc. formally kept at the Operational Archives Branch, Naval Historical Center was transferred to "NATIONAL ARCHIVES II" in June 1996. This includes Action Reports from Commander-in-Chief, Pacific Fleet and Commander, Service Squadron, South Pacific Force.

d) *Department of the Navy, Naval Historical Center, Washington Navy Yard, 901 M Street, SE, Washington, DC 20374-5060;* TEL: 202-433-4132 (Navy Library), 202-433-6773 or 76 (Ships Histories Branch), 202-433-2765 (Photo Archives Section); 202-433-3224 (Operational Archives Branch).

The Deck Log Division of the Ships Histories Branch of the Naval Historical Center has control of all ships deck logs of navy ships dating from 1 January 1962 to present. For that period inquiries have to be made through that office to gain access to the logs. They are stored in the Suitland Records Center.

The Ships Histories Branch also contains data on individual ships filed alphabetically by the name. These files contain a wealth of source material other than deck logs not found in any other Archives. Copies of Citations, Action Reports, War Diaries, etc. may also be found in these files, especially those ships that served in World War II. Files are also kept on unnamed ships, such as LSTs, but these files are not complete.

The Navy Library has extensive collections of World War II publications such as the "Combat Narrative" monograph series (32 booklets), put out by the Office of Naval Intelligence shortly after the battles had been fought; the "Battle Experience" series (26 booklets), put out by Headquarters, Commander-in-Chief, Pacific Fleet and "United States Strategic Bombing Survey" Reports. While the publications are antiquated by research from World War II to the present, they are extremely useful in showing the thinking, policies, impressions, etc. of the time. In addition, they have marvelous illustrations.

Just at right angles to the building, on the right side of Leutze Oark is the Marine Corps Historical Center. Their library, while not as extensive as the Navy Library, is very good for its size and holds Marine Corps World War II publications. If research includes Marine Corps actions in the War, one should visit the library while there and stop in at the Research Branch across the floor from the library. The Research branch also holds valuable data on Marine Corps actions.

A very large majority of all World War II War Diaries, Operational Plans, Action Reports, Damage Reports, etc., formerly kept at the Operational Archives Branch, was transferred to "National Archives II." Call them to see what remains.

2. Other Sources of Information (Textual and Photographic)

a) *History Division, Photographic Section, United States Naval Institute, United States Naval Academy, 118 Maryland Avenue, Annapolis, MD 21402-5035;* TEL: 410-295-1022 or -1020.

This organization has a wealth of photography of U.S. Naval Ships from 1775 to present. It is easily accessible and less costly to purchase photographs from them than it is from "National Archives II." It is recommended that you try here first. A quantity of reference material is also available.

b) *Special Collections and Archives Division, Nimitz Library, United States Naval Academy, 589 McNair Road, Annapolis, MD 21402-5029;* TEL: 410-293-6903.

The Nimitz Library has a wealth of textual material covering all periods. Photographic reference material in the library is very limited. Entrance to the library is supposedly restricted to Naval Academy associated personnel. Anyone else desiring to use the library to conduct research should first write or call to get permission. This is just a formality, but required. Permission is usually given.

c) *Government Photographic Sources*
Department of the Navy, Nimitz Library Special Collections and Archives Division, United States Naval Academy, 589 McNair Road, Annapolis, MD 21402-5029; (301) 267-2220.

National Air and Space Museum, Archives Division, Smithsonian Institution, Washington, D.C. 20560; (202) 357-3133 A3.

Naval Historical Center, Photographic Section, Washington Navy Yard, Building 108, Washington, D.C. 20374-5060; (202) 433-2765. National Archives at College Park, Nontextual Division, Still Pictures Branch (NNSP), 8601 Adelphi Road, College Park, MD 20740-6001; (301) 713-6660.

d) *Veterans Associations and their Newsletters*
Additional information is available through the following newsletters:

1. Four Stack APD Veterans. The *Four Stacker Quarterly.* Annual dues: $15. Phone: (619) 282-0971; Fax: (619) 528-0961; E-mail: apdsec@att.net. Four Stack APD Veterans, Curt Clark, Secretary. 3384 Grim Ave., San Diego, CA 92104-4654.

2. LCT Flotillas of WWII ETO-PTO. Phone: (615) 865-0579; E-mail: hefarmer@home.com. H.E. "Bud" Farmer, Reunion Chairman. 1312 Cheshire Dr., Nashville, TN 37207-1508.

3. Guadalcanal Campaign Veterans, *Guadalcanal Echoes.* Annual dues: $12. Phone: (708) 457-0453. Joe Micek, Editor. 4935 Frank Parkway, Norridge, IL 60706-3231.

4. The Association of Gunner's Mates. *Guns.* Quarterly. Annual dues: $25. Phone: (219)845-3747; E-mail: JPGUNSED@aol.com. Jack Photenhauer, Director. P.O. Box 247, Hammond, IN 46325.

5. United States LST Association. *LST Scuttlebutt Newsletter.* Annual dues: $18. Phone: 1-800-228-5870; Fax: 1-419-693-1265; E-mail uslst@kmbs.com. Website: www.uslst.org. Milan Gunjak, President. P.O. Box 167438, Oregon, Ohio 43616-7438.

6. USS LCI National Association Inc. *Elsie Item Newsletter.* Annual dues: $10. Phone: (717) 684-4785; E-mail: lcipres@juno.com. Website: www.usslci.com. Robert V. Weisser, President. 134 Lancaster Ave, Columbia, PA 17512.

APPENDIX C

Abbreviations and Acronyms plus Ship and Aircraft Designations

The military has a language all of its own. This list includes most of the commonly used World War II acronyms, code-words and abbreviations as well as aircraft, ship and landing craft designations. (Abbreviations frequently used in footnotes by our sources have also been included.)

1. World War II Acronyms, code-words and abbreviations

AA — Anti-aircraft
AAA — Antiaircraft Artillery
AAF — United States Army Air Force
ABDA — American-British-Dutch-Australian
Adm — Admiral
AE — Ammunition Ship
AF — Stores Ship
AGC — Amphibious Force Command Ship
AH — Hospital Ship
AirSols — Air Solomons Command
AK — Cargo Ship
AKA — Attack Cargo Ship
ANZAC — Australia New Zealand Area
AO — Oil Tanker
AOG — Gasoline Tanker
AP — Transport
APA — Attack Transport
APD — Fast Destroyer Transport
APc — Coastal Transport
AR — Action Report
AR — Repair ship
ARL — Landing Craft Repair Ship
Arty — Artillery
AS — Submarine Tender
ATF — Ocean Tugs, Fleet
ATS — Army Transport Service
BB — Battleship
BAR — Browning Automatic Rifle
BGen — Brigadier General
BLT — Battalion Landing Team
Bn — Battalion
Btry — Battery
Bu — Bureau
Buord — Bureau of Ordnance
Bupers — Bureau of Naval Personnel
Budocks — Bureau of Yards and Docks
Buships — Bureau of Ships
BuSandA — Bureau of Supplies and Accounts
CA — Coast Artillery
CA — Heavy cruiser

Cactus — Guadalcanal code name
Cal — Caliber
Capt — Captain
Cardiv — Carrier Division
CB — Large Cruiser
CCS — Combined Chiefs of Staff
Cdr — Commander (also Cmdr)
CG — Commanding General
CinCPOA — Commander in Chief, Pacific Ocean Area
CIC — Combat Information Center
CinCPac — Commander in Chief, Pacific Fleet, (Admiral Nimitz)
CL(AA) — Light Cruiser (antiaircraft)
CL — Light Cruiser
CLEANSLATE — Code name for occupation of Russell Islands
CMC — Commandant of the Marine Corps
Cmdr — Commander (also Cdr)
CNO — Chief of Naval Operations
Co — Company
CO — Commanding Officer
Col — Colonel
COM — Commander
ComAirSoPac — Commanding Aircraft (land based) South Pacific Force
ComAirWing I — Commander Genocide 1st Marine Air Wing
ComAmphibForSoPac — Commander, Amphibious Force, S. Pacific Force
ComGenSoPac — Commander General, U.S. Army South Pacific Force
COMNAVBAS — Commander Naval Base(s)
ComServonSoPac — Commander, Service Squadron, South Pacific Force
ComSoPac — Commander, South Pacific Force
ComSowesPac — Commander, Southwest Pacific (also CinCSWPA)
Cpl — Corporal
Crudiv — Cruiser Division
CT — Combat Team
CTF — Commander, Task Force
CTG — Commander, Task Group
CTU — Commander, Task Unit
CV — Aircraft Carrier
CVE — Escort Carrier
CVL — Light Carrier
DD — Destroyer
DE — Destroyer Escort

DMS — Destroyer Minesweeper
DOW — Died of Wounds
DRYGOODS — Code name for assembly of supplies for New Georgia Offensive, February, 1943
DUKW — Amphibious Trucks
Ens — Ensign
ExO — Executive Officer
FA — Field Artillery
FAdm — Fleet Admiral
Flex — Fleet Landing Exercise
Flot — Flotilla
FMF — Fleet Marine Force
Gar — Garrison
Gen — General
GHQ — General Headquarters
GO — General Order
GQ — General quarters
HMAS — His Majesty's Australian Ship
HMS — His Majesty's Ship
HMNZS — His Majesty's New Zealand Ship
HQ — Headquarters
IJA — Imperial Japanese Army
IJN — Imperial Japanese Navy
Inf — Infantry
Is — Island
JCS — Joint Chiefs of Staff
Lant — Atlantic (Fleet)
LC (FF) — Landing Craft, Flotilla Flagship
LCC — Landing Craft, Control
LCI (G) — Landing Craft, Infantry (Gunboat)
LCI (L) — Landing Craft, Infantry (Large)
LCI (M) — Landing Craft, Infantry (Mortar)
LCI (R) — Landing Craft, Infantry (Rocket)
LCM — Landing Craft, Mechanized
LCdr — Lieutenant Commander (also LCmdr)
LCol — Lieutenant Colonel
LCP (L) — Landing Craft, Personnel (Large)
LCP (R) — Landing Craft, Personnel (Ramp)
LCR (L) — Landing Craft, Rubber (Large)(also Small)
LCS (L) — Landing Craft, Support (Large)
LCT (5) and (6) — Landing Craft Tank
LCV — Landing Craft, Vehicle
LCVP — Landing Craft, Vehicle and Personnel
LSD — Landing Ship, Dock
LSM — Landing Ship, Medium
LST — Landing Ship, Tank
Lt — Lieutenant
LtCol — Lieutenant Colonel
LtGen — Lieutenant General
Lt (jg) — Lieutenant, junior grade
LVT — Landing Vehicle, Tracked (Marks I-IV)
LVT (A) — Landing Vehicle, Tracked (Armored)
MAC — Marine Amphibious Corps
MAG — Marine Aircraft Group

MAINYARD — Code name for Guadalcanal Island
Maj — Major
MajGen — Major General
MARAD — Maritime Administration
MarCor — Marine Corps
MAW — Marine Aircraft Wing
MD — Marine Detachment
MI — Military Intelligence
MIA — Missing in Action
MOB — Mobile
Mm — Millimeter
MSgt — Master Sergeant
MSTS — Military Transportation Service (later Military Sealift Command)
MTB — Motor Torpedo Boat
NAD — Naval Ammunition Depot
NAS — Naval Air Station
NGF — Naval Gunfire
NOB — Naval Operating Base
NSD — Naval Supply Depot
OB — Order of Battle
O-in-C — Officer in Charge
ONI — Office of Naval Intelligence
OOD — Officer of the Deck
OPlan — Operations Plan
PC — Sub-Chaser (steel hull)
PC — Patrol Craft
PCE — Patrol Craft Escort
Pfc — Private, First Class
Phib — Amphibious
Pion — Pioneer
Pl — Platoon
Plt Sgt — Platoon Sergeant
POA — Pacific Ocean Area
POW — Prisoner of War
PT — Motor Torpedo Boat
Pvt — Private
PTO — Pacific Theater of Operations
RAAF — Royal Australian Air Force
RAdm — Rear Admiral
RAF — Royal Air Force
RAN — Royal Australian Navy
RCT — Regimental Combat Team
Rdr — Raider
Reinf — Reinforced
RING BOLT — Tulagi code name
RLT — Regimental Landing Team
RN — Royal Navy
RNZAF — Royal New Zealand Air Force
RNZN — Royal New Zealand Navy
SC — Submarine Chaser (Wooden hull)
SEC NAV — The Secretary of the Navy
SFCP — Shore Fire Control Party
SoPac — South Pacific Area, South Pacific Force

SoWesPac — Southwest Pacific Area (SWPA)
Sgt — Sergeant
SM — Submarine Minelayer
Sqn — Squadron
SS — Submarine
SSgt — Staff Sergeant
TBS — (Talk Between Ships) Voice radio
TF — Task Force
TG — Task Group
TOENAILS — Code name for New Georgia operation
TSgt — Technical Sergeant
TU — Task Unit
UDT — Underwater Demolition Team
USA — United States Army
USAFISPA — United States Army Forces in the South Pacific Area
USAT — United States Army Transport
USASOS — United States Army Services of Supply
USCG — United States Coast Guard
USN — United States Navy
USNR — United States Naval Reserve

USNS — United States Naval Ship
USMC — United States Marine Corps (also
United States Maritime Commission)
USSBS — United States Strategic Bombing Survey
VAdm — Vice Admiral
VF — Navy Fighter Squadron
VMF — Marine Fighter Squadron
VMSB — Marine Scout-Bomber Squadron
VP — Navy Patrol Squadron
VS — Navy Scouting Squadron
WATCHTOWER — Code name for the
Guadalcanal-Tulagi Operation
WD — War Diary
WIA — Wounded in Action
WO — Warrant Officer
WPB — War Production Board
XO — Executive Officer
YMS — Motor Minesweeper
YP — Patrol Vessel
1st Sgt — First Sergeant

2. Aircraft Designations of the U.S. Navy, Marine Corps and Army, circa 1942-1943

A-20 — Boston, Army (2) light bomber ; A-29 — Hudson, Army (2) light bomber*
B-17 — Flying Fortress, Army (4) heavy bomber; B-24 — Liberator, Army (4) heavy bomber (called PB4Y by Navy)*
B-25 — Mitchell, Army (2) medium bomber; B-26 — Marauder, Army (2) medium bomber*
B-26 — Marauder, Army (2) medium bomber
B-29 — Superfortress, Army (4) heavy bomber
Black Cat — PBY equipped for night work
C-47 — Skytrain, Army (2) transport*
Dumbo — PBY equipped for rescue work
F4F — Wildcat; F4U — Corsair; F6F — Hellcat; all Navy (1) fighters*
P-38 — Lightning, Army (2) fighter; P-39 — Airacobra; P-40 — Warhawk, Army (1) fighters*
PBY — Catalina, Navy (2) seaplane; PBY-5A — amphibian*
PV-1 — Ventura, Navy (2) medium bomber*
SBD — Dauntless, Navy (1) dive-bomber*
SB2C — Helldiver; Navy (1) dive-bomber*
TBF — Avenger, Navy (1) torpedo-bomber*

3. Japanese Aircraft Designations, circa 1942-43

"Betty" — Mitsubishi Zero-1, Navy (2)medium bomber*
"Emily" — Kawanishi Zero-2, Navy (4) patrol bomber (flying boat)*
"Helen" — Nakajima, Navy (2) medium bomber*
"Judy" — Aichi, Navy (1) torpedo-bomber*
"Kate" — Nakajima 97-2, Navy (1) high-level or torpedo-bomber*
"Pete" — Sasebo, Zero-o, Navy (1) float plane*
"Sally" — Mitsubishi 97, Army (2) medium bomber*
"Tojo" — Nakajima, Army (1) fighter*
"Val" — Aichi 99-1 Navy (1) dive-bomber
"Zeke" — Mitsubishi Zero-3, Navy (1) fighter (called "Zero" in 1942-43)

* Numerals in parentheses indicate number of engines.

NOTES

Chapter 1. Evolution of Amphibious Operations (p. 1 - 35)

1. George Carroll Dyer, VAdm, USN (Retired), *The Amphibians Came to Conquer.*
2. John A. Lorelli, *To Foreign Shores—U.S. Amphibious Operations in World War II.* (Hereafter, *To Foreign Shores.*)
3. Ibid., p. 13.
4. Ibid., p. 13-14.
5. Ibid., p. 14-15.
6. Capt John V. Noel and Capt Edward Beach, *Naval Terms Dictionary.*
7. RAdm Samuel Eliot Morison, *Operations in North African Waters,* p. 27.
8. John A. Lorelli, *To Foreign Shores,* p. 17-19.
9. Ibid., p. 24-25.
10. CNO Organizational Rosters, 1941-42.
11. Turner memo to Admiral King, 22 April 1942.
12. *Amphibians Came To Conquer,* pp. 212-13.
13. Ibid., p. 213-15.
14. *Joint Action of the Army and the Navy,* 1935, para. 18.
15. *Amphibians Came to Conquer,* pp. 214-15.
16. *King's Record,* p. 320-21.
17. *Amphibians Came to Conquer,* pp. 217-18.
18. *JCS 00581, 2 July 1942.*
19. *Amphibians Came to Conquer,* p. 220.
20. *To Foreign Shores,* pp. 55-6.
21. *Neville* Action Report, 13 Aug. 1942.
22. (a) First Marine Division Operation Orders 5-42, June/July, 1942.
23. COMTRANSDIV to SOPACFOR report, FB7-10/A16-3/Ser 063 of 19 Aug. 1942.
24. Report of Boat Group Commander, USS *Barnett,* 13 Aug. 1942.
25. *Hunter Liggett* War Diary, 7 Aug. 1942.
26. Commander Transport Divisions, SoPac (CTG 62.1) Action Report, 23 Sept. 1942.
27. *Formalhaut* War Diary, 8 and 9 Aug. 1942.
28. *Neville* War Diary, 9 Aug. 1942.
29. *Hunter Liggett* War Diary, 8 Aug. 1942.
30. RKT to Colonel James W. Webb, USMC, CO 7th Marines, letter, 20 Aug. 1942.
31. USS *Charles Carroll* Action Report 9 Dec. 1942, pp. 5-6 and USS *Harris* Action Report 16 Nov. 1942, pp. 4-5.
32. *To Foreign Shores,* pp. 71-73.
33. Ibid., pp. 77-78.
34. Source: *Andrew Jackson Higgins and the Boats that Won World War II* by Jerry E. Strahan, Baton Rouge: Louisiana State University Press, 1994.
35. *Building the Navy's Bases in WWII,* Vol. I, pp. 278-9.

Chapter 2. APD Destroyer Transports (p. 37 - 62)

1. Sources: a) Clark, Curtis G., "All Purpose Destroyer—The Green Dragons;" b) First Shot Naval Vets, *USS Ward Fires First Shot;* c) *Dictionary of American Naval Fighting Ships.*
2. The APD designation stood for A-Auxiliary, P-Transport, D-Destroyer.
3. Hoffman, Major Jon T., *From Makin to Bougainville.*
4. A. S. Lott and R.F. Sumrall, "USS *Ward* Fires First Shot."
5. John D. Alden, *Flush Decks and Four Pipes.*
6. Samuel Eliot Morison, *History of United States Naval Operations in World War II,* Vol.. XV, pp. 93-94.
7. (a) CNO, OP-12, memorandum, 24 Feb. 1940; (b) DWP to Continuing Board for Developments of Landing Boats, memorandum, 23 Sept. 1941; (c) Joint Planning Committee to Joint Board JB No. 355, Ser 687 of 30 Sept. 1941, approved by SECNAV, 3 Oct. 1941.
8. (a) Pacific Fleet Confidential Notice 13CN-11, 1 Oct. 1941; (b) Atlantic Fleet Confidential Memo 10CM-41, 6 Oct. 1941.
9. Unless otherwise noted, most of the following Guadalcanal Campaign information was furnished to the author/editor courtesy of Curtis G. Clark, Secretary/Treasurer, Four Stack APD Veterans Association.
10. *Amphibians Came to Conquer,* pp. 419-20.
11. Ibid.
12. With the loss of *Colhoun, Gregory* and *Little,* off Guadalcanal, the need for additional APDs became obvious, so in late 1942 and early 1943, twelve more flush deck destroyers were rapidly converted. These were: *Talbot* (APD-7), *Waters* (APD-8), *Dent* (APD-9), *Brooks* (APD-10), *Gilmer* (APD-11), *Humphreys* (APD-12), *Sands* (APD-13), *Schley* (APD-14), *Kilty* (APD-15), *Ward* (APD-16), *Crosby* (APD-17), and *Kane* (APD-18).
13. Morison, *The Struggle for Guadalcanal,* p. 366.
14. Morison, *History of United States Naval Operations in WWII,* Vol. XV, pp. 93-94.
15. *Colhoun* and *McKean* were sunk by enemy aircraft, *Gregory* and *Little* were sunk by enemy gunfire, *Dickerson* and *Barry* were sunk by Kamikazes, *Brooks* was damaged by enemy action and later scrapped, *Ward* was mortally wounded by Kamikaze and had to be sunk by U.S. destroyer *O'Brien, Noa* was lost in a collision at sea with U.S. destroyer *Fullam,* and *Greene* was grounded in a typhoon in October 1945.
16. This summary of "Life Aboard a Four Stack Destroyer" was condensed and edited from an article provided by Curtis Clark CWO3, USN Retired, USS *Talbot* (APD-7) and Secretary, Four Stack APD Veteran's Association. (For more information, see "Veterans Newsletters" in the Bibliography.)
17. Morison, *History of United States Naval Operations in WWII,* Vol. II, p. 93.

Chapter 3. Biography of LCT Flotilla Five (p. 63 - 114)

1. Grandson of naval historian Samuel Eliot Morison.
2. McNeill, *The Voyage of the 159.*
3. "The Tin Armada" by Basil Hearde, *Challenge WWII Special,* Vol. 1 No. 2, pp. 26-30, 1944.
4. *Allied Landing Craft and Ships* (Hereafter, "Allied Landing Craft").
5. Official Navy Department Bulletin, "The Indomitable LCTs Never Miss An Invasion," July 1944. Courtesy: Wisconsin Maritime Museum.
6. Harry Denni, Manager, Tank and Refinery Sales, to Robert B. Sahlberg, skipper of LCT-67, letter, 27 January 1961.
7. *History of U.S. Naval Operations in WWII*, Vol. XV, p. 108.
8. *Amphibians Came to Conquer*, p. 464.
9. Ibid.
10. Morison, The Struggle For Guadalcanal, pp. 264-371.
11. Ibid.
12. CinCPAC Report: Solomon Islands Campaign—Fall of Guadalcanal, period 25 January to 10 February, 1943.
13. Ibid.

Chapter 4. Biography of LST Flotilla Five (p. 115 - 188)

1. Martin "Flags" Melkild, Landing Ship Tank USS LST-398 and Flot Five-Pacific Theater World War II, ms., p. 11 (Hereafter "LST-398 and Flot Five").
2. Command History of the USS LST-446, Naval Historical Center.
3. An officer who was formerly enlisted and was not commissioned directly from college or from the Naval Academy.
4. *Bureau of Naval Personnel Information Bulletin, May 1945.*
5. There were 170, 275 total Coast Guard vs. 3, 408, 347 total Navy as of August 31, 1945 according to the annual Report to the Secretary of the Navy, 10 Jan. 1946. A14-15.
6. The LST-396 fire and explosion could also have been caused by a delayed action, armor-piercing bomb or due to shifting explosive cargo ignited by impact or friction.
7. Military slang for situation normal, all "fouled" up.
8. *Reminiscences of John C. Niedermair,* pp. 226-9.
9. Source: Landing Craft and the War Production Board, April 1942-May 1944, War Administration: War Production Board, Special Study No. 11.
10. Bureau of Ships, "Landing Craft Progress Report," July 1, August 1, September 1, October 1, November 1, 1942.

NOTES   Chapter 4 *cont'd* (p. 115 - 188)

11. "Outline of Proposed Scheduling Procedure for Landing Craft Program," August 24, 1942 (signed by J. A. Krug for the War Production Board and Admiral S. M. Robinson for the Navy).
12. "Allied Landing Craft."
13. March/April 1996 LST Scuttlebutt, the official publication of the United States L.S.T. Association (see "Bibliography-Veterans Newsletters.").
14. Command History of LST-446.
15. Rogers Aston, *Memories of War at Sea,* 1942.
16. *Amphibians Came to Conquer,* p. 500.
17. *Memories of War at Sea,* 1942.
18. Melkild, "LST-398 and LST Flot 5."
19. Ibid.
20. Ibid.
21. Ibid.
22. Ibid.
23. APc is the designation for "Small Coastal Transport." Wooden-hulled, and capable of only 12 knots, these ships proved too vulnerable for combat operations. However, they proved valuable as navigational guides for landing craft and often as command ships for LST or LCI flotilla commanders.
24. LST Flotilla Five War Diary, April 1943.
25. Ibid.
26. LST 398 and LST Flot 5.
27. Ibid.
28. LST Flotilla Five War Diary, April 1943.
29. Ibid.
30. LST 398 and LST Flot 5.
31. Building the Navy's Bases in WWII, Vol. II, p. 191-201.
32. LST-398 and LST Flot Five.
33. LST Flotilla Five War Diary, May 1943.
34. *LST-398 and LST Flot 5.*
35. LST Flotilla Five War Diary.
36. Anthony P. Tesori, personal memoirs of World War II.
37. The Trevor and Ward, had been converted from WWI vintage "flush deck" destroyers to high-speed minesweep and transport respectively.
38. LST-398 and Flot 5, p. 97.
39. LST-398 and Flot 5, p. 97.
40. LST Flotilla Five War Diary.
41. Tesori, "Personal Memoirs of WWII."
42. CinCPOA's "Operations in Pacific Areas—June 1943."
43. Dictionary of American Naval Fighting Ships.
44. Commander Kendall King, USN, "LSTs: Marvelous at Fifty," Naval History, Winter 1992.

Chapter 5. Biography of LCI Flotilla Five (p. 189 - 231)

1. A person who was part of the original crew when a ship was commissioned.
2. The (L) which stood for "Large" was used in combined operations to differentiate it from the smaller 105-foot British LCI(S).
3. Robert Weisser and others, *USS LCI "Landing Craft Infantry."* (Hereafter *Landing Craft Infantry.*)
4. *Reminiscences of John C. Niedermair*, pp. 240-42 and 254-55.
5. *USS LCI Landing Craft Infantry,* Vol. I. (Hereafter *Landing Craft Infantry, Vol. I.*)
6. U.S. Navy Division of Naval Intelligence publications ONI/226, 1944 and ONI 226/1, 1945. (Hereafter, "Allied Landing Craft.")
7. *Landing Craft Infantry,* Vol. I, p. 7.
8. Ensign Read Dunn, Jr., *Remembering*, pp. 22-23.
9. *Landing Craft Infantry,* Vol. I.
10. Proper designations by function were LCI(G) gunboat, LCI(M) mortar, and LCI(R) rocket. Also LCI(FF) flotilla flag.
11. USS LCI(L) 334 Combined War Diary and Log, 24 Nov. 1942 – 30 Nov. 1943.
12. *Naval Terms Dictionary.*
13. LCI Flotilla Five War Diary, June 1943.
14. Ibid.
15. *CinCPOA's Operations in Pacific Areas—June 1943.*
16. LCI Flotilla Five War Diary June 1943.

BIBLIOGRAPHY

Bibliographic Note

This volume is based primarily upon four sources of information: official government records, chiefly of the U.S. Navy; published World War II books, especially the naval histories frequently cited; interviews and correspondence with the amphibians who was there; and several privately published memoir manuscripts.

A. Government Publications

Allard, Dean C; Crawley, Martha L.; and Edmison, Mary W.: *US Naval History Sources in the United States* (US Naval History Division, Washington, D.C., 1979).

Allied Landing Craft and Ships, U.S. Navy Division of Naval Intelligence Publications. ONI/226 1944 and ONI/1945. Washington, D.C.

Building the Navy's Bases in WWII, Two Vols. Bureau of Yards and Docks, Washington: GPO, 1947

Dictionary of American Naval Fighting Ships. Naval Historical Center, Washington, D.C.

Dyer, VAdm George C. *The Amphibians Came to Conquer: The Story of Admiral Richmond Kelly Turner.* 2 Vols. Washington: GPO, 1971.

Hoffman, Major Jon T. *From Makin to Bougainville;* (a USMC monograph), Washington, D.C. GPO 1951.

Landing Craft and the War Production Board—April 1942-May 1944. War Production Board, Special Study No. 11. Washington, D.C.

Melson, Major Charles D., USMC. *Up The Slot: Marines In The Central Solomons,* a pamphlet in World War II Commemorative Series, (Washington, D.C.: Marine Corps Historical Center, 1993).

Mersky, Cmdr Peter B., USNR. *Time Of The Aces: Marine Pilots In The Solomons,* 1942-1944, a pamphlet in World War II Commemorative Series, (Washington, D.C.: Marine Corps Historical Center, 1993).

Official Navy Department Bulletin: "The Indomitable LCTs Never Miss an Invasion," July 1944.

B. Interviews and Correspondence

LCTs:

			Jack E. "Cookie"	Johnson,	LCT-182
Carl M.	Barrett,	LCT-322	Ken	Keller,	LCT-158
Edward H.	Burtt,	LCT-68	Thomas J.	McGann,	LCT-377
Robert T.	Capeless,	LCT-62	John A.	McNeill,	LCT-159
Robert	Carr,	LCT-367	John	Morais,	LCT-481
Walter B. "Bo"	Gillette,	LCT-369	Robert B.	Sahlberg,	LCT-67
Robert	Gordier,	LCT-67	Austin N.	Volk,	LCT-60

LSTs:

			William	Jayne,	LST-339
Douglas S.	Adams,	LST-447	Jack	Jordan,	LST-397
Charles J.	Adams, Jr.,	LST-281	Hugh	Kane,	LST-449
Herbert A.	Alhgren,	LST-446	Ruben	Kemper,	LST-447
Robert	Allen,	LST-339	Andrew	Kresnocky,	LST-334
Rogers	Aston,	LST-446	John	La Montagne,	LST-448
James	Baird,	LST-353	John	Lapp,	LST-460
Freeman A.	Ballard,	LST-447	William	Leadingham,	LST-396
Delbert E.	Beardsley,	LST-449	Theron	MacKay,	LST-342
Harold F.	Breimyer,	LST-448	Harry	Mansfield,	LST-460
Dwight	Burt,	LST-460	Martin	Melkild,	LST-398
Robert	Busch,	LST-851	Robert	Menzel,	LST-472
Tom	Byrne,	LST-460	Homer	Mitchell,	LST-446
James	Cogswell	LST-342	Ben	Owen	LST-339
John	Columbo,	LST-396	Thad	Rogers,	LST-399
Hugh	Comer,	LST-446	Lester	Rutter,	LST-396
Don	Connell,	LST-397	Ed	Sargent,	LST-353
Charles	Crane,	LST-472	Frank	Sawyer,	LST-398
Richard	Daspit,	LST-447	Joe	Schmits,	LST-398
Elmer	Froewiss,	LST-472	Miner B. "James"	Stackpole,	LST-396
Harold	Hansen,	LST-448	Don	Sterling,	LST-340
George T.	Heard,	LST-460	Bill	Sutton,	LST-398
Gerhard R.	Hess,	LST-342	Anthony P.	Tesori,	LST-340
Bob	Hilliard,	LST-396	Robert	Thorpe,	LST-339
Gerhard	Hines,	LST-397	Joe	Volcik,	LST-398
Tucker	Hughbanks,	LST-354	William E.	Walsh,	LST-447
Dick	Insley,	LST-460	Richard	Wilson,	LST-398

LCIs:

			Dale B.	Kirkham,	LCI-222
John	Barry,	LCI-66	Thomas	Littel,	LCI-334
William A.	Bertsch,	LCI-64	Fred	Moshure,	LCI-73
Frank	Brady,	LCI-23	Thomas P.	Mulligan,	LCI-334
Donald L.	Brown,	LCI-336	Alfred J.	Ormston,	LCI-334
Bill	Brown,	LCI-327	Elmo	Pucci,	LCI-329
John	Bryne,	LCI-24	Bob	Rosenberg,	LCI-331
Read	Dunn, Jr.,	LCI-335	Homer	Reighard,	LCI-62
Ed	Fincham,	LCI-223	Vince	Robinson,	LCI-336
Harry	Frey,	LCI-70	Mike	Scalpi,	LCI-66
Jack	Higgins,	LCI-67	Bill	Stark,	LCI-23
Ed	Korpinen,	LCI-332	Stephen A.	Wiercinski,	LCI-336

APDs/Others:

Curtis G. Clark, APD-7

Harry Denni, Kansas City Structural Steel

Art Zuehlke, Manitowoc Shipbuilding Corp.

C. World War II Books

Alden, John D., *Flush Decks and Four Pipes,* Annapolis: Naval Institute Press, 1965.

Barbey, Daniel E. *MacArthur's Amphibious Navy.* Annapolis: Naval Institute Press, 1969.

Barger, Mel. *Large Slow Target,* Vol. 3. *A History of the Landing Ships (LST) and the Men Who Sailed On Them.* Carrolton: Taylor Publishing Company, 1994.

Buell, Thomas B. *Master of Sea Power: A Biography of Fleet Admiral Ernest J. King.* Boston: Little, Brown, 1980.

Clark, Curt; McDonald, Johnny; and Witherspoon, Bob, Historians/Collaborators, *The Famed Green Dragons—The Four Stack APDs,* Paducah: KY. Turner Publishing Company, 1998.

Cook, Capt Charles. *The Battle of Cape Esperance.* Annapolis: Naval Institute Press, 1968.

Costello, John. *The Pacific War (1941-44).* New York: Rawson Wade, 1981.

Cravan, W.F. and J.L. Cate. *The Army Air Forces in World War II.* Volume 4. *The Pacific: Guadalcanal to Saipan (August 1942-July 1944).* Chicago: University of Chicago Press, 1950.

Foster, Mark S. *Henry J. Kaiser: Builder in the Modern American West.* Austin, 1989.

  Griffith, BGen Samuel B. II. *The Battle for Guadalcanal.* Philadelphia: J.P. Lippincott, 1963.

Halsey, FAdm William F. and LCmdr J. Bryan, III. *Admiral Halsey's Story.* New York and London: McGraw-Hill., 1976.

Hayes, Grace Person. *The History of the Joint Chiefs of Staff in World War II: The War Against Japan.* Annapolis: Naval Institute Press, 1982.

Hoyt, Edward P. *How They Won the War in the Pacific: Nimitz and His Admirals.* New York: Weybright and Tally, 1970.

Kinderman, Bernard J. and Kenneth C. Swedberg and others. *USS Ward Fires First Shot.* St. Paul: First Shot Naval Vets, 1983.

King, Adm Ernest J. & Cmdr Walter Whitehill. *Fleet Admiral King.* New York: W.W. Norton, 1952.

Krulak, Lieutenant General Victor H., USMC (Ret.). *First to Fight: An Inside View of the U.S. Marine Corps.* Annapolis, 1984.

Lane, Fredrick C. *Ships for Victory: A History of Shipbuilding Under the U.S. Maritime Commission in World War II.* Baltimore, 1951.

Lewin, Ronald. *The American Magic: Codes, Ciphers and the Defeat of Japan.* New York: Farrar Straus Giroux, 1982.

Lorelli, John A. *To Foreign Shores—U.S. Amphibious Operations in WWII.* Annapolis: Naval Institute Press, 1995.

Lundstrom, John B. *The First Team and the Guadalcanal Campaign.* Annapolis: Naval Institute Press, 1994.

Mason, John T., Jr. *The Pacific War Remembered.* Annapolis: Naval Institute Press, 1986.

McGee, William L. *Bluejacket Odyssey—Guadalcanal to Bikini, 1942-1946.* Santa Barbara: BMC Communications, 1997.

Mercer, Bill and others. *USS LCI, Landing Craft Infantry, Vol. II.* Paducah: Turner Publishing Company, 1995.

Miller, Thomas G., Jr. *The Cactus Air Force.* New York: Harper & Row, 1969.

Morison, RAdm Samuel Eliot. *History of United States Naval Operations in World War II,* Boston: Little, Brown, 1947-1990.

_____. Vol. III. *The Rising Sun in the Pacific, 1931-April 1942.*

_____. Vol. IV. *Coral Sea, Midway and Submarine Actions, May 1942-August 1942.*

_____. Vol. V. *The Struggle for Guadalcanal, August 1942-February 1943.*

_____. Vol. VI. *Breaking the Bismarcks Barrier, 22 July 1942-1 May 1944.*

_____. Vol. XV. *Supplement and General Index.*

Noel, Capt John V. Jr and Capt Edward L. Beach. *Naval Terms Dictionary.* Annapolis: Naval Institute Press, 1988.

Potter, E.B. *Bull Halsey.* Annapolis: Naval Institute Press, 1985.

_____. *Nimitz.* Annapolis: Naval Institute Press, 1976.

Smith, General Holland M., USMC (Ret). *Coral and Brass.* New York, 1949.

Strahan, Jerry E., *Andrew Jackson Higgins and the Boats that Won World War II.* Baton Rouge: LSU Press, 1944.

Walton, Francis. *Miracle of World War II: How American Industry Made Victory Possible.* Macmillan: New York, 1956.

Witter, Robert. *Small Boats and Large Slow Targets,* Missoula, Pictorial Histories Publishing Co., 1998.

D. Periodicals

Barger, Melvin D. "Getting the Goods to the Beach." *Surface Warfare.* January/February 1980.

Burck, Gilbert. "Mr. Higgins and His Wonderful Boats." *Life,* August 16, 1943, pp. 100-102, 105-106, 108, 110-12.

Hearde, Basil. "The Tin Armada: Saga of the LCT," *Challenge WWII Special* Vol. 1, No. 2, 1994.

McDonald, Johnny. "Green Dragons Deliver The Goods," *Traditions,* July/August 1996.

Sudhalter, D.L. "How Hurry-Up Henry [Kaiser] Helped to Win the War." *The Retired Officer,* August 1986.

Various Authors. "50th Anniversary WWII" articles. *VFW Magazine,* 1991-1995 issues.

E. Miscellaneous

Clark, Curtis G., *World War II Battle History of APDs in the Solomons, Four Stack APD Veterans Assn.* (Privately published), 1996.

Dunn Jr., Read, *Remembering.* (Privately published autobiography), 1994.

Jordan, Mark H. and others. *Saga of the Sixth, A History of the Sixth U.S. Naval Construction Battalion, 1942-1945.* (Privately published), 1986.

Mason, John T. Jr., "Reminiscences of John C. Niedermair, Architect - Bureau of Ships." Oral History. Annapolis: U.S. Naval Institute, 1978.

"Kaiser's World War II Shipyards." Text of an address by James F. McCloud, retired president, Kaiser Engineers, given at the dedication of the site of Kaiser's Shipyard No. 2 as a Richmond, California, Historic Landmark. 8 May 1992.

McNeill, John A., *The Voyage of the 159,* Whiteville, North Carolina. (Privately published), 1995.

Melkild, Martin "Flags." "Landing Ship Tank USS LST-398 and LST Flot Five Pacific Theater, World War II." (Privately published), 1985.

Tesori, Anthony P., *Personal Memoirs of World War II,* Rockledge, Florida. (Privately published), 1994.

O.K., let's go.

—General Dwight Eisenhower

Index

SAN: 253-2891

Available from your favorite bookseller or by direct mail from BMC

BOOK ORDER FORM

Telephone Orders: (805) 969-5970
Fax Orders: (805) 969-4402
Order on line: www.BMCPublications.com
E-mail Orders: BMCpublications@aol.com
Postal Orders:
BMC Publications
PO Box 5768
Santa Barbara, CA 93150

100% SATISFACTION GUARANTEE
If for any reason any BMC book does
not meet your complete expectations,
just return it undamaged within 15 days
and we will refund your money
or credit your account in full.

❑ Yes! Please send me the following book(s):   Code: 865

Qty	Title	Price/each	$Totals
	Bluejacket Odyssey		
	The Amphibians are Coming!		

Subtotal $ _____

Sales tax: California residents add 7.75% tax $ _____
Shipping: Add $4 for first book/ $2 for each additional book $ _____
(All payments must be in U.S. Dollars)   **YOUR TOTAL is** $ _____
❑ Enclosed is my check or money order for $_____ (Make payable to **BMC**.)

ORDERED BY: *(Please print clearly)*

Name _____

Address _____

City /State /Zip _____

Daytime Phone (___) _____ (in case there's a question about your order)
    ❑ Check here if you would like the author to sign the book(s).

Thank you for your order. (Please allow 14 days for delivery.)

BMC PUBLICATIONS

SAN: 253-2891

Available from your favorite bookseller or by direct mail from BMC

BOOK ORDER FORM

Telephone Orders: (805) 969-5970
Fax Orders: (805) 969-4402
Order on line: www.BMCPublications.com
E-mail Orders: BMCpublications@aol.com
Postal Orders:
BMC Publications
PO Box 5768
Santa Barbara, CA 93150

100% SATISFACTION GUARANTEE
If for any reason any BMC book does
not meet your complete expectations,
just return it undamaged within 15 days
and we will refund your money
or credit your account in full.

❏ Yes! Please send me the following book(s):   Code: 865

Qty	Title	Price/each	$Totals
	Bluejacket Odyssey		
	The Amphibians are Coming!		

Subtotal $ _____

Sales tax: California residents add 7.75% tax $ _____
Shipping: Add $4 for first book/ $2 for each additional book $ _____
(All payments must be in U.S. Dollars)   **YOUR TOTAL is** $ _____
❏ Enclosed is my check or money order for $_____ (Make payable to **BMC.**)

ORDERED BY: *(Please print clearly)*

Name _____

Address _____

City /State /Zip _____

Daytime Phone ( ) _____ (in case there's a question about your order)
    ❏ Check here if you would like the author to sign the book(s).

Thank you for your order. (Please allow 14 days for delivery.)

Available from your favorite bookseller or by direct mail from BMC

BOOK ORDER FORM

<u>Telephone Orders</u>: (805) 969-5970
<u>Fax Orders</u>:   (805) 969-4402
<u>Order on line</u>: www.BMCPublications.com
<u>E-mail Orders</u>: BMCpublications@aol.com
<u>Postal Orders</u>:
BMC Publications
PO Box 5768
Santa Barbara, CA 93150

100% SATISFACTION GUARANTEE
If for any reason any BMC book does
not meet your complete expectations,
just return it undamaged within 15 days
and we will refund your money
or credit your account in full.

❑ Yes! Please send me the following book(s):   Code: 865

Qty	Title	Price/each	$Totals
	Bluejacket Odyssey		
	The Amphibians are Coming!		

Subtotal $ _____

Sales tax: California residents add 7.75% tax $ _____
Shipping: Add $4 for first book/ $2 for each additional book $ _____
(All payments must be in U.S. Dollars)   **YOUR TOTAL is** $ _____

❑ Enclosed is my check or money order for $_____ (Make payable to **BMC**.)

ORDERED BY: *(Please print clearly)*

Name _____

Address _____

City /State /Zip _____

Daytime Phone (___) _____ (in case there's a question about your order)
        ❑ Check here if you would like the author to sign the book(s).

Thank you for your order. (Please allow 14 days for delivery.)

BMC PUBLICATIONS

Available from your favorite bookseller or by direct mail from BMC

BOOK ORDER FORM

Telephone Orders: (805) 969-5970
Fax Orders: (805) 969-4402
Order on line: www.BMCPublications.com
E-mail Orders: BMCpublications@aol.com
Postal Orders:
BMC Publications
PO Box 5768
Santa Barbara, CA 93150

100% SATISFACTION GUARANTEE
If for any reason any BMC book does
not meet your complete expectations,
just return it undamaged within 15 days
and we will refund your money
or credit your account in full.

❏ Yes! Please send me the following book(s):   Code: 865

Qty	Title	Price/each	$Totals
	Bluejacket Odyssey		
	The Amphibians are Coming!		

Subtotal $ _____

Sales tax: California residents add 7.75% tax $ _____
Shipping: Add $4 for first book/ $2 for each additional book $ _____
(All payments must be in U.S. Dollars) **YOUR TOTAL is** $ _____

❏ Enclosed is my check or money order for $_____ (Make payable to **BMC**.)

ORDERED BY: *(Please print clearly)*

Name _____

Address _____

City /State /Zip _____

Daytime Phone (   ) _____ (in case there's a question about your order)
        ❏ Check here if you would like the author to sign the book(s).

Thank you for your order. (Please allow 14 days for delivery.)

BMC PUBLICATIONS